KINDERGARTEN *from* a to Z

Managing Your Classroom and Curriculum With Purpose and Confidence

ALAN J. COHEN

Solution Tree | Press

Copyright © 2021 by Solution Tree Press

Materials appearing here are copyrighted. With one exception, all rights are reserved. Readers may reproduce only those pages marked "Reproducible." Otherwise, no part of this book may be reproduced or transmitted in any form or by any means (electronic, photocopying, recording, or otherwise) without prior written permission of the publisher.

555 North Morton Street
Bloomington, IN 47404
800.733.6786 (toll free) / 812.336.7700
FAX: 812.336.7790

email: info@SolutionTree.com
SolutionTree.com

Visit **go.SolutionTree.com/instruction** to download the free reproducibles in this book.

Printed in the United States of America

Library of Congress Cataloging-in-Publication Data

Names: Cohen, Alan J., author.
Title: Kindergarten from A to Z : managing your classroom and curriculum
   with purpose and confidence / Alan J. Cohen.
Description: Bloomington, IN : Solution Tree Press, [2020] | Includes
   bibliographical references and index.
Identifiers: LCCN 2020019807 (print) | LCCN 2020019808 (ebook) | ISBN
   9781951075095 (paperback) | ISBN 9781951075101 (ebook)
Subjects: LCSH: Kindergarten--Methods and manuals. |
   Kindergarten--Curricula--United States. | Classroom management--United
   States. | Curriculum planning--United States. | Effective
   teaching--United States. | Teacher effectiveness--United States.
Classification: LCC LB1169 .C62 2020 (print) | LCC LB1169 (ebook) | DDC
   371.102/4--dc23
LC record available at https://lccn.loc.gov/2020019807
LC ebook record available at https://lccn.loc.gov/2020019808

Solution Tree
Jeffrey C. Jones, CEO
Edmund M. Ackerman, President

Solution Tree Press
President and Publisher: Douglas M. Rife
Associate Publisher: Sarah Payne-Mills
Art Director: Rian Anderson
Managing Production Editor: Kendra Slayton
Senior Production Editor: Tonya Maddox Cupp
Content Development Specialist: Amy Rubenstein
Copy Editor: Kate St. Ives
Proofreader: Evie Madsen
Text and Cover Designer: Abigail Bowen
Editorial Assistants: Sarah Ludwig and Elijah Oates

ACKNOWLEDGMENTS

Solution Tree Press would like to thank the following reviewers:

Carrie Marshall
Kindergarten Teacher
Glen Stewart Primary
Prince Edward Island, Canada

Donna Hoke Taylor
Alumni BS Education
University of Alabama
Tuscaloosa, Alabama

Danielle Tubergen
Kindergarten Teacher
Lincoln Elementary School
Hastings, Nebraska

Visit **go.SolutionTree.com/instruction** to download the free reproducibles in this book.

TABLE OF CONTENTS

Reproducible pages are in italics.

About the Author xi

Introduction 1
    About Teaching 2
    About Experts and Thinking Critically 3
    About This Crucial Grade Level 5
    About This Book 6

PART 1

Clarity in the Classroom 11

CHAPTER 1
Knowing That Teaching Starts in the Mind 13
    A Good Bus Driver 14
    Characteristics of an Effective Teacher 15
    Mindset of an Effective Teacher 18
    In a Nutshell 21
    Have You Mastered the Chapter? 21
    Answers and Explanations 22
    Skills for the Effective Teacher 23

CHAPTER 2
Working With Administration and Making Curriculum Work for You 25

- Working With Administration 25
- Sticking to the Curriculum or Stick (It) to the Curriculum 27
- Trying Four Ways to Teach Something 34
- In a Nutshell 36
- Have You Mastered the Chapter? 36
- Answers and Explanations 37
- *Four Ways to Teach a Skill* 38

CHAPTER 3
Preparing Your Classroom and Yourself 39

- Getting Ready for the First Day of School 39
- Preparing to Speak to Kindergarteners 45
- In a Nutshell 48
- Have You Mastered the Chapter? 48
- Answers and Explanations 49
- *Preparing for the First Day of School* 50
- *Practicing Kinderese* 51

CHAPTER 4
Employing Practical Classroom Management . . 55

- Why Kindergarteners Misbehave 55
- Strategies for Minimizing Misbehavior 57
- The End Goal of Good Classroom Management 59
- Social Learning Is Discipline 62
- The Three Approaches to Social-Emotional Learning 63
- Effective and Ineffective Disciplinary Tools 67
- Seven Rules for the Teacher 72
- Strategies for Managing Specific Behavior Issues 74
- In a Nutshell 81

  Have You Mastered the Chapter? 82

  Answers and Explanations 84

  Being an Authoritative Teacher 86

  Managing Conflicts. 87

CHAPTER 5
Planning Routines 89

  Fostering Independence Right From the Start 89

  Lining Up 91

  Starting With a Morning Quiz 97

  Getting the Class's Attention 98

  Handling Transitions 100

  Going to the Bathroom. 101

  In a Nutshell 103

  Have You Mastered the Chapter? 104

  Answers and Explanations 104

  Handling Transitions. 106

CHAPTER 6
Managing Whole-Group and Choice Time. . . . 107

  Managing Whole-Group Time. 107

  Managing Choice Time. 112

  In a Nutshell 118

  Have You Mastered the Chapter? 119

  Answers and Explanations 120

  Preparing for Choice Time 121

CHAPTER 7
Making Schedules, Charts, and Plans 123

  Class Schedule 123

  Lesson Plans. 126

  Monthly Calendar 128

  Charts. 129

Homework 132
Parent-Teacher Conferences 133
In a Nutshell 134
Have You Mastered the Chapter? 134
Answers and Explanations 136
Employing Interdisciplinary Teaching 137
Preparing for Parent-Teacher Conferences 138

PART 2

Clarity in Literacy and Mathematics 139

CHAPTER 8
Teaching Literacy 141

Early Assessment 142
Teaching Reading 144
Reading Components 145
Leveled Books 158
Independent Reading 164
Reading Proficiency Help Methods 166
The Writing Progression 167
Independent Writing 169
Fiction Versus Nonfiction 173
In a Nutshell 175
Have You Mastered the Chapter? 176
Answers and Explanations 177
Teaching the Reading Decoding Skills 179
Teaching Each Letter to Mastery 181
Classifying Fiction Versus Nonfiction 182

CHAPTER 9
Teaching Mathematics 183

    Mathematics in Kinderese. 186
    Foundational Concepts. 187
    Teaching Counting 188
    Teaching *More* and *Less*. 189
    Teaching *Same* and *Different* 192
    Teaching Shapes. 193
    Teaching *Left* and *Right* 195
    Conceptual Thinking. 196
    Manipulatives and Other Teaching Tools. 196
    In a Nutshell 199
    Have You Mastered the Chapter? 199
    Answers and Explanations 201
    Preteaching and Spiraling. 203
    Ensuring Mathematics Concept Readiness 204

Conclusion. 205

References and Resources. 207

Index. 219

ABOUT THE AUTHOR

Alan J. Cohen—whose students call him "Mr. A."—is a tenured teacher in the New York City Department of Education. He has taught children from many different socioeconomic backgrounds, including those with processing issues or physical, cognitive, and behavioral needs, and those who are intellectually gifted. His initial position was at a prekindergarten in a low-income neighborhood where his eyes were opened to the unique challenges of the community in obtaining resources and ensuring quality education. He then taught at an early learning center focused on prepping the children for entrance into selective city schools. He began developing a style that combines play, exploration, and academics, and discovered that his method was the best preparation for the students to succeed on the high-stakes entrance tests.

As a proud new father, Mr. A. commuted via subway to the preschool, continuing through the birth of his second daughter, with his youngest in a front pack and his eldest in a stroller. When his children matured, Mr. A. was offered a kindergarten position at a public school near his children's elementary school. He learned that kindergarten is a world in and of itself that requires that much more sophistication in his teaching approach and practice.

Mr. A. has a unique perspective on early childhood education. A keen observer and thinker, with a wealth of experience in the educational system, his teaching techniques follow sound educational theory with a twist, as he has developed his own terminology to describe and implement techniques that cover everything from how to line up students to teaching them advanced concepts of reading and mathematics.

Mr. A. received his bachelor's degree in business at New York University, thereupon realizing that his true calling was teaching. He attended Brooklyn College for his master's degree in education while student teaching kindergarten at a public school.

To learn more about Alan's work, follow MrAKindergarten on Tumblr.

To book Alan J. Cohen for professional development, contact pd@SolutionTree.com.

INTRODUCTION

I was waiting to see my eldest daughter's high school teacher after a parent-teacher conference when another parent introduced herself to me. "This is my son," she said, gesturing toward the teenage boy next to her. "You taught him in preschool—remember him?"

I didn't.

Then she said, "His name is Ilan."

It took a few seconds, and then a flood of memories came back. I could see the Ilan I knew many years ago, transformed into the young man who, at this point, acted as if he were too cool to acknowledge me. I remembered his personality, including what he liked to do, and who his best friend had been. Ilan's mother told me that Ilan was a senior now and applying to colleges. "I wanted to say hello," she said, "so that I could tell you that of all the teachers Ilan had, you were the most impactful and influential in his education journey."

I was overwhelmed. I could see that Ilan's mother was earnest. I didn't know what to say. I tried to be as gracious as I could and wished Ilan luck in college. After they left, I thought to myself, "Is this woman kidding? I was his preschool teacher! Ilan has probably had twenty or more teachers since then. That was years ago. She seems sincere, but this just cannot be true." However, this scenario happened again, and then again, with different variations, to the point where I started thinking that something was there. One parent came to me when his child was in third grade and said, "You know, every time my child learns something new in school, he always says that he already learned it from Mr. A."

High praise? Well, Robert Fulghum (1988) long before noticed this phenomenon, a widespread assertion of the impact of teachers in the very earliest grades, and he made it a theme of his book *All I Really Need to Know I Learned in Kindergarten*. In addition to all of the foundational academics taught in this grade, Fulghum (1988) touches on all the social-emotional learning, such as sharing, being fair, and being balanced.

At my own parent-teacher conferences, parents often ask me what they can do to help their child along his or her educational path. Instead of giving them a handout, I usually explain some of what I know about how students learn, which by now is obvious to me but not obvious to them. I know it isn't obvious to them because I see their widened eyes and gaping mouths. I watch as their brains churn to work out ways they can apply what they just learned to their children.

When a parent, colleague, teacher's aide, or paraprofessional comes to my classroom or on a class trip with me, they often see me do something that looks strange to them but works. Or they see students do stuff they never thought children were capable of doing at such a young age. They ask me about it, and I explain what I do and how I came to this method. Then, typically, they look at me and say, "I would have never thought to do that." Others have said, "Why don't you write a book about how you do things?" So . . . here it is!

About Teaching

As a New York City schoolteacher, I have taught students from every socioeconomic background, from the inner city to the yuppie elite; from many countries, ethnicities, and religions; students with special physical, cognitive, and behavioral needs; students with processing issues; and students who are intellectually gifted. In our school, many of the students are first-generation children with parents from different countries, so a multicultural awareness with a focus on English learning is important. Through all this diversity and variation, every student has presented the same way. What I mean is that every child basically operates on the same principles—even more consistently than do adults. All children need love, affection, attention, and acceptance, and they need to feel special. They are all curious about their world, and although this sounds like a teaching cliché, they all want to learn and can. I have seen absolutely no difference in the intellectual capabilities of students based on their country or ethnic or socioeconomic group—period.

> **I have seen absolutely no difference in the intellectual capabilities of students based on their country or ethnic or socioeconomic group—period.**

Each group I have taught has had essentially the same range of intellectual capabilities. I have also discovered that, although they live in a world full of fantasy and pretend, children are essentially rational and reasonable people. They have a greater ability for representational and conceptual thinking than they are given credit for. They are also way more predictable in their behavior than adults. When I look at something I have to teach, I tend to strip away all I have already learned about the topic and tap into a part of my mind that looks at a situation the same way I would if I were little—but my adult brain is also able to think about it sequentially and analytically, more easily bridging the concrete with the conceptual. How I take students on that journey—from where they are to a step closer to where I am now—is what I call *teaching*.

Some people do this more intuitively than others, but there is no reason a person can't learn to do what some may do largely by intuition. Doing this is not a matter of recovering your *inner child*; that term has so many meanings (and makes me think of adults wearing beanies and licking lollipops while holding a bunch of balloons and singing with Mary Poppins). Rather, it is a matter of having the right attitude toward children and using your adult mind to analyze and observe students to the point where you can relate to them on their terms. It also involves listening intently to what they have to say, both to you and to fellow students. I constantly overhear conversations between students on various philosophical subjects such as good and evil, reward and punishment, and even death. Their thoughts are often far more thought provoking and original than those of seasoned adults.

I once went to a conference at which the whole point was to show how children of today are markedly different from children twenty years ago, ten years ago, and even two years ago. The idea was that it was better in the good-old days. I didn't buy this conclusion because I don't see evidence of it in my everyday work. Perhaps the world into which children are born has changed socially and technologically, but the core of the child, how children go about perceiving that world, what they find stimulating, and the process of how they learn about it do not change.

Human nature does not change, and as valuable as the vast research into this enigma has been, it can only approximate the complexities involved in educating beings as diverse and unpredictable as we are. As a kindergarten teacher, I stay current about the state of the world of children, what the popular toys and movies are, what they are plugged into, and what societal pressures they are under. But in general, as rock singer and lead vocalist for Led Zeppelin, Robert Plant once said, "The song remains the same" (Clifton & Massot, 1976).

About Experts and Thinking Critically

I guess that I can lay claim as a childhood expert because I have an early childhood annotation on my teaching certificate. But a lot of what I know about children comes from being around them, and from having been one myself. I have mixed feelings about the word *expert*. I am still on my personal journey as a teacher. I have my own particular personality, my own strengths and weaknesses and philosophy about life. I can say that every technique I will show you in this book has been authentically research-tested. This means that I have tried these techniques on real children in a real kindergarten class in a real school setting, and they really work (though my methods are backed by research). But this has been with my class with my students. My discoveries are based on the students I have taught, not the students you are teaching. My administrators are not your administrators, my colleagues are not your colleagues, my teaching system is not your teaching system. Because I am confident that the techniques will work for you, I may sometimes sound as if I am an expert. But always keep in mind that I am *my own* expert, based on my own experiences and findings. These are my truths, which I have discovered from teaching.

The purpose of this book is for you to develop *your own* skills, find your own truths, and become your own expert. I encourage you to be a thinking teacher—one who thinks critically. It is misleading on my part to imply that teachers are not thinking for themselves, as almost every teacher I know has strong opinions about how to make his or her classroom a better place for learning. It is more correct to say that a lot of teachers either want to have the freedom to think for themselves or are reluctant to implement new ideas related to their curriculum. They may feel as if they don't have a choice.

The 9th century Buddhist master Lin Chi purportedly said, "If you meet the Buddha on the road, kill him" (Harris, 2006). Lin Chi was not advocating the assassination of spiritual teachers. He was trying to shock people into understanding that at some point, you must make the teachings your own. In other words, it is important to learn all you can from people you may look up to who are knowledgeable. However, if you have become so respectful or intimidated that you can no longer think critically about their ideas, that becomes an obstacle. At that point, you must metaphorically kill your Buddha, so you can free yourself to develop your own unique ideas and insights. That is when you become your own Buddha. This book is not about philosophy or religion. It is about becoming the most effective teacher you can be by applying your unique ideas and insights to your practice.

If you follow this book in a blind and dogmatic manner, you are doomed. This is a book that encourages you to think for yourself as a teacher, about using its ideas to build your own effective teaching methodology and practicum. This book is about always asking yourself—before doing anything—"Why am I doing this?" If the answer to your question does not fall along the lines of, "Because this is going to help my classroom function more efficiently or help students learn more effectively," then think twice before doing it!

Please don't read this book with the expectation of being spoon-fed, as you might be disappointed. This is because my message is to feed yourself. I expect you to think critically about my ideas and develop your own. Additionally, this book is not comprehensive in terms of academic instruction, as that's what textbooks are for. However, I do include my insights on methodology and sequence, as well as a discussion of the conceptual challenges you will find when teaching mathematics and literacy. You should find these very helpful, no matter what curriculum you are teaching. My hope is that after reading the book and taking the time to incorporate its philosophy and techniques, you will get to the point when you are ready to tear up this book and write your own. Then my job will have been done.

About This Crucial Grade Level

Being a kindergarten teacher is difficult, and teachers who teach other grades often don't understand this. Kindergarten is where a teacher lays down the foundation for all the subsequent building the educational system does afterward. Strong foundation, strong building. Weak foundation, weak building. It's as simple as that.

Early childhood is a period of tremendous physical, academic, and social growth. By age three, a child's brain has grown to 80 percent of its adult size, and by age five to 90 percent of its adult size (First Things First, 2020; Penfield & Roberts, 1959). It is well known that vocabulary and reading comprehension are closely related (Alkaboody, 2010):

> **Strong foundation, strong building. Weak foundation, weak building.**

> Young children whose parents read them five books a day enter kindergarten having heard about 1.4 million more words than kids who were never read to, a new study found. This "million word gap" could be one key in explaining differences in vocabulary and reading development. (Ohio State University, 2019)

Kindergarten teachers are responsible for teaching literacy skills in reading and writing, as well as all the foundational mathematics concepts, to a wide range of students. Students go from counting, maybe from 1 to 20, to counting to 100 and beyond, and they come to understand how our system of counting works. They are taught the scientific method—including experimentation. They begin to understand their place in the world and learn the most important social rules of our society.

How long are kindergartener attention spans? How much direction and supervision do they need from you? How many questions do they ask in a span of five minutes? As the teacher, you have over twenty-five very self-directed people who demand 100 percent of your attention, 100 percent of the time. It is your job to manage them and to teach them some of the most important things they will ever learn in their lives.

Teaching kindergarten is so difficult and important that it has been said kindergarten teachers should receive higher pay for the added value they bring to a school. In a *New York Times* article, Harvard economist Raj Chetty and colleagues (as cited in Leonhardt, 2010) estimate "that a standout kindergarten teacher is worth about $320,000 a year. That's the present value of the amount of money a class of students will earn over their careers."

Why is this so? Chetty and colleagues (as cited in Leonhardt, 2010) explain:

> Students who had learned much more in kindergarten were more likely to go to college than students with otherwise similar backgrounds. Students who learned more were also less likely to become single parents. As adults, they were more likely to be saving for retirement. Perhaps most striking, they were earning more.
>
> All else equal, they were making about an extra $100 a year at age 27 for every percentile they had moved up the test-score distribution over the course of kindergarten. A student who went from average to the 60th percentile—a typical jump for a 5-year-old with a good teacher—could expect to make about $1,000 more a year at age 27 than a student who remained at the average. Over time, the effect seems to grow, too.

It stands to reason that with this crucial impact that kindergarten has on students' academic and working careers that administrators put some of their best teachers in this grade and value the special challenges these teachers face.

About This Book

First, this book is designed to benefit prekindergarten, kindergarten, and first-grade teachers in all stages of their teaching careers, but it may feel most applicable to those who are new to the profession. For the teacher who is just starting out, I hope it will serve as your companion, as a trusted teacher friend whom you can go to when you have questions about a certain topic or are questioning some of the methods you have been using or have been taught to use. For the seasoned teacher, this book might help you revisit and rethink your teaching philosophy, approach, and methodology, and help liberate the dynamic teacher within.

Second, I envision the book to be set aside after its initial reading but visited frequently as a resource until it is somewhat worn. At some point it will be very ragged and start to be neglected, as you develop your own insights and develop theories and techniques far superior to those I have outlined. The book will then start to fall apart on its own and finally be trashed, as you realize that you have progressed in your practice way past the book's concepts and methodology. Don't forget to recycle and don't forget to send me a copy of *your* book!

The book is split into two parts. Part 1, "Clarity in the Classroom," is made up of chapters 1 through 7. This part covers the very theoretical ideas of how to approach teaching and why you teach, to all the practical skills you need to hone your craft in general, but specifically for students of this age group.

- **Chapter 1** covers the mindset and skills one needs to have to be an effective teacher and comes to the realization that the thinking teacher approach is the only viable alternative.

- **Chapter 2** veers into the practicalities of teaching, such as developing a harmonious relationship with your administrator while pursuing your teaching goals and understanding how your mandated curriculum, no matter how many times it may change, will not throw you off your teaching track.

- **Chapter 3** details what to accomplish before the school term begins and how to negotiate that crucial first day. It also covers how to speak to these students (in a language I call *kinderese*). You will be introduced to some kinderese phrases, and I have included a practice page for self-assessing whether you are truly speaking kinderese. Over time, you will acquire the tools so that you will speak in a manner implicitly understood by your students.

- **Chapter 4** introduces you to the permissive, authoritarian, and authoritative management styles and discusses what is most effective, as well as seven rules that a teacher must abide by. It also studies classroom management, breaking down effective and ineffective management techniques. You will learn the main reason children misbehave and the end results of effective class management—the hum, controlled chaos, and *wa*, or harmony. It offers practical, effective solutions to real-world problems teachers encounter in their practice, including "They hit me first" and "They don't want to be my friend." It also gives you useful techniques for dealing with a student in the throes of a tantrum. In the interest of helping your kindergarteners see themselves as children and students, instead of boy children and girl children, several sections use the words *they* and *them* as singular.

- **Chapter 5** illustrates how the thinking teacher applies an understanding of student behavior and classroom management to develop routines and transitions that are effective and educational. These will form the bed of consistency and predictability teachers and students will thrive on, and enable teachers to seamlessly achieve educational goals.

- **Chapter 6** is about how to engage all students in whole-group time while catering to each's academic, social, and linguistic level. The chapter discusses everything from rug arrangements to how much time you should allot for this activity, to how best to question students and set up discussions. It concludes with effectively integrating play—otherwise known as *choice time*—into the classroom. I will explain how to offer the most choices possible and how best to manage the flow.

- **Chapter 7** turns to the paperwork involved in being a teacher. I draw a distinction between writing up plans (using plan books and lesson plans) and actual planning and explain how the teacher can maximize the latter while still fulfilling the requirements of the former. I will also illustrate how to optimize student involvement and learning within a mandated schedule and which educational charts are most worthwhile for your room. It concludes with my thoughts on homework and, if you decide to assign it, how best to handle it. I also share my techniques for making parent-teacher conferences smooth as silk.

Part 2, "Clarity in Literacy and Mathematics," is a guidebook to the major understandings and techniques needed to effectively teach literacy and mathematics.

- **Chapter 8** explains how the English language works, details the sequence for teaching reading and writing to kindergarteners, and covers the proper way to teach phonics, sight words, blending, and decoding. I will also describe an easy method for teaching good penmanship. I will highlight the importance of independent reading and writing and explain how best to manage that period of the day by using the technique of speed conferencing.

- **Chapter 9** reveals why kindergarteners often don't understand the mathematics concepts taught in schools. I will offer methods to rectify this using a new, more child-centered approach. I will review some of the basic skills and operations students are expected to learn in kindergarten that many teachers find difficult to teach, such as "How many more?", "How are two objects the same and different?", sorting by two to three attributes, and identifying advanced two- and three-dimensional shapes. You will then learn an effective method to teach students relational words, such as *left* and *right*, and find out about what I think the best manipulatives are for teaching mathematics concepts.

What about science and social studies? I don't devote much time covering these subjects but explain why that doesn't mean that they are any less important than mathematics and literacy.

The conclusion sets you on your way. Throughout the book you will find epigraphs, what I call *one-liners*, that will help crystallize some of the concepts and techniques covered in each chapter.

I would prefer if you read starting from the beginning, because without understanding the book's core philosophy and approach, the practical aspects will only take you so far. A big part of teaching is adapting to the ever-changing teaching landscape. Keeping this in mind, delving into a particular topic of interest, especially if you are more seasoned teacher, would be of value as well.

Sound good? Well then, let's get to it!

PART 1

Clarity in the Classroom

What is teaching about, and how do you approach it? What is more important, the curriculum or the standards? What are standards, anyway? Do you need to follow the curriculum word for word? How much leeway do you have? How do you prepare for the very first day of school? How do you set up your classroom? What do you say when you meet the students, parents, and guardians? I have twenty-five students sitting on the rug in the classroom, what do I do? How do I manage them? What do I do if they misbehave or have conflicts? How do I line up students, transition them between activities, and have them clean up? Do kindergarten students get to play or is it all academics? How do I convert the written curriculum to engaging and challenging lessons that cater to each student's individual needs? How do I write up a lesson plan and deal with other paperwork? What charts should I have in the room? How do I get a raise?

Head spinning yet? I have asked these questions to myself many times and I have found answers that I think will give you a solid theoretical framework and practical skill set that will set you on the path to being an effective and happy teacher with a specialty in teaching kindergarten students. I haven't figured out the one for getting a raise yet, but I am working on it.

So, strap yourself in and let's bring clarity to the classroom!

CHAPTER 1

Knowing That Teaching Starts in the Mind

Your mental approach to teaching is key. Once you have that set, the practical aspects will come easily. Yankees catcher Yogi Berra (as cited in Le Watergate, 1985, p. 18) said about his sport, "Ninety percent of the game is half mental." This is also true of teaching.

It's about mental attitude.

Most teachers adopt the proper attitude toward their students. It probably aligns with my attitude: every child by nature is good, every child by nature is smart and wants to learn and, of course, every child is cute. All of this feels self-evident. As a teacher, you get to be around these lovely creatures all day—not a bad deal. This is the best way to look at the profession, especially on those days you might be having doubts about this. Children are little people who are capable learners. They just need you to show them the way, so don't let them down! They are like puzzles. Some are those easy thirty-five-piece puzzles and some are like a Rubik's Cube, but they can all be figured out. It is your job and your responsibility to do so.

Here are all the codes you are going to crack. You are going to use your mental energy to figure out the students, the curriculum, your colleagues, the parents and guardians, and your administrators. This is not easy, but you are up to the task. Teaching is problem solving. Actually, life is problem solving, but the focus of this book is on teaching. As you read about whether you are a good bus driver (or teaching tour guide), consider what characteristics and mindset make a teacher effective; we'll talk about those concepts in this chapter along with what mindset makes a teacher ineffective.

A Good Bus Driver

In *A Pedagogy of Questioning*, author Gerardo Ivan Hannel (2014) makes a good argument about why there is usually a disparity between the academic readiness of students from different socioeconomic backgrounds when they enter school. The conventional wisdom was that those from a higher socioeconomic status were exposed to more life experiences and diversity. Hannel (2014) argues that it is the quality, not the quantity, of experiences that makes all the difference. He offers the observation that parents of children from higher socioeconomic backgrounds tend to speak to children more frequently, use higher-order vocabulary, and employ experiences as teachable moments (Hannel, 2014). They are, in essence, tour guides for their children in the world. They ask a lot of questions of their children, offer many explanations, make connections between different experiences and encourage their children to do the same, and most of all, they encourage their children to ask questions about anything and everything. These parents, for the most part, do not see themselves as teachers—they are just doing what comes naturally to them. However, they are doing what every effective teacher does—bridge the gap between the adult mind and the child mind by finding a commonality of thought. They are meeting learners where they are in their cognitive development with a goal of facilitating capacity building (Shay, 2017).

Being this kind of teacher can make a difference for your students, of course. And I am not here to overgeneralize or make a judgment about the parenting skills of people of different backgrounds, but I do know that this approach of questioning, describing, thinking, and exploring with students, which Shay (2017) calls the *mediated learning experience* (MLE), has a huge impact on the ability to learn. It gives the student loads of content in all subject areas, analytical tools, social confidence, and excellent literacy skills, like vocabulary and reading readiness (discussed in part 2, page 139).

Who are you as a teacher? You are driving a bus filled with dozens of students, coasting by amazing sights and explaining as you go along, asking questions and answering the barrage of questions coming at you all at once. Yes, I realize I am referencing *The Magic School Bus* (Bastien & Jacobs, 2012), but I am going a step further. You are going to do the MLE so well that each student will feel that he or she is driving alone with you in a small car. Your room setup, your management style, your authoritativeness, your questioning techniques, and your lesson design will all contribute to achieving this desired effect of teaching twenty-five-plus students individually all at once.

Characteristics of an Effective Teacher

Being an effective teacher means you have the ability to observe children and think like a child. In addition to these skills, chapter 3 discusses the ability to communicate with children in the section Preparing to Speak to Kindergarteners (page 45), and chapter 4 (page 55) focuses on the ability to manage young students. But the most important skill is the ability to observe—to see and hear students. Thinking flows from this one, as do communicating with and managing your students. According to early childhood innovators George Forman and Ellen Hall (2005), "It is important for us to know our children deeply, to flow with their currents, and to extend their nascent theories about how the world works."

Observant

Learn the nuances of children's body language, how they talk, what triggers their emotions, and how they think. There are opportunities for this from the moment the students enter the classroom. Don't take for granted the perfunctory times of the day like packing up or cleaning up. You can focus on one student a day throughout the day, a group of students during one activity, or follow your intuition or whatever engages you—but stay engaged throughout the whole day and treat every moment as if you were panning for gold. Constant verbal interaction and genuine curiosity will unlock their thinking patterns. You can ask them open-ended questions like "What does this remind you of?" or "What are your plans?" You are a field researcher and strive to link your observations together to make predictable connections that will make you more knowledgeable about your students. You don't need to know everything there is to know about children, because you never can. You only need to know enough to start your journey and keep adding to your knowledge and expertise.

Observing students requires the teacher to have heightened senses. The sense that usually needs to be developed most is the ability to listen—especially when managing your classroom. You have to work on using this sense more than your sense of sight, which comes naturally. The ability to pick out snippets of conversation, to hear the change in a student's intonation from across the room, to hone in on dissonant frequencies while you have your back turned for a second is a skill that will take you far in your teaching practice.

I would be tempted to say that the best way to develop this skill would be to close your eyes in the classroom, but you should never to that. However, you can close your eyes on a bus, in the subway, on a bench in a park, or in the comfort of your home. Then simply listen, trying to pick out as many different sounds as you can.

When you are in a mall, eyes open, try to shift your listening from the person you are with to people passing you by to people in the stores you are passing, and then to the music playing in the background. Then try to listen to as many of these different sounds at the same time. Now your ear is multitasking. Apply this scanning skill when you are in your classroom—especially in areas where students are not in your line of sight.

Thinking

How can you approach concepts with an adult mind that has childhood sensibilities? The first thing is to realize that we take a lot for granted in terms of our belief systems, cultural cues, language, and number systems. A child is looking at everything from square one. In fact, a child might ask you why a square is called a *square*. When you start explaining the sides of a square and say it has four sides, a child might ask what you call something with two sides or even one side. If you are teaching numbers 1 to 10 and try to give an introduction to place value by saying that we make groups of ten with numbers that we call *10, 20, 30*, and so on, and even demonstrate this with manipulatives, a child might ask you why we don't use groups of eight or six instead. What is the answer to that question?

When you start approaching everything you ever learned as an open book that could have been written in any manner but was presented to you in a certain rigid way, you have arrived at the mind of the kindergartener—the completely open mind that has few preconceived notions or judgments to fall back on.

Going back to the example of place value, the student who was asking about making groups of eight was unknowingly touching on the concept of number bases, which are the number of objects we use to make groups. (Our number system is base 10, so we use groups of ten, but number systems can be base 6 or base 8. Computer systems are built on a binary number system, which is really just base 2. So the child, who does not even know the word *base*, was touching on a deep concept in mathematics and a variation in number systems that we use in our culture.) You are an adult who has to understand number bases before teaching counting. A shallow understanding of the mathematical concepts educators teach can keep them from teaching them effectively (Dixon, Nolan, Adams, Brooks, & Howse, 2016). In part 2 (page 139) of the book, I will give more concrete examples of what to master from these disciplines in order to teach effectively.

What would I say to this student? I would say, "You're right! We don't have to count in groups of ten. We can count in groups of four, six, eight, nineteen, or even twenty-seven." I would use manipulatives to demonstrate this. I would then ask if we could count in groups of zero and try to demonstrate that. The students would be engaged and entertained, learning a mathematical concept, but more importantly, learning how to think. I would then tie everything together by saying that it just so happens that we use groups of ten. No need to digress into a historical lesson about that, no need to teach them binary and no need to mention the word *base*. Stay in the kindergarten world and in their minds, as too much information would overload them. The students will probably accept groups of ten as the basis of our number system, but when they learn about number bases in a few years, they will have you to thank for the ease that they incorporate this seemingly new concept.

> **The ability to think for yourself is most important.**

The ability to think for yourself is most important. Having the commitment and ability to implement your discoveries and insights into your classroom are very important parts of being an effective teacher. If you can do that, you can do all the things you need to in a way that benefits you, your students, and your school.

You may now have a better sense of what this book is about. It's about learning to think for yourself as a teacher, so that you can prune all the weeds from your practice and have your teaching bear beautiful fruit. This is the mindset I will discuss in Mindset of an Effective Teacher (page 18) and it is a thread that permeates this book.

HERE WE ARE TOGETHER

Children play and interact with each other based on their common interests, and nothing more. Yes, they get on each other's nerves, compete with each other, imitate each other, grab things from each another, and know how to get under each other's skin. They are not always friends with each other either (more on that later, in chapter 5, page 89). But the basis for this temporary disharmony is attributable to personality differences.

If one likes playing with building blocks and another likes playing with building blocks, they will both play with building blocks, maybe separately at first (in what's called *parallel play*), but then together (Parten, 1932). In the classroom, you will see students from different ethnicities, cultures, and religions who might never have had the opportunity to meet each other outside the classroom become the best and closest buddies you've ever seen.

I have never had to talk to my kindergarteners about accepting a student into the class who is physically challenged; they have just done it. To them, it's like accepting someone with a different eye color. With amazing patience

continued ▶

and focus, children speak with other children who stutter or have speech issues that make it difficult for me to understand them. If someone has a hard time keeping up with some of the routines, there will always be a student or two who, without any prompting from me, take it on themselves to be that student's buddy and watch out for this other student. The most intellectually gifted student and the student who is struggling the most academically will hook up in the block area and speak to each other like budding architects as they collaborate on a design for a new building.

Babies are very keen about making visual differences and use them to categorize their social world, but they don't have negative thoughts about other groups. However, one can say that young children are therefore primed to exhibit prejudice and can do so if exposed to negative stereotypes as early as the age of six, although that is not their natural inclination (Gjersoe, 2018). In all my years of teaching kindergarteners, I have never seen or heard anything racist, sexist, or otherwise prejudicial based on physical, academic, socioeconomic, ethnic, or cultural differences between one student and another. Students occasionally point out differences between themselves and others, noting differences in skin color, height, gender, and dress, but this is observational and not done in a judgmental fashion. As a rule, in my experience, children just accept each other as they are, as simple and as beautiful as that is.

What happens after students leave kindergarten, I haven't yet figured out! As Rodgers and Hammerstein wrote in *South Pacific* (Adler & Logan, 1958), "You've got to be taught to hate and fear." That culture later shapes and sharpens differences. Representatives from every culture should come to the kindergarten classroom to see how the smallest of children can model the world the way it could be.

Mindset of an Effective Teacher

There are various ways teachers approach their duties and various expectations administrations have. On the ineffective side of the spectrum is the teacher as clerk, taking the curriculum and implementing it. In other words, some educators do only as they are told, no questions asked. Education professor Bill Ayers (2009) sees this, lamenting that teachers often find themselves "locked in situations that reduce teaching to a kind of glorified clerking, passing along a curriculum of received wisdom, predigested and often false bits of information." You can't be an effective teacher if you have a clerk mentality, just doing the job without understanding the importance of being a thinking teacher. Thinking critically, for yourself, is crucial to your effectiveness as a teacher. Chapter 2 (page 25) has information about how to think critically about what you're asked to teach.

Clerking is not the option most teachers want. However, it is a mindset that many new teachers adopt when they feel pulled between the demands of administration, parents, and their own views about teaching. A clerking attitude can also be prevalent among many tenured and veteran teachers. It is not where you are on your career path that determines mindset, but a conscious choice about how you are going to approach your profession. Just as you are never to give your students busywork, under no circumstances are you to engage in it yourself.

Teachers whom professor Dorothy Suskind (2016) might describe as *researchers* or *scientists* approach it this way: they are charged with goals—we call them *standards*—and constantly experiment with creative ways to reach those goals. They do so while learning a lot about the nuances in the curriculum, how students learn, and the best teaching practices. Nothing can substitute for experience and experimentation, but having a cooperative learning group, visiting other classrooms, having a mentor teacher, scouring the web for information, and reading books like this one will give you a leg up in this process.

The reproducible "Skills for the Effective Teacher" (page 23) is something you can use to record what works and what doesn't. The reproducible also offers some of the skills to focus on, which follow.

Teaching can be a very confusing profession. The curriculum that was last year's canon is replaced by new curriculum, which contradicts many of the practices of the old one. Teachers often get conflicting input from colleagues and administrators. "You need to have learning centers in your room," says one administrator. "The last thing you want in your room is learning centers," says a staff developer. "You have to teach lowercase letters in this order," says the grade leader. "Never teach the lowercase letters in that order," says a senior teacher.

Teaching is as much about what you *don't use* as it is about what you do use in your practice. To be a thinking teacher, you may need to subtract as much as you add. If something is working, stay with it. On the other hand, the only way to know what works best is to try things. Often, you will almost get to a point where you see results from a technique you have worked on for a long time when a new one is presented. Don't drop the technique you've invested in to adopt the new method. Work through your current method before jumping overboard. Set high standards by making a list of

> **Teaching is as much about what you *don't use* as it is about what you do use in your practice.**

outcomes you want realized. If your techniques are hitting those points, evaluate the new method and make an informed judgment as to how to go forward. You may not need the new method.

Teachers sometimes get supplies and teaching materials thrown at them. I know that the lack of supplies is a major issue in many school systems, so supplies are a good thing, in general. I am talking about when an administrator finds furniture and teaching materials and dumps them at your doorstep with the expectation that they are appropriate for use in your classroom. You needn't rearrange your classroom or put out the materials the next day unless you are confident that they will result in a positive outcome for the class.

If you get new materials, ask yourself to which curriculum area would they be most appropriate. Do you have better materials that perform the same function? Do the materials fit in with your curriculum and methodology? Try out the materials with your child brain and see if they work for you. Set out the materials on one table to have students play with, and then observe them. You will get a good idea whether to integrate them into your classroom, and if you do not integrate them, you will be able to express cogently why you did not.

You are the gatekeeper of your class, the filter through which only the best ideas, resources, and practices come through. That gatekeeping makes you a thinking teacher. I am not saying that you should automatically reject suggestions or new initiatives. On the contrary, you should definitely look into them and try them out. That is what I spend a lot of my time doing—reading through, trying out, and experimenting with new techniques and resources. It's not about how many resources you have. It's about having resources that work. A teacher is a collector, not a hoarder.

When I was teaching at one school, I realized that the literacy curriculum we were supposed to use would not get students where they needed to be. It was scripted and not very student friendly. I chopped it up a bit, moved some things around, added others, and made it workable for the classroom. I used books of my own choosing, games, computers, and assessments. When administration looked at achievement data, my class was high functioning on all of the assessments. Plus, parents were complimentary about my class and some incoming parents requested that their children be in my class the upcoming year.

Just about every year, the school mission changed, administration changed, the curriculum changed, the content focus changed, the teaching methodology changed, the assessments changed, the evaluative criteria changed, and most importantly, a big part of the teaching staff changed. I just kept chugging along, using what worked and reading through each new curriculum for cutting, pruning, and adding to what I had established, so that it was my own. I took comfort in seeing that what was "radical" on my part the year before was considered a best practice by the next curriculum. My class had a foundation of a clear educational framework, a class setup that fostered positive behavior, practical teaching techniques, and continuity.

In a Nutshell

If you approach your job with a positive attitude, realize that you will be the prime interpreter of the world for each and every student while they are in your classroom, harness your keen power of observing children, become determined to think for yourself, solve your own classroom issues, take accountability for your students, be unafraid to experiment with new techniques, and see yourself as the consummate professional that you really are, then you have all the ingredients it takes to be a successful and effective teacher.

Have You Mastered the Chapter?

Welcome to the formal assessment section of the book—a quiz to test your knowledge of the chapter. You may not proceed to the next chapter unless you have answered all questions correctly. (Just kidding.) Please try the questions. The answers are provided after the questions section for a quick check. I explain the *why* after the quiz, and that is the most important part to consider.

According to this chapter:

1. Teaching starts in the:
    a. Lesson plan
    b. Classroom
    c. Mind
    d. Teacher's lounge

2. An effective teacher resembles:
    a. A gatekeeper
    b. A bus driver
    c. A scientist
    d. All of the above

3. MLE stands for:
   a. Mandated lesson exemplars
   b. Mathematics literacy excellence
   c. Mediated learning experience
   d. More learning examples

4. As a teacher, you should see yourself as:
   a. A clerk
   b. Underpaid
   c. A researcher and scientist
   d. Overworked

Answers and Explanations

1. **c. (Mind)** Planning for lessons and classroom setup is extremely important, but it is the mindset and philosophy behind all you are doing that is the foundation of your craft.

2. **d. (All of the above)** Teachers are much more that any analogy can describe, but the chapter gives the three mentioned in the question to show how they research new ideas, are able to relate to children on their terms, and have the ability to engage all students in their lessons.

3. **c. (Mediated learning experience)** This is the technique teachers use to guide students through the world they are discovering, helping them interpret it and challenging them to think about it for themselves.

4. **c. (A researcher and scientist)** I can't say that many teachers don't feel like underpaid, overworked clerks, but this book is about changing that mentality to empower you with the means to approach your profession as a thinker who knows how to maximize students' potentials while streamlining your workload. I personally think you deserve a raise for that!

Skills for the Effective Teacher

The first column offers some skills to work on in your professional development as a thinking teacher. Record instances you have used each skill successfully and strategies that help you. Skill development is an ongoing process, so keep this chart handy for easy reference and add to it as you continue to grow as a thinking teacher.

Skill	Successes	Strategies
Observation: Heightened senses, especially the ability to listen		
Streamlining: Dealing efficiently with teacher paperwork		
Curriculum: Mastering the curriculum with a focus on the standards		
Gatekeeper: Determining which proposed practices are efficient and effective		
Experimenter: Constantly trying out and evaluating new technique		

CHAPTER 2

Working With Administration and Making Curriculum Work for You

At this point, you might be reflecting on the introduction and chapter 1 and thinking, "I have heard all this before, and I would love to approach teaching in that manner, but there are a few problems. I'm not sure if it's permissible to do this on my own. I have a principal, and she is the boss! Also, I have a curriculum to follow."

This book is not about teacher rights versus administrator rights. It is about looking at your current situation and working to become a great teacher in the classroom—and ensuring your administrator is happy with your performance. This is a tall order, indeed. First, you need to have the right attitude when working with administration. Then, you will understand what it means to *stick it to the curriculum* versus *sticking blindly to the curriculum*. Regardless of what your curriculum looks like, you have four ways ([1] demonstration, [2] example, [3] guided practice, and [4] inquiry) to teach something. This chapter explains these ways and the concepts connected to them so that you can tailor your current curriculum to best fit your class's learning needs.

Working With Administration

The ideal administrator takes time to get to know you, your educational background, and your educational philosophy. He or she learns about the unique challenges each student or parent or guardian brings to your class and is a sounding board and advisor regarding your ongoing questions. This ideal administrator frequently visits your classroom to spend time with you and your students.

But this administrator is the ideal, not always the reality. No matter. Just as your attitude toward yourself is crucial to being an effective teacher, so is your attitude toward your supervisor—regardless of what your administrator's leadership style is. Your attitude should be a positive one. I will explain.

Plenty of administrators have their hearts in the right place. Many principals have concrete teaching experience and have told me that they will always be a teacher at heart. I believe them. But administrators' jobs entail paperwork, evaluations, and supervisory duties. They are often overwhelmed and overworked. Coupled with this, administrators are under the thumb of their own supervisor or superintendent and many have adopted the attitude that teachers have with their principals—don't question the rules, follow them by rote, job security first! These administrators are fearful of breaking the chain, and they simply don't have the time to stay connected to what it meant to them to be teachers. People can't teach out of fear. You can't administrate out of fear—but many do.

The administrator is the big teacher of the school, and responsible for the staff's progress and ultimately for the students' progress. Depending on the size of the school, it can be a very big class of teachers. This awesome responsibility is but one of the administrator's many important duties.

The bottom line is that the administrator's goal, your progress, and the administrator's ultimate goal—the students' progress—are perfectly aligned to yours. This is something that you should always keep in mind. If your class is thriving, and parents are happy, your administrator will be satisfied. You accomplish this by being a thinking teacher. As counterintuitive as it seems, you will end up pleasing administration more if you please yourself as well. You have a lot more leeway in the classroom that you probably think you have.

More likely than not, you will not see your administrator in your room more than three or four times per year. You are on your own the rest of the time. What an administrator wants is a competent teacher in the classroom, pupils who are engaged, learning, and excelling, parents who are happy, and things done according to sound educational principles. If this is what you are doing, the administrator will be in for a quick check and then off putting out the many fires that come up during the day.

The first step is to take sole responsibility for the teaching practices in your classroom. This can be terrifying or empowering. Feel the former but embrace the latter. Remember, principals ultimately understand that following the *principles* of good teaching form the pathway to the school's success.

Thinking for yourself and being persistent will result in you making plans, implementing them, and experimenting for improvement. All of this will give a sense of value to what you are doing. You are likely to be immersed and committed to what you are doing and reap the benefits of feeling ownership and empowerment (Ryan & Deci, 2000). Consequently, a thinking teacher is also highly motivated, hardworking, conscientious, productive, happy, and, most of all, effective. A thinking teacher is an employee any administrator would be happy with.

> **Principals ultimately understand that following the *principles* of good teaching form the pathway to the school's success.**

Sticking to the Curriculum or Stick (It) to the Curriculum

There can be the misconception that teaching is all about following the curriculum. Many teachers, especially new ones, feel they need to follow it like a script. This may work at first, but it ultimately keeps teachers from thinking for themselves and catering best to the needs of their students.

But what is a teacher without the prescribed curriculum? What is the problem with just following it? After all, whole committees of experts worked on the curriculum together and the school spent a lot of money on it! The problem is the curriculum is often written by people who have never been in your classroom, and, as educators Douglas J. Simpson and Michael J. B. Jackson (2003) suggest, trading teacher-driven judgment for prescriptive guidance from those who don't know your classroom can undermine student learning:

> Advantaged and influential individuals and groups unconsciously surrender the individuality, aspirations, and humanity of the child to privileged interests and voices, and in so doing, they unwittingly give or take away the professional roles and responsibilities of educators. That is, educators are frequently stripped of the freedom to think for themselves, to make professional judgments, and to teach in ways that they consider are in the best interest of children and youth, because we wish to prescribe precisely when students learn which specific skills and information. (p. 23)

It is obviously a very important endeavor in the educational field to research and write out lessons for teachers to use when teaching a subject. But there is too much focus on the curriculum being the magic pill that makes students learn. I agree with educational reformer John Dewey (1902, as cited in Simpson & Jackson, 2003):

> Learning needs to be seen as a dynamic, reconstructive, complex, and personal process that cannot be legitimately and thoughtfully legislated by governments, prescribed by policy makers, insisted upon by administrators, demanded by parents, stipulated by curriculum committees, or even required by teachers. (p. 27)

I have sat through many seminars in which the presenter (salesperson) taught us about a new curriculum. Often, the new research-tested curriculum had an opposite methodology to the prior one. Yet all the curricula were developed by an eminent panel of experts, all were research tested or brain based, and all had numerous charts showing the superiority of this method over any other ever developed. Teachers would implement all the practices of the new curriculum, and after the initial euphoria of something new and different to do, the new curriculum would fail as well.

And on and on it went, curriculum after curriculum.

No packaged curriculum will work as is for your classroom. It is better to take any packaged curriculum and adapt it to your classroom than to keep switching from one curriculum to another. The reason lies in the word *packaged*. Given social, economic, ethnic, and geographic diversity, not to mention the variety of school settings and teacher experience levels, it is folly to think that a one-size-fits-all curriculum could ever work. As researchers point out, "Districts, schools, and teachers need the latitude to make professional judgments and to adjust studies for each student if she or he is to learn a great deal of the adult mind in an agreeable and effective manner" (Simpson & Jackson, 2003, p. 27). Other researchers back this autonomy and effectiveness (Weber, Johnson, & Tripp, 2013).

It is better to take any packaged curriculum and adapt it to your classroom than to keep switching from one curriculum to another.

"But it's research tested," you say. Unless you are willing to read through the actual research methodology and findings of each curriculum (any takers?), I wouldn't trust it.

In her book *Language Development and Learning to Read: The Scientific Study of How Language Development Affects Reading Skill*, cognitive psychologist Diane McGuinness (2005) makes a good case for why one should be dubious of any educational research study that claims to have the answers for what to include in the curriculum:

Of the 1,072 studies carried out over the past 30 years on methods of reading instruction, only 75 studies met a preliminary screening consisting of these criteria: publication in a refereed journal, comparison of at least two methods, random selection of subjects into comparison groups, and statistical analysis sufficient to compute effect sizes. On further scrutiny, only 38 studies were found to be methodologically sound. (p. viii)

"But the curriculum is based on the standards," you say. Well, yes, but it is a recommended pathway to the standards, which are, obviously, the concepts and skills students need to know and be able to do by the end of the year. And what should you do if the curriculum is not getting you to the standards? You don't have to ditch the whole curriculum and start over. Just find a detour that gets you to your destination. The following sections can help you get started as I explain my path through the curriculum, the 55/40/5 rule, and the three-year rule.

My Path Through the Curriculum

When I get a new prescribed curriculum, I spend a lot of time reading through it. The whole thing—cover to cover. So, if I have the same curriculum for seven years, I have read it in its entirety once. I will refer to it during the year a lot and will skim it from time to time, especially as preparation before the school year starts, but the major work is done after my initial read. I do this so, at the beginning of the year, I know what the student should be able to achieve academically on the last day of school.

They say that Michelangelo would look at a piece of marble and be able to see the finished image of a sculpture within (Parker, 2013). His main work was done. All that was left was the labor of chipping away at the stone to reveal the image. It is said of filmmaker Alfred Hitchcock that he saw the whole movie in his mind before filming it (as cited in Bouzereau, 2000). While these artists seem to have been born with this gift, a teacher achieves it through the hard work of learning the curriculum and matching it to their everyday real-world experiences. The goal is to know before they even enter the class what the average student will be able to achieve on the last day of school.

I spend a lot of time thinking about this when I read through the curriculum. "What should the students know if I asked them? What skills should they have? What preassessments must I do, and what should I do with the information I get from them?" This is crucial, as it sets my course for the whole year. I work down from the big picture, in a way not dissimilar from Grant Wiggins and Jay McTighe's (2011) backward design.

Reading Methodically

Read through the whole curriculum before teaching the first lesson. Don't jump right into the lessons after doing so, either. Read the curriculum like it is a textbook. Spend a lot of time reading about the standards you will be teaching, the rationale behind the curriculum, and the methods it is using to teach the concepts. When you are done, you will have a good overview as to what it expects from you and the roadmap it is presenting to the standards. This is especially important if you are a new teacher.

Now it's time to do a few sample lessons. You will be using your adult brain and your child brain. As you read through each lesson, understand the concepts and the big picture with your adult brain and then teach it using the prescribed sequence to your child brain. If you are a new teacher, you might need to do a role-play session. This is not the same as practicing your lesson. You can do that with a friend or a colleague. It is thinking through your lesson, so you need to do that by yourself. If you are a more seasoned teacher, you might be able to skip the physical role play and do everything in your mind.

Ask yourself these questions of your child brain: "Am I engaged? What am I understanding? What questions do I have? Does my child brain's understanding match any of the standards the lesson is covering?" If so, check it off. If not, and if your adult brain was unable to adequately answer any of the questions your child brain asked, then you have revisions to do.

As you become more experienced, you will not only role play each lesson to your child brain of the general student, but to the other child brains you have been accumulating as well. Having different child brains is what differentiation is all about. Over time, through activities and keen observation, you will be able to anticipate the needs of advanced students, struggling students, English learners, and any other differentiation adaptations you might encounter. Ask yourself the same questions as with the general student and make additions and adjustments until you feel that your lesson will be appropriate to all of these learners. You may need to change the lesson to provide more background information, you may need to add more visuals, you may need to simplify an activity, or you may need to change the order of the lesson. Find out what additional resources, manipulatives, or activities you might need. You are figuring out what you need to do to reach the goal of the lesson itself—mastery of the standards.

After sampling a few lessons, you will have a good idea as to what general adjustments you will need to make throughout the year. By this time, you should also be developing the picture of what skills and concepts your child brain will be filled with by the end of the year. When the actual brains of the students at the end of the year match the child brain you have developed at the beginning of the year, you have become an effective teacher. Your curriculum and the consistent adjustments you make to it is the bridge between the year's bookends. When it comes time to teach a specific lesson during the year, you will go through that same process but with the added knowledge of your students, knowing what concepts they have mastered, and knowing what concepts they need to work on.

How or whether you document all of this is up to you. Although I have provided a lot of useful reproducibles in this book, they are but starting points and suggestions for your review and are subordinate to the individualized and efficient way you will be approaching your craft. In terms of your career arc, you will probably have to physically document, either by taking notes and marking up texts or taking a quick picture of pages, when you are starting out. As you progress and become more familiar with the standards, and have experimented with the various activities contained in curricula, you will find that it takes less and less time to read through a new curriculum and less of a need for physical documentation. At some point, it can all be stored in the noggin.

Tailoring

When I am done reading through the curriculum, I am ready to tailor it to my teaching style and to the students who are in my class that year—to their abilities and learning styles. This approach is a work in progress and never ends, although I get better at it every year. I add or subtract to the curriculum as needed. I may spend a lot of time supplementing a curriculum with resources it is lacking or subtracting lessons or methods that don't work or are unnecessary.

Occasionally, I can follow the lessons as they are. Sometimes I have to develop more of the curriculum on my own—whatever it takes. Thinking through a curriculum is very hard. But once you have done this, everything else is easy. Blindly following a curriculum is very easy at first, but it makes the rest of your teaching life very hard. A very scripted curriculum is one that I would adapt so I could communicate with students more flexibly. Those curricula that do not differentiate based on the specific academic, cultural, linguistic, or learning styles of students in my class need my personalization. Sometimes curricula lack engaging videos, books, or manipulatives that I can easily access.

When the prescribed curriculum inevitably fails on a school level and the next one is introduced, I say to it, "Nice to meet you, new curriculum; please meet the old curriculum. I am going to make sure that you are friends."

I go through the same process again, by reading the new curriculum cover to cover, but I don't ditch the old curriculum. I take the best of the old curriculum and mix it with what I think is the best of the new one and develop a mental plan for the new year. A note to new teachers: of course, I didn't start out this way. I was terrified to veer off of the curriculum even a tad. It is also hard to make alterations to a piece of clothing you have never worn. I recommend than you read through the whole curriculum as recommended and go through the process as outlined. Your child brain may not be as developed as it will be later in your career, but you can still have a starting point for implementing this methodology. In a later section (page 34), I explain why I think it takes at least three years for a teacher to develop competence in each grade level. You still have a ways to go, but are starting on the right path.

HOW TO SPEND YOUR TIME

How should you spend your time?

- Thinking about and understanding your curriculum (in the ways I describe in this chapter)
- Thinking about and understanding how to teach the curriculum to your students
- Thinking about and understanding your students

I know that many teachers realize how important it is to think about the curriculum, but they truly don't get to engage in this thinking because of the time constraints involved in the teaching profession, many of which (like attending grade meetings, writing up lesson plans, creating assessments, attending professional development workshops, documenting conferences, and recording goals and evaluations) are actually meant to encourage and enhance teacher thinking—that's the greatest irony of all!

If you let the paperwork of teaching sweep you away in a tornado of meaningless work, you will never see the beautiful clear sky that should be your teaching mind. So again, whenever you are asked to do something as a teacher, ask yourself, "Is this going to help me make my room run better, enhance my lessons, or make me teach more effectively?" If the answer is *no* and it is not a requirement, don't do it. If it's possible to make it a low priority, then do so. If it's mandated, then streamlining and efficiency are the key. I go into this in more detail in chapter 7 (page 123), where I discuss lesson plans, room charts, and other items sometimes deemed to be nonnegotiable.

> As a teacher, do what the environmentalists advise: "Think globally but act locally" (Darier & Schüle, 1999). Your world is your classroom; make it a better place to live in. If you keep this in mind and build a classroom that works, you will find out that you were doing exactly what you should have been doing in the first place, although it may not have felt that way at times. In the end, your class will be in accordance with the grandest educational principles all along, your students will be learning to their potential, your parents will be happy, administration will be happy, and you will be a happy and effective teacher.

The 55/40/5 Rule

The paper *Teaching Reading Is Rocket Science* (Moats, 2020) states the following:

> Scientists now estimate that fully 95 percent of all children can be taught to read. Yet, in spite of all our knowledge, statistics reveal an alarming prevalence of struggling and poor readers that is not limited to any one segment of society. About 20 percent of elementary students nationwide have significant problems learning to read. At least 20 percent of elementary students do not read fluently enough to enjoy or engage in Independent Reading.

I took what I learned from this article and applied it to what I was seeing in the classroom and came up with my own 55/40/5 rule of teaching. I am of the opinion that 55 percent of students will learn to read with just about any curriculum. If you present the class with the materials they need to read, these students will pick it up.

Forty percent will not be effective readers unless you do all the super techniques—such as very targeted small-group instruction, focused blended learning, adding extensive visual aids and manipulatives, to name a few—that you are trained and expected to do, and 5 percent of the students will not become good readers no matter what you do, or, stated more properly, these students need special individualized interventions, remediation, and specially designed curricula.

The curriculum developers will insist that their curriculum caters to 100 percent of your students, or that it has accommodations for all learners, but I find that most prescribed curricula are targeted to the 40 percent, whether intentionally or not. So, your curriculum is targeted to a small percentage of your students. Even then, it doesn't mean that it will necessarily work for them.

You don't get a free ride with the 55 percent majority. They will need all your skills, but there will be many things in the curriculum that they will not need. The 5 percent need everything in the curriculum and then some, and you must develop this and might need to seek out intervention specialists based on what is available in your school community. Many schools use response to intervention (RTI), which is a multitiered approach to teaching core instruction and identifying struggling students and providing them with targeted support (Buffum, Mattos, & Malone, 2018). Keep that in mind when reading your prescribed curriculum and remember—you are the curriculum.

The Three-Year Rule

I sometimes think of the prescribed curriculum as *The Cider House Rules* (Irving, 1985). The migrant workers on a farm had a list of rules that were written on the side of the barn that told them how they should do everything. They were written long ago by the managers of the farm who were not there anymore and never had to do the work themselves. No one asked the workers if they agreed with the rules, or if they were effective. No one ever updated the rules. The managers were never out in the fields with the workers. The message was that it was OK to tweak the rules and make them work for you—as long as you didn't break the *principles* the rules were based on. This is what the workers did. The rules are guideposts to the goals and principles. If they don't lead you there, you need to alter them so that they guide you to the end result.

Tailoring the curriculum to your students' needs does not happen overnight. It takes about three years for the thinking teacher to figure this out. It also takes about three years to perfect your management skills, your room setup, your supplies—just about everything. That goes for every new grade that you teach. Each grade is a whole new world—a whole new planet. You are effective from the first day of the first year that you step into the classroom, but there is no way around the learning curve. You can accelerate your development through the techniques taught in this book, being part of a collaborative team, having a mentor, continued professional development, and guidance from administration. That doesn't mean that after three years you are coasting. It means that the major part of the learning curve is done, but the learning curve never ends.

It is important for teachers to know this, but it is even more important for administrators to know it, since they are prone to move teachers around from grade to grade, year after year, for the *good of the school*. With few exceptions, and unless the teacher wants a switch, teachers should be given three years to develop. Why constantly transplant seeds when, left to flourish, they can grow into a field of sturdy oaks?

Trying Four Ways to Teach Something

A curriculum gives you various ways to present content. There are basically four different ways.

1. You **demonstrate** something for someone (Schaal, n.d.).
2. You give someone an **example** (Alford & Griffin, 2019; Bandura, 2004).
3. You practice doing something with someone; this is **guided practice** (Herrmann, 2014).
4. You help someone figure out something for themselves using **inquiry** (Sparks, 2019; Suchman, 1965).

Each of these four ways is an equally valid form of teaching. Together, they represent the gradual release of responsibility model, which suggests these steps as a collective and refers to them *I do it, we do it, you do it together, you do it alone* (Pearson & Gallagher, 1983). See the reproducible "Four Ways to Teach a Skill" (page 38) for guidance on thinking about what skills to teach and how to teach them.

Although a curriculum usually dictates one of these methods for a particular lesson, that doesn't mean that any or all of the other three won't work better, or that you can't use them in combination. So, why not start by following the curriculum's method? If it works, great! If not, don't hit your head against the wall. Try one of the other three ways, try the one that the curriculum was recommending in a slightly different way, or try a combination.

Over time, you will understand which method works best for which lesson and for which student. Now you have used the curriculum as you should. To teach students how to tie their shoelaces, you could let them watch you do it, you can give them examples of the various ways other people do it, you can tie their shoelaces with them and keep practicing with them until they can do it on their own, or you can help them figure out the best way to do it, or any combination thereof.

A method or combination of methods may work for one person but not another. The teacher's essential job is to look at the class and the individual students and figure out which methods will work best and most efficiently. A teacher learns to teach effectively through a combination of experience, trial and error, educated guesses, and intuition. The curriculum is an attempt to figure out for you what *you* must figure out for yourself. It can be very helpful, but the curriculum is not in the classroom. It's as if the curriculum is telling you to teach a student how to tie his or her shoelaces by using *examples* and you have already discovered that it's better to teach it by *practice*. That is why you should not look at the curriculum as a script, but as a guideline.

> **The curriculum is an attempt to figure out for you what *you* must figure out for yourself.**

In a Nutshell

When it comes to your administrator, try to understand where he or she is coming from in terms of new directives, paperwork, and evaluating your classroom. That's the administrator's job. Embrace the supervision but don't assume that it should hinder your role as a researcher and scientist. Both you and your administrator are ultimately after the same goal—creating the best learning environment for students. When it comes to curriculum, do the hard work of developing your own curriculum through an adaptation of your prescribed one. Following an adapted curriculum is still following the curriculum—a pruned rose is still a rose! You will be catering to the specific needs of your teaching situation and personalizing for your students. Isn't that why you have a curriculum in the first place? No prescribed curriculum followed as a script will yield those results. Always think for yourself.

Have You Mastered the Chapter?

Welcome to the formal assessment section of the book—a quiz to test your knowledge of the chapter. Please try the questions. The answers are provided after the questions section for a quick check. I explain the *why* after the quiz, and that is the most important part to consider.

According to this chapter:

1. Don't teach:
   a. Defensively
   b. Social studies
   c. Actively
   d. Middle schoolers

2. Your best teacher is:
   a. Your parent
   b. Your principal
   c. This book
   d. Yourself

3. Your curriculum is:

   a. Your script
   b. Your starting point
   c. Your bible
   d. Your enemy

Answers and Explanations

1. **a. (Defensively)** I know many charming middle schoolers, and social studies is one of my favorite subjects. I also learned how to drive defensively, which is a good thing. However, when it comes to teaching it's all about engagement—yours to the students and the students' to the curriculum.

2. **d. (Yourself)** Parents are a child's first and potentially best teacher. Your principal should be your guiding light. You know that my ultimate wish for this book is that you will tear it up at some point. That leaves you. No one knows you better, and you have to be the one most responsible for learning how to be an effective teacher.

3. **b. (Your starting point)** Scripted curricula sometimes work at the very beginning of your career, but like training wheels, they are a crutch worth removing as soon as possible. Curricula should be your best friend and can be as valuable to you as a bible if you use them as starting points on a pathway for how best to teach standards.

Four Ways to Teach a Skill

When teaching a new skill to students, use this sheet to help you think of additional approaches to supplement what your curriculum prescribes.

Skill to be taught: _____

1. What are two different ways you can model the skill for students?

    a.

    b.

2. What are two different examples of the skill you can provide for students?

    a.

    b.

3. Develop a sequence that would be effective for students to practice the skill.

4. What open-ended questions can you ask that prompt students to think of ways they can acquire a skill?

    a.

    b.

    c.

Kindergarten From A to Z © 2021 Solution Tree Press • SolutionTree.com
Visit go.SolutionTree.com/instruction to download this free reproducible.

CHAPTER 3

Preparing Your Classroom and Yourself

I can't tell you how to design your room, because I don't know your school or what resources you have. I don't know your students or your goals. But you do. I can't provide a communication cheat sheet that makes communicating with your students more effective. However, if you keep in mind all the guidelines outlined in this chapter, you will be totally prepared for that first day and able to use it as a springboard to a great year of learning.

Getting Ready for the First Day of School

After getting a good handle on your curriculum, consider this checklist of what to do prior to your first day in class.

- Know your curriculum (which I discuss in chapter 2, page 25).
- Make sure your room is ready.
- Memorize your students' names.
- Get parents' and guardians' contact information.

After reading through the following sections, the reproducible "Preparing for the First Day of School" (page 50) is a checklist to help you make sure things are in order.

Know Your Curriculum

You do this by going through your curricula as described in chapter 2 (page 25) You don't need to know what you will do every day in each subject. You can't—but knowing your curriculum makes you mentally ready and confident that you are prepared from now through June. You need to have your vision of what your students will look like on the last day of school. You don't need lesson plans (unless they are mandated), but you have to have a master plan in your mind or on paper, in simple form, for what you will do in each subject for the year.

For the actual first day, you need goals and activities. As on any day, always plan more activities than you can ever get to. I usually start with an extended play period, then do a read-aloud or two, show a few videos, do a writing activity, set out some mathematics manipulatives for students to explore, and do another play period.

Make Sure Your Room Is Ready

Your room is your best co-teacher. And your co-teacher must be ready for the big day. It has been said that we are creatures of the places we are in. Professor Andréa de Paiva (2018) asserts:

> Architects have always known the power of their buildings and how they can impact their users. The equation created by the psychologist Kurt Lewin (1890–1947) illustrates the role of the environment on an individual's behavior: $B = f(P, E)$, which means behavior is a function between the Person (a unique individual with his own memories and genetics) and the Environment. By Environment he means not only the social environment, but the physical environment too. Thus, behavior is also influenced by architecture. And this relation between environment and individual happens not only in a cognitive way, but also in an emotional or even instinctive way. (p. 133)

People act and react differently based on the environments they are in and how these environments communicate to them:

> Medieval churches, with their long plans, high ceilings, and stained-glass windows at the top of the walls showed, through architecture, how great divine power can be. The impact of such message to individuals invoked respect and emotion. The classic CEO's room, located on the top floor of the company's building and decorated with marble and wood also shows power and invokes different behaviors on both, the owner of the room and the people who will visit him there. (de Paiva, 2018, p. 134)

> **Your room is your best co-teacher.**

In the planning stages of buildings, malls, airports, and atria, designers apply principles from the fields of architecture, neuroscience, and psychology in order to convey to people the significance and reason for the structure and provide direct and sometimes hidden cues for how they should behave therein. This discipline is called *neuroarchitecture* (de Paiva, 2018). I call it *feng shui for the classroom*.

You can apply these principles when you set up your classroom. It is not about picking a theme or color-coordinating with primary colors and fuzzy tones. These can be components of your design, but they are not the essential parts of it. Classroom design goes much deeper than this. You must design a classroom that can accommodate all the routines and procedures that students attend to throughout a day. The design should allow students to flow easily from area to area and provide the best environment for each subject taught.

I spend a lot of time on classroom design. In every school I've taught in, the first thing I did was redesign my classroom. I would sit in the middle of the room and stare around it. I would measure spaces with my footsteps. I would move the furniture around. I didn't care what I had to throw out or what I had to acquire. I offered furniture to other teachers or left stuff by the door for the custodians. If I wasn't supposed to throw something out, I would sneak it to the basement or leave it in some unoccupied area. If it didn't belong in the room, it wasn't going to be there.

It sometimes took me years to perfect my room. I would find that shelf that I should have used in the first place or see a space that could be used differently. You can get your room to where you want it to be, but don't stop until you do. As you design, consider efficiency (what I refer to as the *five-second rule*) and space (especially where tables are concerned). Even if you do get it to where you want it to be, it will always be a work in progress, like your teaching.

Efficiency: Using the Five-Second Rule

You should have your room set up so that you can access anything you might need or easily direct a student to an item within five seconds of when that student asks you for it. Anything from class materials, tissues, special paper, books, bandages, rubber bands—anything and everything! Your room is not for accumulating materials. It is like a store. After the business day, items are restocked, and everything is set up so it looks just like the day before, ready for business.

The reason your room should be set up this way is because, in my experience, five seconds is the amount of time a student will give you before he or she walks away empty-handed and unattended to. This is the amount of time it takes for another student to come up and ask you for assistance with something else. Patience is usually a virtue, but not in this case.

I am not saying that your day consists of catering to every student's needs at every second. Quite the opposite—the goal is to foster independence. But while you are fostering it, kindergarteners are still dependent on you for many things, so you must follow the five-second rule at all times to ensure good class management.

Space: Considering Tables

I have never had a teacher's desk in any of my classrooms. In fact, that was often the first thing to go. The students need the space to function and to learn—not me. The room is my desk. All the books, documents, paperwork, and office supplies are spread out in the room, and I apply the five-second rule to those items too.

> **PSYCHO ROOM**
>
> Once I had to redesign a room very quickly—but it was worth it!
>
> In preparation for my job as head teacher at an early learning center, I visited the room to observe. I discovered that it was so poorly designed the preschoolers would literally run into one another and constantly fall down going from area to area. There was a lot of chaos but no control. It seems that when the former head teacher left, the way the assistant teacher managed the classroom was by sitting at a huge desk and barking at the students.
>
> I spent the first day taking this all in and figuring out, after talking to the assistant teacher, that she intended to continue in this manner. My job was to help her out. I guess that I was to be the assistant barker. A few days passed like this. Then she told me that she was taking off for a few days.
>
> That evening, I spent a few hours redesigning the entire room. I already had all the ideas in my head from observing. I won't tell you what I did with her desk. The next day, the room was a different place. I had not yet even implemented my management techniques yet, but I didn't need to. The students were settled and playing cooperatively with each other. The room itself was doing most of my job on its own!
>
> The assistant teacher returned a few days later, took one look at the room, and shouted, "This is a psycho room!" I thought, "Oh, you mean it is a room design that is psychologically appropriate to the students' needs as seen by the sudden change in their behavior? Why thank you!"
>
> The teacher didn't last long. Later, I had a wonderful assistant teacher who really helped me and whom I groomed to be a head teacher.

The tables in my room are totally bare. There are no charts taped or glued to the tabletops. Year after year, I see beautiful tables with alphabet and number charts, painstakingly prepared by the teachers, picked at and then destroyed by little fingers gnawing at them day after day. Students need space, and there is too little space on the tables per student as it is. Any chart a student needs is clearly visible on the walls of the classroom. Any chart a student may need that was on the table itself would be under a paper or folder anyway. When they do an activity, they bring all the materials to the tables themselves and put them back the same way. Then the tables are bare again until the next activity.

Memorize Your Students' Names

It is very important to memorize each name—first and last—before you even meet students. They need to feel like you know them, even if you don't yet.

Introductions

On the first day of school, when I see a parent or guardian who has a child in my class, I walk up, introduce myself, and ask the child for his or her name. After the child tells me his or her first name—for instance, "My name is Emily"—I smile with recognition and add the last name: "Oh, you are Emily Bedir. Nice to meet you!" Both parent and child look pleasantly surprised, but more importantly, they look more comfortable. Little do they realize that this small bit of teacher magic was based on my memorizing my class list a few days before so I could recite a student's last name on hearing the first name (and vice versa).

Since I know each student's name already, I spend the day matching the name to the student's face. I am not good with placing names with faces at all, so this is a real mental exercise for me every year. I make name tags for each student and after each tells me his or her name, I put the name tag on the student and take the student's picture. Once I have taken all of the pictures, I scroll through the pictures and match the name on the tag with the face on my camera and the actual face in the classroom. I then keep repeating their names to myself while engaging many students in conversation while constantly referring to them by their names. Once I feel that I have mastered a student's name, I take off the name tag. Usually I have it down by the end of the first day of school, although I sometimes repeat the process the next day. Learning the parents' names and matching them to their children is another story. That takes me a little longer but is not as important as knowing my students' names.

Wordplay With Student Names

Later in the year, you will have ended up calling each student's name hundreds, if not thousands, of times. Eventually you, and your students, need some variation. Some teachers do refer to their students as *honey*, *sweetie*, *sugar*, *baby*, and other terms of endearment. This is fine in the parent-child relationship but not in the teacher-student one. It's generic, one-size-fits-all, and sometimes demeaning in a veiled way (Toor, 2016). No child this age wants to be called *baby* in school, no matter what the intention is.

However, I do think using multiple ways of referring to a student adds spice to the classroom, can raise self-esteem, keeps them on their toes mentally, and can be a great teaching tool. At least that has been my experience. I end up having at least five or six names for each student by year's end—but not by design; it just turns out that way. The names are usually simple plays on first names, created by changing a letter around, or by simply saying the student's last name before his or her first.

In kindergarten, students are at a stage of their language development in which they are into silly language (Segal & Martin-Chang, 2019). Wordplay is a way for them to play with language and realize that there is a lot of variation in the way we pronounce things. Making minor changes to your students' names is one way to introduce them to wordplay. If you do something as simple as change the vowel pronunciation of a word from a short to a long sound, students hear it and react with feigned shock, surprise, and giddy laughter. They feel as if you are breaking the rules of language in a good way. By doing this, you are subtly teaching them that the rules of language and therefore anything they are going to learn are not set in stone and can be mentally played with. You are setting them on the road to be inquisitive and flexible thinkers—all by just having a little fun with their names.

Some of the ways I add spice to addressing students is by referring to a particular quality, interest, accomplishment, or family relationship, as in, *Kid Who Just Learned to Snap Her Fingers, Pokémon Shirt, Brother of Shawn, Mr. Red Hair, New Sneakers Kid, New C Reader, Cool New Haircut Kid,* and so on. You are obviously always going to keep it positive and focused on something the student takes obvious pride in, and not single out what may be considered unflattering qualities. My students get into this as well and turn it back on me all the time, which I enjoy. My favorites were when one student started to refer to me as *Mystery,* and another *Mr. Egg,* instead of *Mr. A.*

Playing with sounds, words, and concepts makes students pay attention to you whenever you start to speak, because you are essentially sending out a puzzle they need to figure out, and for which they might be the solution. Doing this educates students as to their own uniqueness and that of each of their classmates. It also promotes the class *wa* (or harmony, page 60) and adds fun to the day.

See how much teaching you can get done with only the students' names!

Get Parents' or Guardians' Contact Information

The second-most important thing you need to accomplish before the first day is getting the parents' contact information—most importantly, their email addresses. Set up an email group for your class based on the system at your school for this. If you can't have this done before the first day of school, then have this done by the end of the first day—OK, at least by the end of the first week. Don't wait longer than that. Knowing each email gives you access to students' parents, and more importantly, it gives them digital access to you, which is comforting to them. You can email the group to communicate what the class is up to throughout the year, and send individual emails to deal with student-specific issues.

These are the equations that guide me when interacting with parents.

>Informed parent = Happy parent

>Happy child = Happy parent

Once I know each student by name and have all the parents' emails, the rest is gravy.

Preparing to Speak to Kindergarteners

Everything in your classroom is designed to be age- and developmentally appropriate, and language is no exception. The language of kindergarteners is something I call *kinderese*. Over time, I have learned to speak it with a certain fluency. Some old television personalities, such as Art Linkletter of *Kids Say the Darndest Things* (Linkletter, 1945–1969), and Allen Funt of *Candid Camera* (Funt, 1948–1992), spoke it. My mother-in-law speaks it. I can't define it exactly, but I know it when I hear it.

When I took a course about how people acquire language, we learned the specific way parents, especially mothers, speak to their babies. We have all heard it. It involves a higher pitch, a lot of body language, simple words that are used repetitively, and so on. It is spoken naturally by parents and is the perfect way of communicating to little brains for them to understand the rules and nuances of their native tongue. It is called *motherese* (Nelson, Hirsh-Pasek, Jusczyk, & Cassidy, 1989), and parents will add new lingual challenges and complexities as the student masters new language skills. Students in kindergarten are past this stage, as they are obviously not babies. On the other hand, these children are far from being young adults. All of this is based on my observations of the level of engagement and comprehension I see when someone speaks to kindergarteners on a childish level and on an adult level.

When special guests, who are adults, come to do presentations to the class, they usually do one of two things: (1) speak in motherese or, more commonly, (2) speak in purely adult language. In the latter case, they will use college-level words the students have never heard before and somehow think that they have knowledge of all the underlying knowledge on which the presentation is based.

The way the guests convince themselves that the students have internalized the lesson is by asking a leading question that the students can answer without having to know anything. From a lesson on computer coding, "So do we move the cursor vertically (wink, wink, nudge, nudge) or laterally (straight-faced)?" This is a question directed to students who never heard of the term *cursor* and don't even know left or right. But they all get the answer correct.

It's OK for guests to do this, as they are trying their best. But on the whole, students of this age are often not spoken to in a language they truly understand—and that's not OK. Research shows that humans are biologically programmed for motherese, as they do it naturally (Piazza, Iordan, & Lew-Williams, 2017), but I don't see that people naturally speak the language that best suits students in their preschool and kindergarten years. Some parents intentionally speak to their children in adult language, assuming the children will grow into it. For a child of six years old, I think that this is like reading *War and Peace* (Tolstoy, 1968/1869) to them instead of a picture book.

I know that kinderese is as much a listening process as it is a speaking process, because people who have mastered it really listen to what the kindergarten-age child is saying and respond on point to what they have heard. They introduce sophisticated words to the conversation, but then explain them, use them in context, give an example, and weave them throughout the conversation.

People who speak kinderese mind the following.

- **Do not talk down to or over a kindergartener's head:** They speak exactly *to* the student's comprehension level. They will back off a new concept if they know a student does not yet have a frame of reference for it or doesn't understand its underlying assumptions and they will work backward until the student does. If I were told to teach a student I'd never met about punctuation, I might prepare a lesson to do that, but if I mentioned the term and the student wasn't familiar with it, I might not use the word *punctuation* again but instead show the different forms of punctuation. That way I could see if the student could name the marks or if he or she understood how the marks are used. If he or she couldn't do this, I would test print concepts and sentence structure comprehension and work my way up until I could possibly introduce the concept of punctuation.

- **Use any word necessary to get a concept across:** This applies even if a word has never been used before in that context. They will create new words if they need to. This is why children relate to Dr. Seuss's inventive words so well. That is why I call the vertex of a shape an *ouchie*. I will go more into why I do this in chapter 9 (page 183), but the point is that the actual word is always subordinate to the concept you are trying to get across. If the proper terminology gets in the way of that, find or create a word you can use on a temporary basis that relates to the concept until the concept is acquired and then scaffold up to the proper term when you see the student is ready. Another option is to have the student restate the concept; he or she may come up with a word that will help make the association (Marzano, 2009, as cited in Alber, 2010):

> *Step one:* The teacher explains a new word, going beyond reciting its definition (tap into prior knowledge of students, use imagery).
> *Step two:* Students restate or explain the new word in their own words (verbally and/or in writing).
> *Step three:* Ask students to create a non-linguistic representation of the word (a picture, or symbolic representation).
> *Step four:* Students engage in activities to deepen their knowledge of the new word (compare words, classify terms, write their own analogies and metaphors).
> *Step five:* Students discuss the new word (pair-share, elbow partners).
> *Step six:* Students periodically play games to review new vocabulary (Pyramid, Jeopardy, Telephone).

- **Know that they must sometimes bend the rules of grammar and word order:** This is in favor of communicating an idea. Kinderese is dynamic and grows in sophistication as the student matures. This includes phrases particular to my classroom that I created by necessity for efficiency and the ease of concept comprehension that might not conform to standard English. For instance, I might refer to the *ball* we are living on (later *sphere*). I might not be able to utter a complete sentence in the middle of a lesson, so might blurt out, "Fast, go, back, tag," which means that the student should go to the bathroom, return immediately to the classroom, and not forget to take the bathroom pass. If a student were reading a sentence and I reminded him or her to "eat the words," the student would know to work on blending consonant-vowel-consonant words—more on that in chapter 8 (page 141).

You can't learn kinderese from a book, and it doesn't come naturally to most people—even teachers. You learn it from speaking to children and using your sophisticated adult brain to analyze how they are communicating, break it down, and figure out how best to communicate with them. The reproducible "Practicing Kinderese" (page 51) can help you begin thinking this way, as it offers vocabulary and asks you to define it as a two-year-old, an adult, and a kindergartener.

In a Nutshell

The best way to ease the jitters of the first day of school is to be prepared for the *last* day of school, when your vision of students who have mastered the standards will have been realized. Put yourself at ease by being confident about your curriculum from the get-go. Put your students at ease by knowing their names, giving them a few easy welcoming activities, and speaking to them in a language they intuitively understand at that age. Put the parents and guardians at ease by opening a permanent line of communication that shows you are available and attentive to their questions and concerns.

Have You Mastered the Chapter?

Welcome to the formal assessment section of the book—a quiz to test your knowledge of the chapter. Please try the questions. The answers are provided after the questions section for a quick check. I explain the *why* after the quiz, and that is the most important part to consider.

According to this chapter:

1. The most important way to think of your classroom is as:
    a. Your home away from home
    b. Your co-teacher
    c. A place full of charts and student work
    d. A work in progress

2. Your ability to access items quickly in your classroom is called:
    a. Something that is impossible to do
    b. The five-second rule
    c. Being a super teacher
    d. Fostering independence

3. Before the first day of school you should have:
    a. A good idea of what your students will know on the last day
    b. Your students' names memorized
    c. Read through all of your curricula
    d. All the above

4. Kinderese is a language that:
    a. Is spoken in Kyrgyzstan
    b. Should be taught in dual-language programs
    c. Is a step up from motherese
    d. Is easy to learn

Answers and Explanations

1. **b. (Your co-teacher)** Your classroom can be your home away from home; it is usually filled with charts and student work; and it is always a work in progress, but if you take the time and put a lot of thought into your class setup, it will function as an additional cueing system to students about the way they should act and the goals you aspire to. It is as if you have a second teacher in the room.

2. **b. (The five-second rule)** If you can access anything that you or a student in your classroom needs in five seconds or fewer (which is a very doable objective), it will help foster students' independence. That may sound counterintuitive, and you are obviously a super teacher for doing this.

3. **d. (All the above)** All are the necessary preparations you need to complete in order to start your school year the right way.

4. **c. (Is a step up from motherese)** I am sure there is a form of kinderese spoken to kindergarteners in Kyrgystan, and kinderese should be used in dual-language programs. Kinderese is a very advanced form of motherese (baby talk) that is appropriate for children of kindergarten age and is very difficult for an adult to learn, as it takes time, observation, and experimentation to get this form of communication just right.

Preparing for the First Day of School

After setting up your classroom before the start of the school year, use this checklist to be sure you've covered everything.

- ☐ I have a strong preliminary understanding of each curriculum and the related standards.
- ☐ I am happy with my room setup as a starting point for the year.
- ☐ I can access any item I am asked for within five seconds.
- ☐ I have each student's first and last name memorized.
- ☐ I have planned a few ice-breaker activities for this day.
- ☐ I have a plan for how to obtain contact information for each parent or guardian within a week.

Practicing Kinderese

Work with a partner and write how you would explain the following to a two-year-old and then to an adult. Now picture a kindergartener in front of you and explain the same thing. Note changes in your vocabulary, grammar, body language, and intonation between the three approaches. Have you created child-friendly terms or bent the language to get your point across to the younger set? What visuals and manipulatives are required for each audience?

1. How to draw a square
   Two-year-old:

   Adult:

   Kindergartener:

2. What clouds are made of
   Two-year-old:

   Adult:

   Kindergartener:

3. Why it is important to brush your teeth
   Two-year-old:

   Adult:

   Kindergartener:

4. How big the Earth is
   Two-year-old:

   Adult:

   Kindergartener:

5. Summarize a picture book
   Two-year-old:

   Adult:

   Kindergartener:

6. The difference between a two-dimensional and three-dimensional shape
   Two-year-old:

   Adult:

   Kindergartener:

7. The concept of one-half
   Two-year-old:

   Adult:

   Kindergartener:

8. The differences between the seasons
   Two-year-old:

   Adult:

   Kindergartener:

9. Why families are important
   Two-year-old:

   Adult:

   Kindergartener:

10. What a map is and how it is useful
    Two-year-old:

    Adult:

    Kindergartener:

CHAPTER 4

Employing Practical Classroom Management

Understanding good class management is but a first step to teaching in a high-functioning classroom. The challenging part is applying all the techniques of good class management to the rules and routines in your classroom so that all are learning to their full potential. In addition, aside from being fair, flexible, predictable, and observant, you sometimes have to be stubborn and patient.

In this chapter, you will learn why kindergarteners misbehave, the end goal of good classroom management, the three approaches to discipline (otherwise known as *social* or *social-emotional learning*), effective and ineffective disciplinary tools, and seven rules for the teacher.

Why Kindergarteners Misbehave

I don't have a license in special education, but I have taught students with a range of behavior and varying needs, including students who had fetal alcohol syndrome, autism spectrum disorder, Down syndrome, oppositional-defiant disorder, and so on—almost always in a general education classroom. I believe children are reasonable and logical and, for the most part, nonjudgmental and cooperative.

If you want to get control of your classroom, you first must identify who is cooperative and who is not (with no judgments, please). You need to encourage the cooperative students to keep doing what they are doing and put a lot of energy into setting up activities, scenarios, and educational opportunities to establish the positive atmosphere in the room. In every teaching situation I have been in involving a general education classroom, the following usually holds true of the class.

- About a third are there to listen to you and accept your authority.
- About a third don't yet get what school is about. Either they find it hard to follow directions, have poor socialization skills, have a short attention span and are impulsive, or look at you as a barrier to doing what they want to do when they want to do it.
- About a third are sitting on the fence. They can go either way and are watching what will ultimately happen in the room.

Students who misbehave are not bad children. They misbehave for many reasons. Some of the reasons include attention seeking (acting out), limit testing, or coping with an underlying mental issue (Morin, 2019). Effective teachers are like good doctors. They analyze the symptom, try to find the underlying cause, and then apply the appropriate medicine—in this case, a discipline strategy.

> **Students who misbehave are not bad children.**

Of all the reasons for misbehavior in the classroom, I have discovered that in most cases you can narrow it down to two causes. While I never rely exclusively on these two reasons, I begin with the assumption that the misbehavior is caused by one of them or a combination of the two. If I am wrong, I look for alternatives. But these assumptions hold true most of the time.

In my experience, I have found that most students misbehave because of one of the following reasons.

1. **They are not fully aware of the classroom rules:** Usually, I can resolve a behavior problem by simply reminding a student of a class rule and the reason behind it. So, if a student grabs a bin of toys during reading time and starts playing with them, I explain that we have a time for that later and that I will bring out that particular bin for him or her to play with then. The student will usually return to what he or she is supposed to be doing.

   The best way to communicate the class rules is by modeling them, assessing how well students have incorporated them; revisiting through whole-class, small-group, and individual instruction; reassessing; and so on—the same way you would teach any subject, through instruction, gradual release, and assessment. So, the first thing to do is make sure that students know what the classroom expectations are and to make sure that the expectations, or class rules, are fair, clear, and consistent. This is a little easier than dealing with the following issue.

2. **They are still working on their impulse control, or lack thereof:** Put a lot of focus on immediately working with the students who need help exhibiting positive social skills and win them over. The fence sitters will follow along. Handling impulsivity will go a long way toward establishing classroom control, as "impulsivity is the tendency toward rapid, unplanned reactions to internal or external stimuli without regard to the negative consequences of those reactions" (Carver & Johnson, 2018). This trait is obviously not exclusive to children, but at the kindergarten level it is evident in repeated behaviors. The cerebral cortex, which helps control impulses, is not fully developed until the mid-twenties (Wallace, 2018). Kindergarteners are about twenty years removed from that.

Examples of impulsivity are too numerous to mention, as it is a hallmark of children at this age. Some more extreme examples of this trait would include a student who grabs an item from another student because he or she wants it, a student who runs up and breaks a structure another student has been working on, and a student who pushes bins of books off tables to see what happens. For a kindergartener dealing with impulse issues, the impulse will take precedence over any rule—even if he or she is aware of it (Carver & Johnson, 2018). Different students have varying degrees of impulse control, and one student's abilities may vary in different situations.

Strategies for Minimizing Misbehavior

The following strategies offer ideas for a variety of design routines and activities that will lessen misbehavior resulting from impulse control issues.

- **Offer choices:** Give students options whenever possible, even simple ones such as choosing between markers and pens for writing or even different colored markers.

- **Make things fun and engaging:** Incorporate visual aids, videos, art, music, and most of all, humor, in to your lessons and activities.

- **Give opportunities for movement:** *Always keep them moving* is a good mantra. Although many students can sit attentively for long periods, adding a dramatic activity, a discovery walk through the classroom, or a dance break will keep them on their toes.

- **Learn through play:** Incorporate a lot of guided discovery materials such as open-ended manipulatives into your activities. When you are using more targeted manipulatives, such as interlocking cubes, always set aside a few minutes for students to explore them before using them in a specific manner during a lesson.

- **Differentiate lesson plans:** When you are planning a lesson, take into account the other points mentioned here so that you address the behavioral modifications necessary for a successful lesson.

These are super techniques and very effective—up to a point. There will always come the time when the class is doing an activity and each student will need to conform to it, like it or not. There will be times when safety is an issue, such as fire and lockdown drills, and the student needs to simply follow the directions. Then, you will have to deal with impulsivity head on, as in, "I know that you want to do this right now, but you can't because the class is doing something else at the present time." If you read on and learn the Seven Rules for the Teacher (page 72) and when and how to use positive and negative consequences (page 67), even very impulsive students will eventually follow your teachings of positive behavior and improve their self-control to the point where they will be cooperative learners. Harvard Medical School instructor Karen Postal (2011) might describe this as the teacher acting as the child's *external frontal executive network*, literally lending the student his or her own brain's ability to modulate emotions, resist impulses, and plan into the future. Students are appreciative for that loan until the day they can do those on their own, as you will soon see.

Teaching a student about prosocial behavior is very demanding work. I have had to work very hard, day after day, with many students over the years, patiently redirecting them, modeling prosocial behavior, and keeping a special eye on them throughout the day. I always thought that when a particularly challenging student moved on to first grade, that perhaps he or she would feel a lingering resentment or annoyance about me and would just dart out the door without even a goodbye. I learned many years ago that what the student actually does is quite the opposite.

One year, on the last day of school, the moment came for each student to see me for the last time as his or her teacher. One of the most challenging students from that year looked over at me from across the room. I was ready for the student to give me a limp wave and exit quickly. Instead, he ran across the room and gave me one of the longest and strongest hugs I have ever received as a teacher. I knew instantly what he meant by that gesture. This happened year after year with difficult students with whom I had worked very hard on social skills. The more difficult the student, the bigger, stronger, and longer the hug. It is one of the most rewarding moments you will ever have as a teacher. I realized these students actually loved me. "But for what?" I thought. I figured that they realized that I gave them a great gift. It was the gift of self-control that they never had. It must be hard going through life being ruled by your impulses. Self-control is a powerful thing. So, these students were thanking me for that gift. Of course, they had self-control in themselves all along!

> **Self-control is a powerful thing.**

The End Goal of Good Classroom Management

What is the end goal of good class management? What does a well-managed kindergarten classroom look like? In my opinion, what you are going for is a combination of the following two things: (1) controlled chaos (and here, you'll learn why it works) and (2) the hum and wa.

Controlled Chaos and Why It Works

A roller coaster would be boring if it went five miles an hour in a straight line, but it would be terrifying if it seemed at any point it could fly off the rails. What makes it so much fun is that you feel you are in danger but know that you actually are not. Roller coasters are an example of controlled chaos. Once you know that you are safe, you can let loose and really enjoy the unpredictability of the ride. You can experiment with new things like raising your arms or crouching in a turn. One of my daughters was reluctant to go on a roller coaster when she was young. I said, "Watch the people on the cars. They always come back safely." She has loved roller coasters ever since.

I was always told that children crave predictability, structure, and routine. I never understood this, because it would seem that students like when things are different, spontaneous, and unpredictable. The answer is that they like both, but it begins with predictability. Predictability and routines help a child feel safe and lowers their anxiety, as they know what to expect (Center on the Developing Child at Harvard University, 2017). This is the kind of predictability children thrive on. What if when you hit the *y* key on your computer keyboard, it typed the letter *r*? What if the next time you did this, it typed the letter *h*? What if you opened a can of corn and there were peas in it? Getting corn when you open a can of corn is predictable in the same way that we rely on the laws of science, like gravity or magnetism, to help make our lives as safe as possible. *That* is the kind of predictability children want in their environment and in the people they deal with. Your classroom has to have certain rules that always work the same way. In some ways you are like a robot or a computer keyboard. Press the *y* button, and you will always get a *y*. You are not a slot machine but an automated food kiosk—pressing a certain button will always give the same snack—for anyone who presses it.

Your classroom environment, rules, and management techniques give kindergarteners predictability, structure, and routine. (Chapter 5, page 89, has more on those.) They provide the rails of the roller coaster. What happens is that once students understand them, once they feel and experience them, they become comfortable, cooperative, and receptive and use them as the springboard to inquisitiveness, innovation, and creativity. Knowing they always have a cushion to fall back on allows them to be bold, imaginative, and experimental.

Controlled Chaos and the Wa and Hum

A teacher is part mentor, part clown, part psychologist, part motivator, part diva, part interpreter, part cop, part judge, part researcher, part pacifier, and part agitator. You are the counterweight, always trying to keep the room's wa in balance. *Wa* is a Japanese term that means group harmony and unity, peaceful coexistence (Veltri, 2016). Your job is to foster and maintain class wa as much as possible. The best form of wa is controlled chaos.

When students are engaged, excited, motivated, happy, and learning they emit a communal hum, like the purr of a cat or the buzz of a beehive. It has a certain frequency—I don't know exactly what it is, but I know it when I hear it. It is a beautiful sound and very soothing to the soul. It probably has the same frequency as that of the universe. As a teacher, I am like a musician who is constantly trying to tune my room to that frequency. Some refer to this hum as *flow*—where a person is fully immersed in what he or she is doing right then, and losing track of time (Csikszentmihalyi, 2008). But you will only get the hum if you are doing everything you need to do as a teacher. You don't have to be doing anything fancy; the hum can be heard during routines as well as exciting projects. The students will not emit it unless the teacher is doing all the things he or she is supposed to be doing. Have you ever heard the hum in your classroom? It's beautiful music.

> **A teacher is part mentor, part clown, part psychologist, part motivator, part diva, part interpreter, part cop, part judge, part researcher, part pacifier, and part agitator.**

You can walk into two rooms. In the first, young students are walking in various directions, narrowly missing each other. They are talking with loud voices, pulling materials out of the cabinets, pushing items off the tables, maybe even standing on chairs. In the second one, they are doing the same thing. The first room is an accident ready to happen, a dangerous place, but the second is a place of learning and discovery. The first room is chaos, and the second room is controlled chaos. It is a culmination of all of the techniques discussed after this section. It is hard for an outsider to really tell what is truly going on in a classroom.

The difference between the two rooms is the teachers. The difference is that a student in the second room will tell you that they are walking around with a craft stick so they can compare its length to those of other objects in the classroom and a student in the first room would be walking around with a craft stick with no purpose. Students in the chaotic room would be sliding random objects around the room for fun and students in the controlled chaos room would be doing the same in order to better understand the concept of friction. The difference is that the second classroom has the hum and the first does not. The difference is that at the end of the day, the teacher in the first room is filling out three accident reports, and the teacher in the second room is planning for the next day.

The other thing about a controlled chaos room is that it doesn't always look chaotic. Sometimes it looks more controlled than the most controlled room ever looks. And it can be anywhere in between. You can walk into my room at 10:00 a.m. and think I am the strictest teacher in the world, leave, and return at 10:05 a.m. and conclude I am the most permissive. You can walk in at 10:10 a.m. and think that it is a very teacher-directed room and walk in at 10:20 a.m. and be convinced that the students make all the choices.

In the classroom, it is as if you are at the beach and each student is in a life preserver with a string attached to it. The student can go wherever he or she wants on the beach and the string is held so loosely and the life preserver is so comfortable that the student can go swimming and diving and try out new nautical tricks even in the deepest water without even thinking that you are around. Even so, the minute the student is in danger or doing something wrong, you can pull on the string and bring him or her back to shore. In the classroom, you are holding twenty-five-plus strings at the same time. Although the students may be engaged harmoniously in a class activity, I monitor them constantly using the observation skills I mentioned in the introduction. They are comfortably aware of my presence. A quick signal such as a clap, countdown, or even a quick look alerts them that I need their attention. A person watching the students from the shore doesn't notice the strings or the life preservers, and it looks like the students are one gulp away from drowning. You know they are not. That is controlled chaos.

It reminds me of when I was at the Prospect Park Zoo in Brooklyn, New York, and found myself by the baboon exhibit. It consisted of a very long pane of glass from which you could watch a troop of baboons in their habitat. Some of the baboons came very close to the glass, which was very exciting. They seemed very uninhibited and engaging. Some baboons were playing with each other, some were resting, some were eating, and some were doing their own thing. I noticed that one baboon in the back, far away from the glass, sitting alone and, from my perspective, looking bored.

I asked one of the zoo attendants about this and she said, "Oh, he is the leader. He has to protect the clan from any danger, so he is constantly looking around for predators on the ground and from the sky. He especially keeps an eye out for the babies in the group because they are the most vulnerable" (J. Eaver, personal communication, September 2016).

She continued by saying that if any of the group's members were not getting along or if one member was harassing another member, the leader will intervene, and quickly. But he doesn't have to jump up and run toward anybody, because everyone in the troop knows he is there. All he needed to do is shift his eye position, perhaps glare, crouch up a little bit, cock his head, turn his hand over, and they will get the message (J. Eaver, personal communication, September 2016).

I watched the group for about an hour and everything the attendant told me was absolutely true. The other baboons were playing as if he weren't there, but only up to a point. They felt the leader's presence, I'm sure. I guess the baboons know a little about controlled chaos too.

Social Learning Is Discipline

So how do you manage students in a way that leads to controlled chaos and wa? Well, we have to use that word *discipline*. Its meaning is not by its nature harsh. It comes from the Latin *disciplina*, which means knowledge or instruction ("Discipline," n.d.). The student is your disciple. When you are disciplining students, you are teaching them. You are teaching them the norms of behavior in our society. It is a subject like any other that you teach. Children have a right to know the acceptable rules of behavior, and once they move on in their lives, they can eventually accept or reject them—as with anything else they learn from you. This is all part of *social-emotional learning*, and you should regard it as one of the subjects you teach. But you cannot teach it the way you teach mathematics or literacy. Students have to live it, each and every day, in a consistent manner, led by your actions.

Discipline is a subject, like any other. You are teaching it to the class. Social-emotional learning *is* discipline. I have been asked to implement many schoolwide social curricula, such as anti-bullying campaigns. One dictated that everyone in the school had to say "Hi" to everyone else. One had everyone find someone sitting alone at lunch and sit next to him or her. Another time, students had to act out a word of the week, like *empathy* or *compassion*. There was also the curriculum in which we read about an extraterrestrial who came to the class and had to learn how we act nicely with each other here on Earth. In another, you had to find a student in the act of doing something nice for or to another student, write it on a piece of paper, and put the paper in a bucket to be displayed against the buckets of the other classes. The class that had the most populated bucket got a prize. (I think the only learning going on in this approach was competitiveness.) As with many other prescribed curricula, I appreciated the effort; they were well intentioned. They were also addressing a real problem. Some initiatives even worked, temporarily. Everyone did say "Hi" to each other the day they were supposed to, and it felt really nice. However, the next day everything went back to the way it had been.

The truth is, the social learning curriculum cannot be restricted to a singular learning block in each day (unless the learning block is the complete day). Students are engaged in social-emotional learning on their own every second of the day, and you should be teaching it every second of the day, through demonstration, example, guided practice, and inquiry. It is probably the most important subject you are teaching. I hope that by reading this book you will understand this and be able to make it part of the fabric of the classroom.

The Three Approaches to Social-Emotional Learning

According to developmental psychologist Diana Baumrind's (1971) seminal research, parents usually follow one of three approaches in managing their own children. Because of commonalities between parenting and teaching young students, this approach can be generalized to classroom-management styles teachers can utilize. These styles harken to the porridge in *Goldilocks and the Three Bears*—one is too hot, one is too cold, and one is just right (Baumrind, 1971; Bernstein, 2013).

1. **The first one is *permissive*:** Lax and lenient best describe this approach (Barnas, 2000; Baumrind, 1971). The children are given the freedom to follow their impulses with low regard for rules or consequences. This usually results in children who are spoiled, self-centered, and have trouble following rules.

2. **The second one is *authoritarian*:** This is the strict, oppressive dictator who is unyielding and more interested in power than fairness. This usually results in one of two extremes—overly submissive or rebellious children.
3. **The third one is *authoritative*:** This parent—or teacher—has high expectations but conveys these expectations with warmth. This is the just-right approach that you should be using with your students.

You can see how the styles intersect with discipline in figure 4.1.

TEACHER INVOLVEMENT

		Low	High
DISCIPLINE	**Weak**	Permissive or Neglectful	Permissive or Indulgent
	Strong	Authoritarian	Authoritative

Source: Adapted from Baumrind, 1971.

Figure 4.1: The intersection between teaching styles and discipline.

Being Permissive or Authoritarian: Negative Outcomes

It's obvious why it's easy to be permissive. Not so obvious is how easy it is to succumb and become an authoritarian teacher. As an adult, you have no idea how much power you have to control and manipulate students—if you wanted to go down that dark path.

> ### LORD OF THE BUNK
>
> When I was in my late teens, I was the counselor of a group of young children at a sleepaway camp. Each group had a cabin, and an additional counselor would stay in the bunk. We had the swimming counselor in our cabin. Once, the swimming counselor did something stupid that irritated the kids, so I decided that we should make a circle around his bed when he wasn't there and start chanting insults about him. Yes, it was a stupid idea. I learned my lesson, as you will see.
>
> It started out as a lot of fun and we kept making up new and louder chants. Then the counselor himself walked in. He looked really annoyed, but we thought it was funny, so we kept escalating and chanting more. He

> then looked distressed, but that just egged us on even more. I felt like Jack in *Lord of the Flies* (Golding, 1954), although by nature, I am actually more like Ralph or Piggy.
>
> At some point, I was about to say, "OK, guys, now let's get him," when something inside me snapped. I realized how absurd and irresponsible I had become. I could have had the children flip his bed over. I could have had them throw things at him. I could have told them to charge the counselor, and they would have.
>
> Boy, did I learn a lot from that experience. I really apologized all I could to the counselor about my behavior. I feel bad thinking about it as I relay the story to you. But I learned that, as an adult, you have a lot of power over children. That is why teachers are highly trained, go through background checks, and are monitored, as they should be. The proposition that an adult can't control kids or that the kids are running the classroom does not bear out.

If teachers really wanted to, they could be harsh, punitive authoritarians and have students line up like soldiers, sit with hands clasped with nary a peep, and have them walk up and down the room from wall to wall for no reason the whole day (Baumrind, 1971; Bernstein, 2013). It's pointless and abusive, in my opinion, but easily doable. It is the teacher, not the students, who has the power in the classroom. It is the teacher whose power must be held in check. My three points on this follow.

1. It is easy and cowardly to be an authoritarian teacher—don't fall into that trap! Is all the control of the room in your hands? Are your rules meant to suit your needs only? Compare this approach with a description of the techniques of the authoritative teacher to make sure that you have the right balance in your classroom.

2. If you are a permissive teacher because you feel that you can't manage your classroom or that the personalities in your room are too strong for you to handle, then you need to know who, by far, the most powerful person in the room actually is.

3. If you take the cynical route and become an authoritarian teacher, the students will blindly listen to you—up to a point. They are cooperating because they trust you to lead them. Once you lose that trust, your power crumbles like a cookie. This is because the ultimate truth about authority is that it flows from the students to you—not from you to the students (Wells, 2016).

Students confer authority on the teacher in the same way that people confer authority on political figures. When people realize that their government is corrupt and not working to serve them, the government ultimately collapses. This concept of *consent of the governed* (Wells, 2016) works in the classroom as well in the political arena. Students will accept your authority only if you are also fair, reasonable, predictable, and flexible. The authoritarian teacher does not exhibit these qualities. In the same way that tyrants fall from their perches into the dustbin of history, the authoritarian teacher will follow the same path.

If I had to characterize each of the three methods on the continuum of love versus respect, I would say in the simplest terms that the permissive teacher wants to be loved, the authoritarian teacher wants to be respected, and the authoritative teacher wants to be loved and respected in equal measures at all times.

Being Authoritative: The Method That Is Just Right

The best kind of approach to effective class management is for the teacher to be authoritative—amazing what the change of a few letters at the end of a word can do. This is the *just-right* approach, but also the hardest to master. An authoritative teacher is the self-appointed authority in the room. Like the authoritarian teacher, this teacher makes the rules—but that is where the similarity ends. The authoritarian is cold and punitive, whereas the authoritative is warm but firm (Baumrind, 1971). Unlike the permissive teacher, the authoritative teacher retains the ultimate control.

The authoritative teacher is like the tightrope walker. He or she needs to be in perfect balance all the time and is constantly fine-tuning him- or herself and the environment to achieve that end. He or she makes the rules, but the rules are fair and purposeful. They are negotiable, but not until the class has integrated them into its everyday routines. The teacher uses a mixture of rewards and consequences to enforce the rules. The authoritative teacher has the power of a dictator but does not want to exercise this power. This person would rather everyone have freedom and make their own choices. This teacher actively moves the class toward these goals, modeling and then gradually releasing (Fisher & Frey, 2008; Pearson & Gallagher, 1983), so that students can govern on their own. But kindergarten teachers are dealing with young children. They still need to hold the reins. This always needs to be in the undercurrent of the understanding between you and the students. Often, being a good, authoritative teacher means that you have to outstubborn a student. You have to be the rock and the hard place. You have to be the unstoppable force and the immovable object. If it comes down to a battle of wills, your will wins. But do it like Gandhi did it—quietly, subtly, nobly, justifiably, and with principle—but immovably. Never be like The Zax (Dr. Seuss, 1961), going face-to-face with a child and seeing who blinks first.

The authoritative teacher approach is embedded in all of the topics of the book that give practical examples as to how to resolve issues between students, manage routines and activities, and actively teach. You will see that consideration is taken to balance students' needs with classroom goals and that rules are fair, flexible, and consistent.

Effective and Ineffective Disciplinary Tools

Here is what I have learned about rewards and consequences when managing students in the classroom: it is a great idea to use positive reinforcement (Kirkham, n.d.). A teacher should be a fountain of positivism, with compliments and exhortations dripping all around the room. The best positive reinforcement is when a teacher shows true appreciation for a student's behavior.

Then why use consequences? Because consequences have their place. Even negative emotion has its place.

As a teacher, you have to be dispassionate, but that doesn't mean that you have to always suppress your emotions. You shouldn't be this phony, always bubbly, happy mannequin, smiling throughout the day—while underneath you are not a happy camper. Keep it real. You can let your students know, in a polite way, if you are annoyed, angry, or frustrated—usually through body language. I sometimes use a pose of disapproval. It could be resting my hand on my chin, a quick or prolonged glare, rubbing my nose, furrowing my forehead, or waving my finger as in "No, no." Once a student gets the message, I often resolve the pose into a comical one so all's well that ends well. Remember to always to keep your emotions in check, but you don't have to hide them.

> **The best positive reinforcement is when a teacher shows true appreciation for a student's behavior.**

Every child at home and at school will at some point receive a consequence for misbehaving. It would be nice if rewards worked all the time, but they don't. The one flaw that positive reinforcement has is that children will keep upping the ante for the same behavior. They start negotiating for a behavior that is expected of them. Jim Taylor (2009), who specializes in the psychology of parenting, says that if used improperly, positive reinforcement can have the opposite effect. It can contribute to very undisciplined behavior, as can harsh consequences.

We're back to permissive versus authoritarian. The fact is, it isn't just about the kind of reinforcement you use. Although positive reinforcement is absolutely the preferred method, it's very much about how and the circumstances in which you use either kind of reinforcement.

The primary ways in which you manage students who are young is through the following.

- **Room setup:** You can read more about this in the section titled Space: Considering Tables (page 42) in chapter 3.
- **Classroom-management style:** That's what this chapter is all about—being an authoritative teacher who is in charge but caring, intentional, and personable.
- **Ability to motivate and engage them:** These include learning through play, incorporating movement activities, and setting up learning options, as well as other techniques, as discussed in the section titled Why Kindergarteners Misbehave (page 55).

You should rarely have to go into your toolbox to pull out a strong consequence, but know that they are available if necessary.

What follows is a discussion of some of the major consequences at your disposal. These include sharp tongue, time-out, time away, physical escort, and restraint. These are your management tools. Just because you have a tool in your box *doesn't* mean you have to use it. I have Allen wrenches in my toolboxes that I have never used, but they are there if I need them. You would never use a tape measure if a project calls for a wrench, and you would never use a hammer to fix something if you could accomplish the same thing with your finger.

All the management tools should be available to a teacher to use appropriately and when necessary. If teachers do not know about the tools, or when and how to use them appropriately, they should be trained and trusted to do so.

Ineffective Methods

Ineffective methods, including a sharp tongue or a time-out, do not work to produce the desired outcome.

Sharp Tongue

Some teachers will keep their hands behind their backs but will use their mouths as tools of discipline and punishment—ineffective tools. These teachers may feel helpless, so they use sharp language, insults, and threats to control their young students. Their words inflict mental scars that will affect these students for the rest of their lives (Streep, 2016). And frankly, they hurt.

We must treat the issue of mental scarring as seriously as we treat the issue of physical scarring. Any consequence that leaves a scar is abusive.

To the extent that consequences have to be used, they have to be used as teaching tools. If there is even the slightest chance that a consequence will leave a mental or physical scar, it is inappropriate. When you give a student a consequence, it's all about you understanding what the student did and the student understanding what he or she did, why it was wrong, and what he or she needs to do to fix it. Sociologist Mike Sosteric (2012) explains that if a child gets a consequence and knows he or she did nothing wrong, the child will feel violated. If a child knows he or she did something wrong and gets a consequence that is fair and helps him or her act more positively, the child doesn't mind the consequence.

Before I give a student a consequence, I must know what the student did. I always give the benefit of the doubt—especially when I didn't see the incident. In those cases, I will seek out other evidence, but unless it is compelling, I will usually let it slide (possibly with a raised eyebrow). This is why the difficult students don't resent me at the end of the year.

Time-Out

This is a very difficult topic. I don't like the term *time-out*, as it is associated with a lot of cruel teaching practices. I have been in meetings where I was told that under no circumstances should it ever be used and in others where it was the most encouraged form of consequence.

In the time-outs I have witnessed, students are told to sit alone if they have done something wrong. However, "time-outs frequently make children angrier and more dysregulated, leaving them even less able to control themselves or think about what they've done" (Siegel & Bryson, 2014, p. 24). Often, they don't know what they did. They sit alone for an undisclosed period while the teacher ignores them. It is meant to be a form of punishment and the student understands that. At this point, the ignored student may use it to his or her advantage and find something to play with. So, to the extent that it is meant as punishment or time for reflection and learning, it doesn't work. He or she will play until bored, then will feel isolated and either become more disruptive because annoyed, or will stare into space. I don't understand the value of anything that goes on with this method.

When you give a time-out, you are playing with dangerous medicine. According to parenting expert Justin Coulson (2016), "Time-out is a polite term for solitary confinement." People are social beings, so to isolate them is a serious thing. While I wouldn't make a direct analogy between the two, consider the warning of Harvard Medical School psychiatrist Stuart Grassian (2006) who tells us that solitary confinement can cause severe psychiatric harm. I think time-outs are an ineffective tool.

Effective Methods

Time away is a general in-class method that is effective if applied judiciously. Physical escort and restraint are only to be used in emergency situations, like when a person is in physical danger.

Time Away

I don't use time-outs, as I consider them authoritarian. However, I sometimes have students take *time away*. This is the authoritative approach that I created so the intended effects of the time-out (lesson learned, behavior change) can be realized without all of the ancillary psychological damage the time-out can potentially inflict.

In this method, I also give the student a spot to sit alone. It sounds the same as a traditional time-out, except the student sits close to the others. I constantly interact with him or her. I watch to see if the student is sitting nicely. As a student is sitting, he or she watches the others work or play to pick up cues as to what proper behavior in the classroom looks like. The student having time away remains engaged with the others.

Time away is not a time for play. I want the student to realize that he or she is there for a reason. I approach the student and ask why he or she is sitting in the chair and not playing with the other students. Some know right off, some of them don't know and have to figure it out, and some of them know but don't want to say. If the latter is the case, I sometimes have them act it out or draw a picture, but it usually doesn't take long for them to open up. The urge to return to the herd is strong and, as I mentioned, a student wouldn't be in this situation if I hadn't observed the behavior first and explicitly worked on it beforehand with the student.

The fact is that by the time the time away is over, students do know why they are there. They also figure out, or I help them understand, the way they can fix their behavior, so it doesn't happen again. It becomes a discussion and learning experience. It is as much work for the teacher as for the student, so both end up wanting to avoid this scenario at all costs. The student understands that a temporary break was necessary.

If administered properly, the time away is an effective classroom-management tool.

Physical Escort

A teacher (or parent) rarely needs to do anything more extreme to control even the most difficult student than to give a physical escort. The escort is not considered a form of physical restraint. As defined by the U.S. Department of Education (2012), "Physical escort means a temporary touching or holding of the hand, wrist, arm, shoulder, or back for the purpose of inducing a student who is acting out to walk to a safe location" (p. 14). It is simply taking the student by the hand and leading him or her away from the present situation. It is not to be used to pull a student or to squeeze a student's hand. If you find yourself doing this, stop—you are hurting the student!

A physical escort is appropriate when a kindergartener is in danger of hurting himself or others, including you. Your goal is to redirect the student and eventually—when everyone is calm—get to the root cause of the behavior. You may lead the student to another area, or to a time away. You may lead the student around the classroom, so he or she can see how the other students are playing, or you may even have to lead the student to the principal's office.

Physical escort is a very tricky technique and needs to be done appropriately and only when necessary. It lasts only a few seconds but is a useful tool that will help the student regain self-control.

Restraint

The U.S. Department of Education (2012) provides guidance and describes principles that states school districts, school staff, parents, and other stakeholders will find helpful on the use of restraint in schools. According to the U.S. Department of Education (2012), restraint should occur only if a student is in imminent danger of harming him- or herself or others.

I have had to use restraint a few times, and it is not a pleasant experience. It was usually in extreme cases, like when a student in my class had oppositional defiant disorder (discussed more on page 79). One such case happened during the middle of an activity—one student suddenly punched another very hard, sending the other keeling over in pain, and then continuing to punch. I ran over and wrapped my arms around the aggressive student from behind to restrain him from moving and being able to use his arms. I then held on for dear life as administration was called.

I understand that some teachers are reluctant to restrain a student when necessary. If this is the case for you, keep trying one of the other acceptable tools for discipline or find someone in your school who can restrain a student appropriately. But this technique is time dependent, so it's best if you learn to do it and employ it when necessary. Hopefully, you will never be in a circumstance where you have to do so.

Seven Rules for the Teacher

It may seem that the authoritative teacher is always making the rules, but the toughest rules to follow in this model are meant for the teacher. That is because with the right to manage young students comes responsibility and accountability. See the reproducible "Being an Authoritative Teacher" (page 86) for an exercise that requires reflecting on a less-than-successful classroom incident that could have been resolved more effectively with an authoritative approach. See the reproducible "Managing Conflicts" (page 87) for a conflict checklist.

Here are the seven rules the authoritative teacher needs to follow.

Rule 1: Always Be Predictable

The rules and their enforcement have to be predictable and consistent, because the "more you're consistent, the less tantrums, meltdowns, and negative behavior you'll see" (Alison, 2020). Children like to go off the rails and be spontaneous. They like surprises and doing everything the opposite way, but here is the key: they love spontaneity, but only if it sits atop predictability in their environment (Schimmer, 2011). The classroom-management techniques in chapter 4 (page 55) are one way to establish this predictability. Spontaneity is a variation from the norm, but the norm

> **With the right to manage young students comes responsibility and accountability.**

has to first be established—by you. Employing an authoritative approach and establishing classroom routines (page 66) go a long way toward establishing this norm.

Rule 2: Make the Consequence Fit the Incident

The degree of the consequence should match the degree of the incident—it should be the least restrictive available. For example, an authoritative teacher is more prone to briefly discuss the incident on first occurrence, rather than disciplining a student. And "to be effective, the consequence needs to fit the behavior in a logical way so that the child associates the consequence with the behavior choice" (Allen & Boelter, 2016). If someone smashes a cookie that was on the floor, that person cleans it up. He or she is not put in time away. If the consequence cannot match the incident, you can give a different consequence. If you saw a student hit another student, the consequence will obviously not be hitting back. It would be something else (maybe your school uses restorative practices), with the understanding that it is a consequence for the hitting. The consequence should not be excessive and must have to do with the particular student and situation.

Rule 3: Never Threaten a Student

Not threatening a student means a few different things.

- Don't speak to a student in a threatening manner. This includes words, tone, and body language. Please refer to the Sharp Tongue section (page 68) for an example of this. However, matter-of-factly laying out a student's choices, and the consequences related to each, is not a threat.
The Time Away section (page 70) and the upcoming section where I outline common scenarios of student behavior and how to deal with them (page 74) give you tools for acting appropriately in these situations.

- Don't make an incident a personal one between you and the student. It isn't about you.

- Don't tell a student he or she will experience a consequence if you know you won't follow through (Erwin, n.d.). You don't want to have to eat your words. It hurts your credibility. For example, if you know that every student has to go on a class trip, you wouldn't tell one of them that if he or she is not ready by a certain time, he or she can't go.

Remember that "it is essential you take steps to deal with serious anger and to get help if you can't do it by yourself" (Hayes, 2002, p. 22). The serious anger I am talking about here is potentially yours. Monitor your feelings when you are in a stressful situation and stay in control always.

Rule 4: Ensure That Yes Always Means Yes, and No Always Means No

This is related to the previous concept. Always carry out your word. If you promised a student a reward, then you had better make it happen. If you said no, stick to it. Consistency leads to credibility. If you say no and renege, students realize they might be able to manipulate you.

Rule 5: Don't Reward a Student for Negative Behavior

I have seen the practice of making the difficult student into the special helper. The idea is that it gives the student something to do, so he or she is occupied with needed attention. In my experience, this is not a good technique at all. In fact, "if primary schools want to nip negative behaviour in the bud, then they have to stop rewarding students who behave badly" (TES Professional, 2015). Why? Read on.

A student becomes my helper as a reward for *good* behavior. All a difficult student learns from becoming a special helper is that misbehavior is rewarded. The other students pick up on that too. The difficult student, as a special helper, becomes exempt from learning and that is exactly the opposite of what this student needs to be doing, which is learning to behave and learning to learn.

Rule 6: If You Didn't See It, You Probably Shouldn't Give a Consequence

You have to always be observing. Always presume innocence unless you know otherwise. Be very reluctant to give a consequence based on a student's reputation or another student's word. If you did not see what happened, you should try to get to the bottom of what occurred by gathering evidence and questioning the students. If this gives you a reasonable idea as to what actually occurred, that is fine. You really shouldn't give out a firm consequence if you haven't witnessed the event or if you doubt what really occurred. In those cases, make sure that the students are put in a situation so that the situation doesn't occur again. Separation and redirection usually work best. Make a mental note or document the event so that you can be on the lookout for the same situation occurring again and, if it does occur again, you have a good background on it.

Rule 7: Don't Force Apologies

Never make a student apologize to you or to another student. If someone does not feel sorry, saying so will not make him feel it. The forced apology will not make the victim feel better, either, because she'll know a real "I'm sorry" from a phony one. You are just making a student do something he or she doesn't want to do, and students will resent you for it. Routine apologies "do nothing to address the situation or behaviour, yet they remain the standard apology that children continue to use into adulthood" (Rifkin, 2019).

The victim student is more interested in justice and security, so that whatever happened will not happen again. The teacher needs to find out what prompted the action and find that solution. In the process, the student who did the action might start to feel sorry for what he or she did, and that is the time to encourage the student to say "sorry." It would be nice if this happened, but it is not the end goal of the process.

Strategies for Managing Specific Behavior Issues

Let's go over a few real-world situations that typically occur in a kindergarten class and see how the authoritative teacher might handle them. I will talk about how I react when students do the following. As always, it is a combination of what I have learned from research and, as I mentioned at the beginning of the book, being a teacher who acts as a researcher or scientist—from my own experiences and discoveries.

The following sections explain what to do if students do the following.

- Say, "They hit me first!"
- Say, "But—!" simultaneously
- Say, "They don't want to be my friend!"
- Have tantrums
- Display behavior based on oppositional defiant disorder

What to Do When a Student Says, "They Hit Me First!"

A popular answer that kindergarteners give if you ask them why they hit another student is "They hit me first"—as if that gives them license to hit the other person. Then the other student says, "They hit *me* first," creating an endless circle of accusations and self-righteousness. In my experience, children are more interested in justice than in hitting other students. So, if you appeal to that sense and explain that there are other ways to achieve justice other than hitting, they start to listen attentively.

My answer to the first person who says, "They hit me first" is "Why did you hit them back?" followed by a stupefied look.

> **In my experience, children are more interested in justice than in hitting other students.**

"But they hit me first," the student will say again, a little flustered because I did not immediately confront the other student.

My answer—"Why didn't you tell the person who hit you to stop? Why didn't you walk away? Why didn't you go to the teacher?"

I follow this by giving the student another stupefied look, and I continue: "If you'd told them to stop, they might have stopped. If you walked away, they might have stopped. If they followed you, they should have followed you right to me, and I would have taken care of it. *They* would get a consequence, and you would still be playing. Now they are getting a consequence because they hit, and you are getting a consequence because you hit."

By this point, I don't have to display the stupefied look anymore. They get it. I then talk to each student to see what prompted the hitting and to try to work it out so it doesn't happen again. The person who did the initial hitting, and sometimes the person who hit back, feels sorry for what they did, so I might suggest that apologizing is a nice thing to do. Sometimes they do, and sometimes they don't. It's nice if they do, but it is secondary at this point, and, as I said earlier, not something that should ever be forced. Children are reasonable, logical people. They pick up on this idea very quickly and stop the behavior.

What to Do When Students Say, "But—!" Simultaneously

Sometimes when students are unable to settle disputes on their own, the teacher helps resolve verbal disputes between them. Two students will run up to you and plead their cases at once, each shouting louder than the other. Things you do prior to this are important, including setting up your room and managing student behavior properly. By setting the stage for good student behavior, you will minimize the number of disputes you have. If you remember the first quality of teaching—observing—you should already know what is going on (or at least be aware that a dispute is brewing).

The first thing to realize when the students approach you is that their dispute has reached the point where they cannot resolve it on their own.

The second thing to realize is that both students will try to plead their cases as hard as they can.

The third thing is to listen to the student who is not dominant. The dominant student usually wins, which is why you should always listen to the other one first. Act like a courtroom judge, silencing the dominant student with a wave of your hand or a glare whenever they inevitably try to interrupt and take over the proceedings. After the first student finishes, you are ready for the dominant student to speak—and boy, are they ready! You are teaching the students about procedure.

You can usually get a good grasp of what occurred and what to do about it after you hear both sides individually. If you are still not satisfied, you can gather evidence, question witnesses, and come to a verdict.

What to Do When a Student Says, "They Don't Want to Be My Friend!"

If a very agitated student runs up to you and says, "They said they aren't my friend!" or "They don't want to play with me!" you might feel an instinct to go to the offender, give a stern look, and say, "We are all friends here. Play together."

On the other hand, this is my usual response: "OK. They will probably be your friend later. So, find another friend to play with now."

I don't follow the dictum that all students in a class always have to be friends with one another. Students get annoyed at each other, grab from each other, and even hit each other. Those are not friendly acts. Being someone's friend is voluntary. One of the worst things that you can do is to force someone to be another person's friend (N. Johnson, 2019). At one school where I taught, we were supposed to always address the students as *friends*, as in, "Listen, friends, we are going to do this activity now." You were supposed to put the word *friends* into every sentence. It was as if the act of repeating something made it come true in real life. It sounded hollow and never worked. Yes, students have to respect one another and get along, but they don't always have to be friends.

I have no problem assigning partners for a school activity, because you don't have to be friends to do that; you just have to get along with each other. That's what I explain if students don't like a partner assignment. But if a student does not want to be another student's friend, most of the time it is because the first is just not in the mood to play with the other student—at that time. This mood is usually temporary. Also, the one who was rejected forgets about the former friend when playing with a new friend. When both students see each other subsequently, everything goes back to normal—friends again!

The students who come to me with the complaints don't know this, but I do. They are distressed, but if I remain calm, slightly sympathetic, and reassuring, they start to feel calmer. Once they learn that when another kindergartener says, "I don't want to be your friend," it doesn't mean forever—it only means right now—they are less likely to get distressed or come to me next time. They either play alone happily or find a new friend to play with.

What to Do When a Student Has a Tantrum

What do you do if a student is having a tantrum? In general, I let students tantrum all they want—within reason. If the tantrumer and no one else is endangered, and class materials are not being ruined, someone can go for it. A tantrum is usually "a way a child communicates his or her feelings" (Stanford Children's Health, n.d.). My favorite was the student who threw shoes.

Crying, which often happens in tandem with a tantrum, is a form of communication (Provine, Krosnowski, & Brocato, 2009), as well as stress relief and emotion regulation (Rivera, 2015). Don't demand that someone stop crying; that is the opposite of the kind of safe classroom

> **Crying, which often happens in tandem with a tantrum, is a form of communication.**

you want to create. If you want a student to stop crying, deal with the issue they are crying about. Then teach that there is a more efficient way to solve a problem: talk about it! Children are reasonable, rational, and efficient at heart. They won't disappoint you in that regard.

If a student is in danger or endangering another during the tantrum, you must restrain the student (page 71). However, in my experience, very few tantrums fall into this category. A tantrum usually follows this pattern: someone gets upset and starts to tantrum. The student is so into his or her tantrum as to not even know what he or she is doing—but usually has the sense not to endanger themselves or others.

Clinical psychologist Jacqueline Sperling (2020) recommends actively ignoring tantrums, as attention only feeds the behavior. When a student launches into a tantrum, I go about my business while keeping the student in the corner of my eye and, of course, using my Super Teacher sense of hearing. The student will keep tantrumming and, at some point, give me the *look*. I often make a game with myself to see how long it will take until I get the look, but it always comes. The look is the student saying, "Here I am having a tantrum. What are you going to do about it? I'm sure you want me to stop. I will, if you give me what I want."

My response, usually sent by body language, is along the lines of "I'm not going to do anything about it, and I'm not going to discuss what you're having a tantrum about until you stop. You must be expending a lot of energy and getting tired, but when you're done, I am here and will talk to you." This elicits one of two reactions.

- **The student calms down:** If he or she calms down, then the game is over.
- **The tantrum escalates:** If the tantrum escalates, the student will eventually give me the next look, which says, "Well, how about me now? I bet you didn't think that I could scream this loud or cry this hard, did you? What's your next step?"

At this point, some of the other students usually get annoyed at the situation and cover their ears or ask me to make the tantrumming student stop. But I know that if I stay calm, the other students will stay calm. Ignoring the behavior is another option (Watson, Watson, & Gebhardt, 2010). I tell the students that at some point the tantrum will be done. Once students understand the duration of the tantrum, which is usually not prolonged anyway, it becomes a non-factor.

To the tantrumming student, I give the same message I did before: "You can scream, yell, cry, shout bloody murder, whatever you want to do for as long as you want to. When you're done, I'll speak to you. By the way, we're having a fine time here doing a great activity. You must be really tired now that you have expended even more energy. You would probably be having more fun if you were playing with us." This is usually communicated via the body language, but once in a while I will have to explicitly say this—in kinderese of course. That usually finishes it, but you never know. A persistent student may further escalate or may go down a notch to conserve energy but stay at it.

It may take a few rounds with the most persistent student, but the tantrum will end. Then the student's natural sense of reasonableness and logic return, and I can work out the problem that initiated the tantrum in the first place and give the student more fruitful alternatives to tantrumming. (In extreme cases, you will want to contact your school's counselor, social worker, or psychologist, and the parent or guardian. There could be something going on with which the student needs help.)

The student has learned from this experience that a tantrum is a dead end that's using up a lot of energy that could be used for other things in the student's best interest—at least that's the way it's going to be in school, with this teacher. The tantrum will stay in the student's toolbox of effective strategies only if it proves effective with parents or other teachers.

Sometimes a student has a tantrum as an attempt to avoid a consequence for a different behavior (Teaching Tolerance, 2016). After the tantrum is over, I give the consequence right away. It takes a lot of courage to do this, but it should be done. If you truly feel that carrying out the consequence right away will cause another major blowout, you can defer the consequence, but *let the student know you are deferring it* and don't delay in giving it more than one day. You will be surprised how quickly, easily, and cooperatively a student will usually accept the consequence. Never teach from a place of fear—fear of students, fear of parents, fear of administrators. The only fear you should have is for the safety and learning of your students.

In case you're wondering, I don't give a student a consequence for having a tantrum, as it is simply a form of expression. On the other hand, a student will bear some responsibility if he or she harms others or property during that time.

What to Do About Oppositional Defiant Disorder Behaviors

None of your class-management tricks are likely to work with a student who has oppositional defiant disorder (ODD; Johns Hopkins Medicine, n.d.). ODD is a "recurrent and developmentally inappropriate pattern of angry/irritable, negative, defiant, disobedient, and hostile behavior toward others that causes functional impairment; and this pattern persists for at least 6 months" (as cited in Lin et al., 2019). It is no wonder; the disorder has them specifically challenging authority figures (American Psychiatric Association, 2013).

I outlined in chapter 4 (page 55) the predominant reasons most children misbehave, but these are not commonly applicable in the case of ODD. Children with ODD seek out confrontation. ODD results not only in confrontation but also in escalating to the most extreme level as quickly as possible. Restraint may turn into a fight. You need to have a lot of self-control when you are working with someone who has ODD. If you don't, the person can lure you into using physical force.

In all my years in education, I have only taught two or three students who had this disorder. Statistics are only estimates, and they vary, with researchers saying that between 2 percent and 16 percent of children have the syndrome (Mishra, Garg, & Desai, 2014). However, you do yourself a grave disservice if you quickly label a student who presents difficulties, even the *most* difficult student, with the disorder. Don't throw up your hands the first time you encounter a challenging student and convince yourself he or she has ODD.

Students who have ODD need services—usually a one-to-one paraprofessional with them at all times. You should definitely document all incidents of misbehavior a student who has ODD presents and seek out resources from your administration so they can start evaluating the situation and, hopefully, request a psychological evaluation.

Struggling with this student doesn't mean you are a bad teacher, or that your methods don't work, or that you are powerless. Your goal is to give students what they need. Follow your school's procedures for an evaluation referral and possibly related services, such as a dedicated paraprofessional or a transfer to a more appropriate educational setting.

STUBBORN BELIEVER

A new student walked into class late nearly all the way through my first year teaching. Soon, it was obvious to me that I was in the presence of someone who had ODD. He threw the whole balance of the room out of whack within thirty minutes of entering, trying to hit other students, succeeding in hitting them, cursing, throwing things, and so on. The teaching year was put on hold. I was rattled a bit, but I am stubborn, and I believe in children.

> I didn't have to find out what would happen in the long run. I discovered the next day that he would calm down a bit if I held his hand as if he were my partner for the day, so that is what I did. I could have a conversation with him, and he could do some activities with my assistance. All was going well. I felt like Mr. Super Teacher. Then, out of nowhere, he leaned down and took a big chomp out of my hand. Ouch!
>
> I never saw that student again. My guess is that when the administration reported this to the parents they put him into another school. I wish I could have warned that next teacher what to expect.
>
> A few years later, I encountered another student who had ODD. This student climbed on shelves, yelled at her teacher, and could not be reasoned with, in addition to throwing things and hitting others. She repeatedly ran out of her classroom, with teachers trying to chase her down. So, she was put in my class and had a paraprofessional who stayed with her throughout the day. It turns out that the consistency of my class, along with the special attention from the paraprofessional, worked. When I say *worked*, I mean that she made observable progress over a long period of time. As the layers of defiance peeled away, she revealed her talents, interests, and humor. It was a very rewarding teaching experience, and I grew to really like her.

What do you do until the cavalry comes? That's a very hard question to answer. Think class safety above all else. I have seen incremental improvement in students with ODD using the management techniques I have outlined in this book, but you will feel like you are going into battle every day until they have received the proper support services they need.

In a Nutshell

In order to be an effective class manager, you must adopt the role of the authoritative teacher and be bound by the many rules you need to follow in order to gain the trust and cooperativeness of your students. Understand that impulse control is a major challenge for children of kindergarten age and this contributes to what we perceive as misbehavior. The gift of self-control, which students will attain in an environment where consistency, predictability, and fairness are the norms, is one that they will truly cherish and appreciate.

Once you understand the many techniques (and their limitations and benefits) at your disposal to foster positive behavior in your classroom, and apply the teacher's seven rules to yourself, you will be able to approach class management with confidence and skill.

Have You Mastered the Chapter?

Welcome to the formal assessment section of the book—a quiz to test your knowledge of the chapter. Please try the questions. The answers are provided after the questions section for a quick check. I explain the *why* after the quiz, and that is the most important part to consider.

According to this chapter:

1. The best positive reinforcement for a student is when a teacher:
    a. Gives the student a sticker
    b. Shows genuine appreciation of the student's act
    c. Points out the positive behavior to the other students
    d. Calls the parent to tell them about it

2. A good class manager needs to be:
    a. Predictable
    b. Fair
    c. Stubborn
    d. All of the above

3. Those most bound by classroom rules are:
    a. The students
    b. The classroom pet
    c. The teacher
    d. The principal

4. A major behavioral issue with many kindergarteners is:
    a. Having impulse control
    b. Following a sequence of directions
    c. Remembering the rules
    d. Hitting other students

5. The true meaning of discipline is:
    a. Knowledge
    b. Obedience
    c. Cooperation
    d. Directing

6. It's OK:
    a. If a student doesn't say "I'm sorry" to another student
    b. To let students go to the bathroom if nature is calling, no matter when it is
    c. If a student doesn't want to be another student's friend
    d. To let a student tantrum unrestrained

7. One end goal of good class management is:
    a. The hum
    b. The buzz
    c. The twist
    d. The purr

8. In relation to teaching, a roller coaster is a good example of:
    a. Your typical school year
    b. Your relationship with parents
    c. A well-run classroom
    d. All of the above

9. In the classroom, the term *wa* specifically alludes to:
    a. Class attentiveness
    b. Class harmony
    c. Class freedom
    d. All of the above

Answers and Explanations

1. **b. (Shows genuine appreciation of the student's act)** I am not a big fan of stickers, although I admit that they are popular and have their place as a reward. All students want their classmates and parents to know how smart and talented they are. However, when a student feels truly appreciated by someone as important as a teacher, it is a very powerful reinforcement indeed.

2. **d. (All of the above)** Students thrive on predictability and fairness in a teacher. Sometimes being an authoritative teacher means having to let them know that you will consistently stick with your principles and, if necessary, outstubborn them.

3. **c. (The teacher)** Rules, rules, rules—everybody's got to follow them. Well, maybe not the classroom pet. The principal has loads of rules to follow but we're talking about the classroom here. If you expect students to follow rules, you are bound by even more rules yourself to ensure that you are predictable and fair in your practice.

4. **a. (Having impulse control)** Most behavioral roads lead to issues with impulse control, which at the kindergarten age is totally within developmental expectations. Hitting other students is often an example of that. The other behaviors listed might be attributable to a student not being familiar with rules and routines or other developmental factors.

5. **a. (Knowledge)** Obedience and following directions are part of discipline, but that's not to say that it should be done in a blind manner. Discipline is about conveying the accepted cultural rules of society in a rational way to act cooperatively with others.

6. **a., b., c., and d. (All OK)** These are all OK. First, the feeling of being sorry has to come from inside a person. Give the student time. Usually students will want to say they're sorry voluntarily. Not letting someone go to the bathroom because it's outside a set time is an authoritarian practice. If nature is really calling, it needs to be answered. Give students the freedom to express how they feel about others and give them space and respect if they need a break from each other. You'll see that most often this is a fleeting emotion and they will play together soon. Though sometimes a student in a tantrum needs to be

restrained (if the student or someone else is in danger of being hurt), for the most part, you can let a student tantrum and reason with him or her after the histrionics are over.

7. **a. (The hum)** I use the term *hum* to describe the way it sounds in a classroom when students are challenged and engaged. I guess you could also call it a *buzz* or a *purr*.

8. **c. (A well-run classroom)** I hope that after reading this book you will acquire techniques that make your school year and relationship with parents and guardians as smooth as glass. If you start to think of a roller coaster as a fun ride that is both chaotic but predictable and incorporate these ideas into your practice, your classroom will feel both free and controlled at the same time.

9. **b. (Class harmony)** Wa is all about harmony. Harmony is calm, peaceful, and stress free, and that is what you want your classroom to be. A harmonious classroom has attentive students and a sense of freedom permeating the air, but these are just aspects of wa.

Being an Authoritative Teacher

After dealing with a specific classroom incident that was not resolved effectively, use this checklist to help compare your actions with the Seven Rules for the Teacher. Check off the rule (or rules) that would have resulted in a better outcome. Think of ways you can be more consistent in following this rule in the future and note them after the rule.

- ☐ **Rule 1:** Always be predictable.
- ☐ **Rule 2:** Make the consequence fit the incident.
- ☐ **Rule 3:** Never threaten a student.
- ☐ **Rule 4:** Ensure that yes always means yes and no always means no.
- ☐ **Rule 5:** Don't reward a student for negative behavior.
- ☐ **Rule 6:** If you didn't see it, you probably shouldn't give a consequence.
- ☐ **Rule 7:** Don't force apologies.

Managing Conflicts

Use this checklist to help manage classroom conflicts between students.

	Yes	No
Did I see what happened?		
Are all students safe?		
Did I need to use any physical methods? ____ Physical escort ____ Physical restraint		
Did I listen to each student's version of what happened?		
Did I determine whether a consequence was necessary?		
Was the consequence fair and reasonable?		
Did I make sure not to force one student to apologize to the other?		
Did I stay calm, cool, and collected throughout the whole affair?		

CHAPTER 5

Planning Routines

You are now ready to apply the thinking teacher's philosophy along with your understanding of effective class management to the practicalities of running your classroom. The chapter starts with how to foster your students' independence. Independence empowers students with a sense of responsibility, control, and accomplishment and frees you up to focus more on the act of teaching. This correlates directly with the frame on which your instruction lays: routines and transitions. I review some important routines such as unpacking in the morning, starting days with a morning quiz, lining up students, getting the class's attention, and bathrooming.

Fostering Independence Right From the Start

Independence is a big theme in kindergarten when trying to avoid conflict and establish routines. Here are two quotes from esteemed educational pioneer Maria Montessori (as cited in American Montessori Society, 2019) about the subject: "The child looks for his independence first, not because he does not desire to be dependent on the adult. But because he has in himself some fire, some urge, to do certain things and not other things," however, the "child's individual liberty must be so guided that through his activity he may arrive at independence." With all this in mind, it has to be firmly understood that while kindergarteners want to be independent and have that capability, they are still very dependent people, especially at the beginning of the year.

We move them toward independence over time. Reading books to students about becoming independent, or instructing them to act independently, will not work alone. Fostering independence, like any other subject, involves gradual release (Fisher & Frey, 2008) and all the processes that go along with good teaching. When you do something for students, it is not with the mentality of a servant. It is with the understanding that you are showing or modeling for them how to do it. The second they are able to do it alone, it becomes their job.

At the beginning of the school year, you are going to do everything the students have not yet learned to do or cannot yet do for themselves. If you want a totally independent room by the end of the year, where students are doing most everything for themselves, including making their own decisions, this is where you start. Think things through.

A major classroom routine is what to do on entering the classroom. Before telling them to unpack their belongs at the beginning of the day, ask yourself, "Do they know where their cubby spots are? Do they know how to take off their jackets, to hang up their backpacks, what needs to be taken out of the backpacks, where the rug is, what to do when they get there?"

At the beginning of the year, I try to give students the illusion that school is one big choice time. Then I slowly wean them off that notion and choice time becomes one period a day. So, on the first day of school and thereafter, until they can do it on their own, I go over every item to unpack and start their day. I work with each student individually. While I do this, I have the other students do the one activity they can do intuitively and cooperatively, with the least direction possible. I simply have them play! It's choice time until I'm done. I do the same at the end of the day when they need to pack up. One might say that this is a lot of time and effort for something that is basically procedural. But procedure and routine are the bed of rice on which you are going to lay the spontaneity and creativity.

Also, this method serves as a great initial individual assessment of each student. I learn about their fine motor skills, verbal skills, ability to sequence and follow directions, academic preparedness, and most importantly, their personality. No, I don't write any of this down—I am too busy teaching them what to do. In turn, the students get to learn about my personality and see me as a nice person who is there to help them throughout their day.

> **Procedure and routine are the bed of rice on which you are going to lay the spontaneity and creativity.**

As the days progress, I let students assume more responsibility for unpacking their own belongings. They know that they are expected to do this on their own. They have my model to refer to as well as the other students' models, and they know that the quicker they get it done properly the more time they have to play. They also are aware of my powers of observation and authoritative approach, so if they didn't unpack properly, they will be fixing the issue. In short time, more students can do the complete task independently and with my confidence that it is done according to my expectations. After only a few days, choice time period dwindles down to about fifteen minutes. I then phase out choice time in the morning entirely and start the day with the morning quiz (page 97).

> **STAYING THE COURSE**
>
> In my first year of teaching kindergarten, I was blessed with seven or eight students with significant behavioral issues. In my opinion, most of them would have qualified for behavioral individualized education plans (IEPs) and should have been in a class with a higher teacher-to-student ratio, a special education expert, and a personal paraprofessional attendant.
>
> These students threw sharpened pencils around the room; tried to run out of the room; had angry tantrums, turning over and throwing chairs, or punching other students in the chest; exhibited inattention and hyperactivity; and so on. Welcome to teaching! Also, in the middle of the year a student diagnosed with oppositional defiant disorder, which results in argumentativeness, vindictiveness, and an easily lost temper (Mayo Clinic, n.d.), joined the class.
>
> Anyway, I stayed the course. I didn't send any of the students to the principal's office and was not on the phone with the parents every day about their children. I basically used the educationally sound, appropriate ways I previously mentioned as well as the tips in the next section about discipline to help the students modify their behavior. I taught my tail off right through the very last day of school, but I had these students pretty much under control in a few weeks. As this was my first year of teaching kindergarten, I thought that this was the norm.
>
> That was by far my most challenging year of teaching. Every year since has been smooth sailing by comparison. The point is that I took it on myself to manage my class. I was green, with no experience teaching kindergarten, but I did it—and so can you!

Lining Up

I find that a line is a wonderful social and academic learning tool. Students are lined up constantly during the day: to go to another room, for lunch, for fire drills, and for dismissal. Because lining up is a brand-new concept for some students, and because it's such a common part of the school experience, I talk about why to line up, how to line up, how to handle stairs with kindergarteners, and how to handle students who talk in line.

Why to Line Up

Kindergarten-age children are used to holding a parent or caregiver's hand. When walking with the parent, a child is free to let his or her eyes and mind wander around to whatever strikes his or her attention. Take away the parent and give the child the hand of another child. Now both are walking around with wandering minds. Now, multiply that by twelve, and you have an idea how a kindergarten line looks at the beginning of the year.

The most important benefit of lining up students is that they develop what I call *line awareness*—the ability to recognize where they are in space and to know the surrounding environment. The way to teach line awareness is to keep the students on their toes, so they have to be aware—no autopilot here. I gather my students from the auditorium in the morning, and we line up to go to the classroom, which is one flight up. Once I establish a simple route I almost never take the same route twice. That would be too predictable and therefore decrease line awareness. I might even go up to the second floor and then come back down with them to our floor. This not only develops line awareness but overall awareness of the school environment. A lot of students know their school only by the specific pathways they take to the class, gym, cafeteria, and auditorium. Now they are discovering multiple paths around the school and their minds are being exposed to flexible thinking, all by this routine that is often overlooked.

I also do line tricks to develop line awareness. I may have the students walk backward, turn around 180 degrees, and other types of things. It's a lot of fun, and the turning around part comes in handy when we find out we are going the wrong way, and also during fire drills.

While the students walk in the line, I reinforce concepts I have been teaching (as in Teaching Left and Right, page 195). I can have the line leader stop at a certain shape, number, or letter he or she sees, or at a certain number of tiles, for example, or the leaders walk until they see a feature of the school, such as a fire extinguisher or an exit sign. Later in the year, I can incorporate addition and subtraction problems, left and right, and just about anything else I have taught. When the students get good at recognizing and understanding these concepts, I can start coding with them. This is where I give them a sequence of directions to follow.

I usually don't stay in a particular place in the line. If I am in the front, I am usually walking backward—a skill I had to develop. I make sure that each student is holding his or her partner's hand without a gap to the next pair of partners. On the staircase, I stand at the midpoint, so I can see the whole line as it proceeds up the stairs.

How to Line Up

You have some options at your disposal, and like discipline, some of them work and some of them don't. The following sections explain the ineffective and effective ways of lining up.

Ineffective Line-Ups

The following sections reveal pros and cons of lining up student with partners, by height, by gender, and with the rope technique.

With Assigned Partners

My second teaching job was as a preK teacher in an early learning center. I started there in February, so all the routines had already been established. I watched how they lined up the students. It took at least fifteen minutes. A student would be paired with another student, and the two would start arguing. The pair was then switched. Then someone would say he didn't like his partner, so they would be switched. Then someone would say she had the same partner yesterday, so they would be switched. The negotiations dragged on and on until, finally, the line was ready to go.

You might think this experience caused me to always assign partners. I never do assigned partners. First of all, you have to memorize them, and your brain is busy enough already with more worthwhile things. And one or more students being absent causes problems and delays. But the main reason that I don't assign line partners is that I am then randomly assigning a student a partner for most or all of the year. And the students cumulatively spend a lot of time in the line throughout the year, for better or worse.

By Height

Some teachers have their students line up by size. This means that as they are walking, the same students will always have the same perspective of the line. It doesn't seem fair to me that the shorter students will not know how it feels to be at the back of the line and that the tall ones will never be line leaders (or vice versa).

By Gender

One of the more popular ways teachers line up their students is to have a line of boys and a line of girls. The boy holds hands with the girl he is next to, so it's a line of boy-girl, boy-girl. This assumes an equal number of girls and boys, which never happens. However, this is not my main issue with this method. I do find this method to be the fastest to line up the students, so I do use it—for fire drills, and then only out of necessity. Otherwise, I don't, because it highlights and focuses too much on gender differences and assumes a person's gender based on appearance.

Remember that I said that children notice differences but they don't judge them? When you start lining up in this way or make groups based on gender, you will invariably start saying, "The girls lined up so well today." Or "Come on, girls, let's move it!" and so forth with the boys. The students start seeing themselves as *boy* children with certain characteristics, or as *girl* children with certain characteristics, as opposed to seeing themselves as simply as children and students. This type of talk can also exacerbate a gender gap in academics.

You must cater to all your students. A certain small percentage of your students may not conform to what one might see as traditional gender roles. This small but significant percentage can suffer under circumstances that emphasize gender divisions because students with a nonbinary identification who question their gender may feel forced to select one group or the other. When confronted with such a choice, no safe space exists for these students. Research also confirms the psychological damage this causes (Martin & May, 2020).

With the Rope

At one of my preschools, they had a different method for lining up. It was known as *the rope*. The practice was to have a huge rope with handholds. The teacher would hold the handhold at the front and each student would take his or her own handhold. I assume they did this because they thought it was the safest way to have a line. But what is to keep a student from letting go of one of the handholds? I would rather have another student who can talk to, hold, and restrain an antsy student than a piece of twine.

I tried the rope once. I took hold of the lead handhold and it was like pulling seventeen students who were sitting in a cart as opposed to a teacher facilitating the students' journey through their environment. Line awareness? There was none. Then I thought, "What if a child actually ran off the line?" If I have a line of students holding each other, there is an automatic control on each. If a student runs off this line, I have to drop the rope. I just dropped sixteen controls right there! I ditched the rope and had a beautiful group of line-aware preschoolers walking around in no time.

Effective Line-Ups

The following sections explain the effective three-by-three method and my preferred method, by random partner.

Three-by-Three

An assumption exists that students must walk in line as pairs. However, if safety is of paramount concern, such as when you are on a trip, you can always have them walk as trios. This makes the line very compact, so it is easier to manage. To achieve the safest line, you should put the most line-aware students in the middle positions and have the less-aware students hold either of their hands.

Random Partners—Preferred Method

This is how I fixed the line situation in a school I used to work at. I simply assigned random partners every time the students lined up. When students said that they didn't like their partners, I responded that they didn't have to. This was not their friend—it was their partner. They usually accepted this logic.

In no time, the students got the idea that they were stuck with their partners, but only temporarily, and it was in their best interest to get along. They then started finding ways to get along with anyone who was their partner. Over time, they were able to get along with any other students they lined up with. Class wa was on its way. We lined up quickly every day, with no issues, and were efficiently on our way to the next activity.

I simply call the line. This is where nicknames get put to good use. Each student is on his or her toes trying to figure out who I am actually calling and who will be his or her partner for that particular line. No one knows who will be the line leader or the "caboose" until I start calling out names. It's a fun process and takes about one minute.

Having a random line means new line leaders every time. This is a very responsible position, because I usually don't stand in front of the line. It is a job like any other job in the classroom, so if they can't do the job, they lose it. They will get another chance soon enough. In the interim, all the students watch and learn from those who know how to do it.

These are the reasons I think that this line-up approach works best: within a few weeks, every student has been partners with all the others, has been in every position in the line, and has been a line leader. No, I don't have a systemized checklist and probability randomizer to make sure that this works out scientifically. But with 180 days in the school year and about five line-ups per day, I am confident this is the case. In a very short time, I have a class of line experts, which is a good thing to have—especially when it comes to emergencies.

How to Handle Stairs

When working with kindergarteners, you will notice one thing on the staircase, especially at the beginning of the year. A few students need to get both feet on the next step they are going to before they can proceed to another step. They find it difficult to step over by putting one foot on a step and the other foot on the following step. As in most things students learn, it's usually a matter of their being taught how to do it and practicing. It takes more time for young and small students to master this because it is a big distance for them, and they are still developing their gross motor skills. Work on having these students step over from one step to the next, both for going up and going down, since they are separate skills. My kinderese term for this is *going one step*. That is the goal for most kindergarteners who don't have physical limitations.

I differentiate and give those who need it special attention until they acquire that skill. So, some of my tutoring time on my prep might be taking a student to the stairs and teaching how to do *one step–one step* using the usual teaching methodologies of example, demonstration, and guided practice.

Table 4.1 is what I sound like when my class is walking up the stairs. I am behind everyone so I can see all of them ascending.

Table 4.1: Directing Students Up and Down Stairs

WHAT I SAY	WHAT I AM DOING
"OK, go to the top and stop."	Instructing the student at the head of the line to ascend the staircase until he or she reaches the first step with the rest of the class following
"One step, one step."	Instructing students to remember to step over each step as they walk up (instead of having both feet on one step at a time)
"No spaces."	Instructing students to walk up with their partner to the step that is directly behind the partners in front of them, so that every pair is on an individual step, with no step unoccupied
"I'm on the left." or "I'm on the right."	Telling students that I am walking up from behind on their left or right side and that they should move slightly over to let me through (sometimes for a little fun, "I'm coming up the middle" for relational word instruction)
"Go to the next."	Instructing the line leaders to go to the top of the next staircase, but using a different phrase that relates to sequencing comes in handy when teaching *first*, *next*, and *last*—especially when it comes time to teach writing genres

Of course, these are all kinderese terms, and while I am saying these phrases, students are chatting among themselves and I am having fun observing and interacting with them.

How to Handle Talking in Line

Do I let the students talk when they are walking in the line? Of course I do! I encourage it! Talking fosters an exchange of ideas and social interaction. What is bad about talking? I expect the students to be quiet and listening during many parts of the day for different purposes. I don't see the purpose for this in a line. The default should always be the freedom to talk. Students can speak even while they are developing line awareness.

I can regulate the volume by teaching that my hand is the volume control, then showing them their current level and where they need to be. If they are near volume level ten (they would go to eleven if allowed to), I simply put my hand to my forehead and slowly move it downward to my neck, and it's really like using the volume knob on my stereo system.

The only time the students have to be quiet in the line is when there is a fire drill. In this case, my index finger on my lips is the signal for total quiet. The other time total silence is required is if we are passing the class of a particularly irritable teacher who left his or her door open and cannot tolerate anything but complete silence. Then it's like a bump in the road—finger on my lips for five seconds and hand back to my chest.

Starting With a Morning Quiz

Once the students have mastered the art of unpacking, they learn about the quiz. Every morning when they enter the class, they stay in line. I am usually sitting on a table near the rug area. Each student comes to me, one by one, and I ask a question. The question might be based on a concept or skill we just learned, or it might be preteaching. The questions vary from day to day and can be in any subject area. I tailor the question to each student's skill level.

So, if it is a question on counting and a student can count to 10, I might ask him or her what number comes after 8. If the student can count higher, I might ask what number comes after 18. I might ask what number comes before another number, or I might ask a student to count backward. If I will be teaching about 3-D shapes in a few weeks, I might have a few shapes in front of me and see which ones each student can identify.

This serves many purposes.

- I get a lot of academic information about each student individually and about the class as a whole.

- I see how everyone is doing emotionally.
- I check for visible bruises or things of that nature that I need to be concerned about.
- This staggers the students, because the next thing they do is hang up their coats and unpack.

You might think the students would be impatient standing in line—my philosophy is always to keep them engaged and moving. However, they don't mind. They use the time, consciously or subconsciously, to do the following things.

- Become reacquainted with their friends.
- Pay attention to what I am doing so they are prepared for when they get to me.
- Get in the right mindset, so that when they step over the threshold of the classroom, they are immediately in a learning environment.

I can do nearly a whole lesson this way, and it only takes a few minutes.

Getting the Class's Attention

The first thing to remember is that there is no one way to get every student's attention. At one school I worked in, the administration insisted that every teacher use the method of clapping three times to get the students' attention, so that any teacher or substitute could walk into any class and apply the magic method and it would work. I remember being asked by a principal to substitute for a few minutes in a class in which the teacher had an emergency. I tried the schoolwide magic method (clapping), and it worked! For about a full second. Then the students resumed talking among themselves. When the principal came in to check on the class, her mere presence stopped the talking dead in its tracks. The effectiveness of any method is totally contingent on who is using it. The students didn't know me but they were used to the method. So, they reacted to it and then resumed their business. However, they knew the principal and understood the consequences of misbehaving, so the principal didn't even need to use the method at all.

> **The effectiveness of any method is totally contingent on who is using it.**

Some teachers turn off the light to get students' attention. Others carry an implement, like a bell or whistle. Those are great techniques, but they have their limitations. I tried the light switch technique when I first started teaching and found myself sprinting across the room to the switch when I wanted the students' attention. When I was in the hallways or outside with the class, this method was not usable. I also tried the whistle method but after finding myself constantly fumbling through my pockets and then sometimes realizing that I had misplaced it, I aborted. I wasn't too interested in wearing a whistle necklace. Some teachers use a cute rhyme or a soft song to capture attention. Great idea on paper, as poetry and music should be an integral part of your classroom. But what if you have a fire drill, or a lockdown, or a student is about to do something unsafe? A cute ditty just won't do at that point.

Your goal is to get students' attention as quickly and authoritatively as you can. From that point on, your message can be funny, informative, or serious—whatever you needed their attention for in the first place.

I use a simple countdown. I usually start from ten, but I can start it from any number I wish, depending on how quickly I want their attention. A note about this method, if you decide to use it: your voice must be calm but firm, and you must count down evenly. Let's say the class is at the rug, and you are ready to do a read-aloud. You will start at ten and count down evenly to one. A lot of teachers will start the countdown, and when they get to the number three and see that the students are not ready, they will start going "*three*," then "*two*." Then they will sometimes pause and do the popular "*one and a half*" and then wait until they think the class is ready and then go, "*one*." If the students aren't ready, they will do the countdown again, or say the infamous, "Well, I'll just sit here and wait until you are ready." This is backward teaching. You have just changed the whole dynamic from the students taking your cue and getting ready for a reading session to you taking their cues. You have to count down to one only once and do it evenly.

What happens if the students are still talking when I get to one? Then the *unhappy* authoritative teacher emerges. There are times of the day when you are facilitating the students or are lurking in the background while the students work independently. This is not one of those times. This is a time when you are front and center and you demand attention. Unhappy teacher will point out in a matter-of-fact, nonjudgmental way by name who is doing the right thing, but also who is not.

A lot of teachers are taught that you have to work only in the positive. For example, if a student is not sitting properly, you don't address him directly but point out another who is sitting properly and the other student will do the same because he wants a compliment too. This works sometimes, but sometimes the student who is not sitting properly couldn't care less what the others are doing. So, you have to keep it real and let everyone know what you expect of them and that if they persist, a consequence is coming. Unhappy teacher is like that. A few countdowns like this and when you get to "one," everybody will be sitting like angels. Just kidding. These are children. But they will be very close to sitting angelically.

Some teachers count down evenly and then start the activity whether the students are ready or not. The idea is that the students will come around to you and start paying attention. Unfortunately, this technique often doesn't work. If you start your activity when students are talking, the student who is talking thinks that it's OK to do this when you are ready to teach.

I look at whole-group time as if the students are the orchestra and I am the conductor (*conduct* or . . . Get it?). At least at its outset, the conductor will tap the baton to alert the musicians that the piece is ready to begin and will not start until every musician is in tune and ready to play. You do the countdown, make sure the students are ready, and begin. Let the music play!

Handling Transitions

Transitions are, of course, the times of the day where students end one activity and move to another. Transitions are a stressful time for many teachers. They are the times when the teacher feels that he or she has the least control of the room and when there is the greatest chance of mischief. Transitions occur multiple times throughout the day, so a teacher who does not have a good handle on managing them will indeed have little control over a room of potentially mischievous students. Here are some tips to handle them effectively. See the reproducible "Handling Transitions" (page 106) for a checklist.

- **Avoid rushing into a transition without preparing students for it:** Start prepping them for the next activity long before the present activity ends. Begin prepping while the students are in the midst of the present activity. It's a form of preteaching. You are putting a little arrow in their head that points them in the next direction. You can do this by mapping out the various parts of the day. They won't remember each activity specifically or be able to recite them back to you, but you have planted the seed.

- **Have a worthwhile activity lined up:** That motivates students to move to it. It's like they are at the amusement park and one ride has just finished and there is another just starting. They will want to race from one to the other. The activity can be as simple as having a video projected on the SMART Board or working on whiteboards. Stagger the transition by allowing students who are finished within a few minutes of the activity's conclusion to move to the next one. Tell those who are still working that they have a few minutes left and count down minute by minute until there are no minutes left.

- **Make any cleanup as simple and quick as possible:** If they are writing, they should put the writing utensil into the bin and go. If they are working with mathematics manipulatives, just let them leave the table and go to the rug. You are teaching them about transitions, not cleaning up. One teaching point at a time. Your job, at this point, is to hustle everyone to the next activity, so they learn that as soon as they finish cleaning, it's time to move on. Cleaning up has to be kept as simple a job as possible. Who finishes the cleanup, then? You can, at first. Later, you will have helpers to do the work for you. I will discuss how you divvy up jobs in chapter 7 (page 123). This way, you can have three students cleaning up instead of twenty-five. Learning to clean up after oneself is a great exercise in responsibility, but we are after maximizing efficiency and learning during lessons.

Going to the Bathroom

And now the thorny issue of bathrooming. There are a few common paths teachers usually take when asked this question. When a student asks, "Can I go to the bathroom?" some teachers always say yes, and others always say no. Some say, "We'll see," and still others have students attend the restroom on a schedule.

Always "Yes"

Teachers who always say yes do so because they feel they have no right to keep a young student from going to the bathroom. Their worst fear is that a student will pee on him- or herself. It seems like sound thinking, but it really isn't. Going back to the class-management models, I would characterize this as permissive.

This is what happens with this model: the student goes to the bathroom and immediately another hand pops up. Then another. This will go on throughout the lesson, so that if a teacher is reading a book, he or she is reading it to a constantly rotating group. There will be no continuity or focus during any lesson because it will be constantly interrupted. If the bathroom is outside of the class, a student or groups of students will constantly be in the hallways without any supervision.

Sometimes, the permissive teacher will start to say no after a few students have gone to the bathroom. The idea is that this has now gotten out of hand and needs to be stopped. This teaches the students that the next time you want to get out of class, you need to put your hand up as early as possible. That is why the minute this teacher's lesson starts, the hands go up immediately. Also, you now have the situation in which a student who really has to go raises a hand and gets a *no* answer.

Always "No"

The teacher who always says no is following the model of the authoritarian teacher and this is downright cruel. The teacher will usually announce before a lesson that no one is permitted to go to the bathroom during the lesson, using the phrase "Don't even ask." This results in the usual scenario for the authoritarian teacher. Some students will squirm and hold on for all they're worth, and others won't even try and will relieve themselves in the classroom. Neither outcome is acceptable.

"We'll See"

As you know, I take the authoritative approach, which is the hardest approach to implement because it takes a lot of thinking, planning, observing, and decision making. But it gives the same results the authoritarian teacher wants with the empathy of the permissive teacher—you just don't have to go to either extreme.

Whether I say yes or no depends on a lot of factors. I will describe them in the next section. However, if a student asks to go to the bathroom, and it doesn't look to me like an emergency, I will usually say, "Do you really have to go?" or "Can you wait for a few minutes?" The reason is that I implement a schedule before we get to that point.

On Schedule

Yes, kindergarteners will have to go to the bathroom throughout the day, but it can be minimized if you put them on a schedule, especially at the beginning of the year. I also teach them that sometimes you get a sudden urge and then it passes.

If you have a bathroom in your classroom, you can stagger use during a specific time of the day. If you have a bathroom outside of the room, especially one with multiple stalls, you can have bathroom time once in the morning, once at lunch (usually under the supervision of a teacher's aide), and once in the afternoon. The whole procedure can be done in ten minutes or less.

Students at this age have pretty good control over their bowels, and they usually don't need to go this frequently (Everyday Health, 2018), so you can adapt to that as the year goes on. They will get used to the schedule, and your lessons will be disruption-free. But if they get the urge to go while they are getting used to the schedule, they will ask permission.

When this happens, you are going to consider the particular student, assess the situation, and make a decision. Unless I can tell that the need is immediate (the usual shaking of the knees, scrunching of the face, and putting their hands in front of themselves), I will ask the student to wait a bit, but I always follow up with the student a few minutes later. I will know that the student never had to go in the first place if I follow up, and he or she is engrossed in an activity and looks up at me as if to say, "What's your problem? I'm busy." On the other hand, if I follow up and the need is obvious, then obviously I let the student go.

There will always be students who will have to go to the bathroom in the middle of lessons, no matter what the schedule, and they will of course be allowed to relieve themselves. But your job is to make sure that the need is there and to teach the students that they do have body control in this area. The student who waited a bit and realized it was a false alarm learned that the need was not immediate and that this provided an opportunity to play with a friend. That was an important lesson in body control.

Have I ever made mistakes? Yes, and I don't feel good about them. This includes preschool, where the need to go is higher and the control is not as developed. It is not in my best interest to have students wet themselves. What about an angry parent? To the level that a mistake occurs, most parents understand, so they are not angry. There isn't a parent out there, including myself, who hasn't made a mistake, and we all feel bad about it. At the beginning of the year, I ask the parents if their children have any bathrooming issues, and I am communicating with them via email, so I already know about the special cases and accommodate them. Even so, I look at these students as works in progress and work with them over the course of the year so that their situations improve. It is like an advanced form of toilet training.

It is the same methodology if someone tells you that he or she needs a drink of water or a snack, or needs to eat lunch right away. The needs of learning have to be balanced with the student's individual needs.

In a Nutshell

Once the school year starts, you will begin immediately working on the students' age-appropriate independence skills. You will also be developing routines that are both efficient and educational. Keep experimenting until you find the right balance between your classroom goals and the needs and capabilities of the students in your class. Once established, you and your class will have built the vehicle that will drive you smoothly through the school year.

Have You Mastered the Chapter?

Welcome to the formal assessment section of the book—a quiz to test your knowledge of the chapter. Please try the questions. The answers are provided after the questions section for a quick check. I explain the *why* after the quiz, and that is the most important part to consider.

According to this chapter:

1. Sometimes the best response to "Can I go to the bathroom?" is:
    a. Yes
    b. No
    c. We'll see

2. The morning quiz lets you:
    a. Assess students academically and emotionally
    b. Perform a brief visual physical wellness check
    c. Stagger students as they put things away
    d. All of the above

3. The recommended way to line up students is:
    a. Randomly
    b. Boy-girl
    c. Height order
    d. Assigned line spots

Answers and Explanations

1. **c. (We'll see)** A *yes* answer can sometimes prompt a stampede, while a *no* answer might discourage students who really need to go. We all know what happens then. The thinking teacher evaluates every situation on its own and makes an informed judgment that can be changed when the circumstances warrant.

2. ***d. (All of the above)*** The morning quiz is a valuable tool for setting the academic tone for the day, making sure each student is physically and emotionally ready for a fun day of learning, and getting a quick one-on-one with the teacher.

3. ***a. (Randomly)*** The name of the game is to keep students guessing and engaged and letting them experience things from the most perspectives possible. Line-up is no exception. Choosing randomly every time you line up will accomplish these goals.

Handling Transitions

Use this checklist to determine whether you are managing transitions as well as possible.

- ☐ I prep students for the next activity long before the present activity ends.
- ☐ I have a worthwhile activity lined up.
- ☐ Our cleanup routines are as simple and quick as possible.

CHAPTER 6

Managing Whole-Group and Choice Time

You have twenty-five students sitting on the rug staring at you. What now? Welcome to whole-group time. It is a part of most every lesson and this chapter is about setting up properly, managing behavioral issues, and presenting lessons and materials in the most effective way so that students understand the concepts and skills you are targeting and so that the classroom is set up for a related activity afterward.

Mr. Rogers (as cited in Callahan, 2015) said it best: "Play is really the work of childhood." Play, or choice time, is essential to your class. It's everyone's favorite part of the day—unless you are not allowed to have one. I remember one consultant who, when asked about it, responded, "They don't need it. The children have played enough. They need to start learning at this point in their lives." We will pay that comment no mind. Every second of choice time is precious, and you should pack in as much play as possible into that period.

Managing Whole-Group Time

A lot of teaching theory and practice is about differentiating to reach each student through small groups and individualized instruction. These are effective ways to attain that goal. However, whole-group time is also very important and beneficial to students' learning and provides an additional and often overlooked way to differentiate. Early childhood consultant Judith Colbert (2008) says, this "time may be such a familiar part of the day that its full potential as a tool for teachers remains unrealized." Please make sure that this potential is realized, along with other methods of instruction, to ensure a well-balanced learning environment.

I think of whole-group, or circle, time as a form of small-group instruction, although my small group is then very large! I can review or introduce new material, initiate conversations, sing, or read a book, while at the same time observing each student and gauging the effectiveness of my teaching. This gets my gears working for setting up more individualized instruction. This time builds a sense of community, fosters language development through questions, answers, and class discussions (Scull, Paatsch, & Raban, 2013), and gives the class a focus for the day.

The following sections talk about how much time to allocate for whole group, differentiation in whole group, dance breaks, rug arrangements, and questions and discussions.

How Much Time

It is conventional wisdom that students at this age shouldn't sit for more than about ten minutes and therefore it follows, on its surface, that whole-group time should not exceed that amount of time. It is true that a five-year-old's attention span is about ten to fifteen minutes (Neville, 2007). However, I don't feel that the act of having students sit more than ten minutes is wrong or hurtful, which is sometimes the implication.

The real issue is that children shouldn't sit for more than short periods of times if they are not engaged during that time—in other words, when they are being lectured to. I do cringe when the art teacher, music teacher, or a guest comes into the room and drones on and on even as students start squirming and rolling their eyes. Yes, students have short attention spans and are highly distractible, but like the successful concert and movie, the teacher can change topics quickly and reset the ten-to-fifteen-minute span. I guess that you could call these a sequence of micro-lessons. Distractions (surprises and humor, for example) are built into the presentation. If students are engaged in this way, it is OK to go over that limit to a certain point.

Differentiation

To have a successful whole group, you must be able to differentiate within the group. The idea is that you are teaching each student individually all the time. You have to be like *Bugs Bunny* (Avery & Givens, 1938) or *The Simpsons* (Groening, 1989). Let me explain. My daughter loved *Barney & Friends* (Leach, 1992) until she was three years old, and then it was over. I can't watch *Barney* at all as an adult. But we could always watch *Bugs Bunny* or *The Simpsons* together at any age. That is because *Barney* emits on one frequency—very young child—while *Bugs Bunny* and *The Simpsons* emit on many frequencies, ranging from child to adult. The children won't necessarily get all the humor in these cartoons, but they will get some. These cartoons are firing on all cylinders—and they provide differentiated entertainment that engages viewers of many ages.

To differentiate during whole group, you might throw out a high-level concept or statement that will go over the heads of all but a few of the students but is still accessible to the students who don't understand it fully. You might then find an entertaining way to reinforce a concept that most of the students have mastered but specifically target it to struggling students. As I explained in chapter 2 (page 25) in regard to preparing a lesson from your curriculum, you can use videos, a song, movement, props, or even a silly voice, pose, or walk. Differentiation informs the philosophy for doing an effective whole-group lesson or activity. Chapter 2 also explains how you read through each lesson and prepare it for differentiation. Here is where you get to do it. You have to speak to students at their different levels at the same time.

It takes time and trial and error to develop this skill, as with most teaching skills. However, no matter how engaging you are, there will come a time when the students will need a break from sitting. And that is where the musical dance break comes in.

Dance Break

Even the most engaging and entertaining whole-group lessons have a limit. If you plan well, you will have moved to the next activity before reaching it, but if you see a few students losing focus—shifting positions frequently, becoming easily distracted, and chatting among themselves (especially after sitting more than the benchmark ten to fifteen minutes)—it is usually a sign that mental or physical fatigue has set in. It is time for a dance break. It is time for some music and exercise. It is known that "exercise increases brain serotonin function in the human brain" (Young, 2007, p. 396) and "listening to the music you love will make your brain release more dopamine" (Dolan, 2019). These are feel-good hormones. In the dance break, the students' brains feast on a double whammy of neurotransmitters that play an important role in our cognitive, emotional, and behavioral functioning.

> **No matter how engaging you are, there will come a time when the students will need a break from sitting.**

When I say *break*, I mean a real break—not a structured one. I simply put on a piece of music that lasts three to four minutes. Even during this fun time I am trying to educate my students, so I expose them to music of different genres and cultures, but usually something kindergarteners can dance to. There are dance programs where the students stay at their spots on the rug and copy the performers on screen. This is just an extension of whole-group time. We want to have a break from whole-group time at this point.

The students can go off and do what they want, with a few simple rules concerning chasing and running, of course. The students don't have to stay on the rug at this time. When the first student sheepishly takes a step off the rug and I encourage going to the rest of the room, the student looks at me incredulously and then goes. The others soon get the idea and follow. Once everything is established, controlled chaos ensues. Some students walk around, some talk with each other, some lie on the rug, and some even dance. Many times, they form their own dance circle or conga line—with absolutely no prompting from me!

After the song or musical piece is over, the students return to the rug all refreshed and ready for more learning fun. I might do a little more of whole group or we might transition to an activity or independent work—whatever is called for.

I might do one break a day, but not more than two a day. It just turns out that way. Sometimes there are no breaks. Breaks are never planned. It is simply another teaching tool that requires an awareness of your students and the atmosphere in your classroom to gauge when best to use.

Rug Arrangements

I have seen teachers arrange students in different ways on a rug. One popular way is to have them sit in a big circle. It's like a round table with everyone facing each other. It seems very egalitarian, and "it supports whole-class as well as pair-wise dialogue" (Yale University, 2019). I call it the *Kumbaya* seating plan. I like this way of arranging the students, but it doesn't work with my objective of having all students engaged all the time.

Instead, I always have the students sit in makeshift rows facing me in more of a traditional model. I sit on a child-sized chair. It is high enough so that all the students can see the book I am reading and low enough where I am not towering over them. I don't stay in the chair for long, as I frequently stand up to access the SMART Board or to demonstrate something to the class. It's the eyes-on-me part of the day for them and eyes-on-them part of the day for me, and this is the best seating arrangement for that. Other parts of the day I am inconspicuous, but not at whole-group time.

I don't have a rug spot for each student for the same reason that I don't assign line spots. I used to assign spots when I started teaching, but quickly found out that it was just another high-maintenance and low-reward system that was not necessary at all. The students sat just fine without assigned spots. They like to sit at different spots with different neighbors at different times for different reasons. I trust and give them the benefit of the doubt.

The only time I assign a spot is if a spot they have chosen hampers their ability to fulfill the expectations of the whole-group time. So, if a spot at the back doesn't work out, I will move them to the front and vice versa. Sometimes a student does better at the side than in the middle. Sometimes when two particular students sit next to each other, they become disruptive. In this case, I will tell them to separate either just for that day or for a longer period. I will also do this during the activity, especially if a student is persistent about not being cooperative.

If a student is continually disruptive, I will politely ask him or her to leave the circle. It doesn't work to send a student back to his or her seat, because if there are other disruptive students, you may wind up with a community of children populating the tables while the teacher caters to the survivors on the rug. The students sitting at their seats at the tables are the forgotten ones. They spend their time trying to amuse themselves or the others while the rest of the students are learning. Not good.

When I ask a student to leave the circle, I have the student sit on the periphery, right outside the circle. It is a form of *time away* (page 70) but applied to this specific context. He or she is is still expected to participate in the lesson and to use that space to learn. Although a student on the periphery is literally four inches from the next student, it can feel uncomfortable being there. The other students will usually pay no mind, as they are engrossed in the lesson, so this student does not feel singled out or shamed. I will continue the lesson, teaching to this student the same as the others, but the student is in a different spot. At this point, the student's motivation is to get back to the school of fish, not swim away from it. I give my subtle encouragement to continue in that vein. When the student is ready, which usually doesn't take too long, he or she is invited back to the circle and takes a spot without any fanfare.

Questions and Discussions

During whole-group time, I present a topic, concept, or skill for the students to master. At some point students will ask me questions, and other times I question the students. I teach that raising a hand to answer a question is very nice, but even if they don't raise a hand, they should still be thinking of an answer, because I may call on them anyway.

Students do *not* raise a hand for a few reasons.

- **They have not thought of an answer:** I sometimes call on someone who is not raising his or her hand to find out why and work with that student, so that he or she will engage with the learning that is going on. For example, if I call on a student who has not yet thought of an answer, I will say, "OK, I will get back to you." I always get back to the student.

- **They thought of an answer, but they think it is wrong:** If I call on a student who is reluctant to raise his or her hand because he or she thinks an answer is wrong, I will offer reassurance and ask him or her to share what he or she thinks. The student then finds out that either he or she was not wrong or that it was good that he or she was wrong (if it was a factual question), because that gave me an additional teaching point for the lesson. And of course, I let students know "There are no wrong answers."

- **They have a worthwhile answer, but are shy about raising their hands:** If a reluctant student gives me a great answer, I will say encouragingly, "That is a great answer. Why didn't you raise your hand in the first place?"

- **They are not paying attention:** If I call on a student and he or she has no answer because of not paying attention, I will tell him or her to start paying attention. Not participating is not an option. To engage a reluctant student, you must first present the student with engaging material, and the student has to then feel he or she is on call at any moment.

Managing Choice Time

The underlying rationale of choice time is for the students to have freedom, choices (hence its name), and fun! Almost every early childhood educator recognizes the importance of play, but it pays to repeat the words of child psychologist David Elkind (2008), who says that:

> Most of us engaged in the study of play consider it a form of exercise for creative dispositions—for imagination, for curiosity, for fantasy. We believe it has a vital role in human development. Through play, children create new learning experiences, and these self-created experiences enable them to acquire social, emotional, and intellectual skills they could not acquire in any other way. (p. 1)

Every second of choice time is precious, and you should pack in as much play as possible into that period. So, here's how to do choice time. First of all, get your mind right. Children can play. Children will play. Children *are* play. I have never met a child who did not know how to play. The sun shines; children play. Children do not have to be taught to play—they will teach you how to play. Yes, there are types of play and stages of play. Each child will master them over time—but just let them play enough and they will go through them all.

After that, consider station numbers and options, rules, start and end times, and cleanup. The reproducible "Preparing for Choice Time" (page 121) is a checklist that will help you get ready.

Station Numbers and Options

To have a successful choice time that students look forward to and excel in, you have to have many more choices than there are students. The one-child-one-choice model simply does not work. What if you went to a diner with two other people and there were three plates in front of the three of you—one was chicken, one was beef, and one was vegetarian? The waiter asks one of you to choose a plate, then asks the second person to choose, and of course, the third has no choice at all.

> **Children can play.**
> **Children will play.**
> **Children *are* play.**

My general rule is double the total number of students in the class to figure out how many play spots the room needs. If I have twenty-one students in my class, I have eleven different activity areas for them to choose from and a total of forty spots available every day. I would have more if I could've thought of a way to do that. I offer the following options as well as others.

- **Manipulatives:** I spend time trying to find new educational, open-ended, and challenging manipulatives. I now have a kid-tested collection, including Magna Tiles, Gear Builders, Snap and Build Blocks, and Marble Run. I have been around a lot of toys in my career and am always finding new ones for choice time. Lakeshore Learning (www.lakeshorelearning.com) and Constructive Playthings (https://constructiveplaythings.com) are popular and good resources to start with. You can also put out almost any of your mathematics manipulatives (page 197). Watch as students reinforce and extend the concepts that you have taught with them or retool the manipulatives for a use you never dreamed of.

- **Sand or water tables:** Why do children love the beach? The beach is just one big sand table that is connected to a big water table. I have separate sand and water tables and students often cite them as not only as their favorite choice time activities but their favorite school activities of all. I embrace the sandy and watery mess when they are engaged in communal play that accentuates mathematical skills such as measuring and volume. It is a small price to pay for such engaged learning.

- **Toy garage, farm, or playhouse:** I have one of each. I can add almost any small manipulative—animals, people, counters, craft sticks, or cotton balls

- **SMART Board:** I have transformed the SMART Board into a play area for two by simply letting students access its paint feature so that they have a big electronic canvas to be creative with. They can also access educational programs such as ABCYa (www.abcya.com), Raz-Kids (www.raz-kids.com), and Starfall (www.starfall.com) on the SMART Board.

- **Computers:** These consist of four laptops on a table that have access to open-ended educational games in literacy, mathematics, music, and art programs. It is a very social area, and students do all the things we hope that they would do in independent work, such as working as partners, bouncing ideas off one another, and instructing each other.

- **Creative ventures:** One toy towers above them all in terms of holding the students' interest and in helping them be creative, cooperative, and analytical. I can always count on building bricks, like Legos. I don't put them out every day, but I could if I wanted to, and I would always have a few takers. Every student of every generation I have taught has the same engaged and positive attitude about building blocks. The kitchen area comes in second, and clay, or Play-Doh, comes in third. For art, I can simply put out watercolors and paper or collage materials and glue. If you put out some markers and paper, you have an instant writing station and see that period of learning extend through choice time, which frees students from writing in the curriculum focus or genre you are currently exploring.

What if an area is available and nobody is using it? This tells me that area is not popular—at the moment. I can wait until it catches on, I can initiate play in that area and see if any student picks up on it, or I can get rid of the area. It's as simple as putting the bin in the closet and taking out another one.

HOW NOT TO DO CHOICE TIME

Once, a staff developer came in to teach us how to do choice time. She showed us a video that outlined how important instinctive play is. The play was not planned and, on its surface, was seemingly without purpose. All good—let's play! But at that point, we were also told that the students did not know what it is to play. They don't play at home, no one has taught them to play, and if you give them a toy to play with, they don't know what to do with it.

> This now gave the staff developer purpose: choice time turned into another subject, complete with lesson plans, minilessons, documentation for what stage of play and type of play each student was engaging in, a plan for moving them to the "next level," and the share, where we would discuss, as a class, how the play went that day. The staff developer also noted that playing on a computer was not real play because computers are not hands-on enough.
>
> Then we were introduced to the choice time chart, on which the teacher would make a picture of each play area along with one spot for each student. The staff developer showed the students the choice time chart and had each of them pick their spot. They didn't really know what they were choosing because they had not played a lot of these games before. The students would sit and wait until everyone made a choice. The staff developer told the students that they had to stay in the area they chose for the whole time because that would build up play stamina. This was an important aspect of play that she described to us earlier. As this process dragged on, I saw a lot of impatient and antsy students. The last five students had little choice at all because there were not many places left. This procedure took more than twenty minutes.
>
> At last it was time to play! The teacher said, "OK, students, you can go now." Twenty-five-plus students stumbled to their choices. Many had already forgotten what area they had chosen or did not make a correspondence between the chosen area and the actual area. Some did not like their chosen areas and proceeded to a new one. Others played in the area they chose, got tired of it, and wandered to a new area or simply drifted around the room. The staff developer seemed oblivious to this. In about seven minutes, the staff developer exclaimed, "Cleanup time!" No kidding—I timed it. Cleanup was long and chaotic. It took a Herculean effort to get everyone back to the rug for sharing. "Share what?" I thought.

Before choice time, I simply go to the closet and choose the games for the day. I do it quickly, but these are not random choices. I put a lot of thought into it. I consider which ones students are getting tired of, which are currently riding a wave of popularity, which coincide with the concepts I am teaching and the units I am doing, and so on.

Rules

There are only two rules.

1. **Each area can have only a certain number of students:** The number of students to an area usually depends on how many spaces, usually chairs, are available at the table where it's set up. If it is a rug activity like the

blocks, it has more flexibility, but the rule is about four students to an area. It is very easy for a student to figure out how many students an area can handle. You see a chair? That is one spot. You see four chairs? That is four spots. The activity is on the rug? I'll tell you before choice time begins, or ask a student in the area, or ask me.

What if someone comes to an area that he or she wants to play in and all the spots are occupied? I ask the student to make a different choice. What if he or she really likes the area and can't wait to get in? The student can watch for when somebody leaves and then go for it, just like we do when we want to go to an area that is occupied by other adults, but no waiting around; find another area and keep an eye on the area you want to get to.

2. **No dumping:** Don't come to an area and flip over a bin. Just take what you need. You don't even have to clean up your area if you leave it. Someone else is going to take over anyway, so why not leave things out? The last person to play in the area will clean up, and it is a very easy job to do.

Start and End Times

What if you went to a theme park and were told to stay on one ride for the whole day? What if you had to pick your major before you entered college and were told that you could not change it? With those thoughts in mind, the other choice I give is how long someone can play in an area. I let everyone play for as little or as long as they want to. Some students play in an area for five minutes and then seek new horizons. Others stay the whole period. The average kindergartener in my classroom will play in two to three areas over the course of a forty-five-minute period. In fact, once students know they can leave an area any time they wish, they stay in it longer.

I trust the students. They know what to do. They know what choices to make and why they are making them. I start choice time by simply having students sit at the rug area. I might explain a new game that I'm introducing that day, but most likely, I will have the students discover it on their own. I simply call them one by one and they find an area they want to play in. No waiting: "Go ahead. Find an area and start playing."

Everyone wants to be first, or at least be one of the first called. How does that happen? It comes when they do the *right way* during the day. That is kinderese for being attentive, cooperative, and following all the class rules. What if someone had difficulty doing the right way? Then that student will probably not be in the first ten called. Even so, the last student called still has about sixteen play spots to choose from. What if a student *really* didn't do the right way? That person might have to wait a little longer. It is a mini time away and I will say, "Let's figure out what happened and how we can fix that so tomorrow, perhaps you can be the first one picked." Within two minutes, I can get all the students up and playing. It turns out that being last is actually not much of a wait at all.

There is no pomp and circumstance when singling out who did things the right way that day and who didn't. Everything is subtle. The students figure out the scheme of things very quickly by observing the consistency of the daily method. I do give compliments and admonishments from time to time, but my focus is getting the students playing as soon as possible.

During choice time, students are bustling about, working together, doing things alone, focusing, exchanging knowledge, laughing, and engaging. Controlled chaos at its best! The hum is louder than ever! Why? The main reason is that they are playing for about forty minutes of the forty-five-minute period. They know the rules, so they have the bed of stability and are free to explore and fulfill the meaning of the simple word *play*.

I always have choice time as my last period, whether it is on the official schedule or not. It is a fitting culmination of the day. I also integrate snacks into this period. An official snack time eats too much of the day and most of the students are still digesting their lunch at the time when snack time might fit in. At choice time, everyone is free to snack and play. My students need to be packed up for dismissal at 2:30 p.m., so I simply start calling them one, two, or three at a time to pack up and then go back to what they were doing. Cleanup, which we'll discuss next, takes about five minutes, so I can have the students playing until about 2:25 p.m. for a 2:30 p.m. dismissal.

Cleanup

Toys, table games, and manipulatives take different amounts of time to put away. Cleaning up blocks or clay may take up to five minutes, cleaning up the kitchen area or building bricks may take three minutes, and cleaning up the sand table or the computers may take a minute or two.

Observe who is playing in which area to learn who the fast and slow cleaners are. Armed with this knowledge, you stagger the efforts. That's right, there is no announcing, "OK, it's cleanup time now!" Of course, you will prep the class as a whole and in each area about how long they have left to play, but as an example, you will tell students playing with blocks and clay to start with five minutes left to play; two minutes later you alert the Lego and kitchen areas; and right before choice time is over, you will tell those at the computers and sand table to wrap it up. You can then give each area a reminder at three or two minutes (whatever you deem appropriate), and then, of course, at one minute, give one last heads up. Everyone finishes cleaning up at about the same time and you don't have anyone waiting on others to finish cleaning.

I used to think it was so clever of me to turn the cleanup for the block area into a sorting activity, so that each piece would be put into its proper place—until I learned that it takes kindergarteners about twenty minutes to sort the blocks, and that is if they are staying on task. I learned my lesson. Cleanup for the area now simply consists of putting the blocks randomly into a large bin as quickly as possible. Students will exercise their sorting skills another time.

If you use bins for your games, make sure they are big, and teach the students to simply get the toys into the bins and then move on. No disassembling—they can do that at the start of next choice time, if they want to. There is no need to have the students return the bins to a storage area or shelf. If you do, there will be arguing about who should take the bin, bins dropped with the tiny manipulatives falling on the floor, and bins stacked in precarious piles just waiting to topple. The students should just leave the bins on the tables and you or your helpers can take care of it. Cleanup this way won't feel like a chore at all, and you will be able to maximize students' playtime, as well as their happiness and yours.

In a Nutshell

You will be doing whole-group time every day, many times a day, and it is rightfully a crucial period that is a core part of your teaching. Design it as a series of micro-lessons that are educational and entertaining so that students can be attentive for extended periods and assimilate new concepts and skills before doing independent and group work. Develop the ability to differentiate within the whole group. Use whole-group time to promote verbal language skills and comprehension by having group discussions and expecting everyone to participate when questions are asked.

In many ways, choice time is the essence of kindergarten, and it's unfortunate that in some schools, students are deprived of this most important part of the day. During this period, students communicate with each other, exchange ideas, experiment with newfound discoveries, focus, and engage—what's not to like? Don't get bogged down in any procedure that will take away from even a moment of this precious time.

Make sure that the choices you set up far outnumber the students in your room and give them the freedom to make or change their choices with as few limitations as possible. Work on making clean up a snap with the preceding techniques and join in the fun yourself!

Have You Mastered the Chapter?

Welcome to the formal assessment section of the book—a quiz to test your knowledge of the chapter. Please try the questions. The answers are provided after the questions section for a quick check. I explain the *why* after the quiz, and that is the most important part to consider.

According to this chapter:

1. The most important word that should pop into your head when you think of choice time is:
    a. Fun
    b. Choices
    c. Manipulatives
    d. Play

2. At choice time, it is best to:
    a. Assign students to a play spot
    b. Have students choose a play spot and stay there for the whole period
    c. Have students choose a play spot and remain there as long as they wish
    d. Spend a lot of time with setup and cleanup tasks

3. The longest part of choice time is:
    a. The cleanup
    b. The playing
    c. The setup
    d. The students choosing where to play

4. It's OK to call on a student:

    a. If a student is not raising a hand

    b. If a student is not listening to the lesson

    c. If a student just answered a question

    d. All of the above

5. If a student at first seems disinterested in your lesson:

    a. Tell the student to pay attention

    b. Keep on going, unfazed

    c. Immediately change your lesson

    d. Give the student a movement break

Answers and Explanations

1. **d. (Play)** That's what it's all about! With lots of choices and excellent manipulatives, choice time will be a time of learning and fun.

2. **c. (Have students choose a play spot and remain there as long as they wish)** Having limited choice at choice time defeats the purpose—it doesn't even live up to its name. The less time it takes to set up and clean up, the more time there is to play.

3. **b. (The playing)** Yes, the playing! All the other choices—setup, cleanup, and choosing—should take fewer than five minutes.

4. **d. (All of the above)** If a student is not raising a hand or not listening to a lesson, all the more reason to get him or her involved and engaged. If a student just answered a question, why not give a follow-up to expand understanding, provide challenge, and promote discussions in the classroom?

5. **b. (Keep on going, unfazed)** Be confident that your lesson is developmentally appropriate and engaging. Consider the students who are disinterested initially as those who will be enraptured and involved very soon. You won't need to tell them to pay attention. They will do it on their own. Of course, if your lesson is just not working, you should alter it midstream. A movement break is always welcome after students have been sitting for a while.

Preparing for Choice Time

Use this checklist to see if you have set up your choice time to be one of fun, play, and learning for students.

- ☐ I have set up enough activity spots for twice the number of students in my class.
- ☐ Each activity area is designed for a specific number of students.
- ☐ I have utilized every space available in the room for activities.
- ☐ I have minimized the time it takes for the students to make their choices.
- ☐ I have maximized the amount of playing time in the period.
- ☐ I have communicated the simple rules to the students—no dumping the toys, no excess people in areas.
- ☐ I have minimized the amount of time needed for cleanup by giving the students a heads-up that it is coming and staggered the cleanup accordingly.
- ☐ I had fun with my students during choice time!

CHAPTER 7

Making Schedules, Charts, and Plans

Conventional wisdom defines a big part of teaching as writing up plans, documenting, physically cutting, pasting, and taping. These things are indeed part of the job, but they shouldn't be a major part. I would like to address some everyday teacher responsibilities that many may see as time-consuming and think restrain their ability to teach effectively.

I mentioned before that I spend a lot of time thinking about how I can streamline my work duties while still fulfilling the expectations of administration so that I can find the time to think about, work on, and progress in my teaching practice. Here are my thoughts and practices related to how to spend your time, as well as how to handle your class schedule, lesson plans, monthly calendar, charts, homework, and parent-teacher conferences. Some of what you will read may sound unconventional because it is. I always prefer what works, and hey—why not start a new convention!

Class Schedule

I post a schedule in my classroom, and it has cute clip art representing every part of the day coupled with the time of each activity. It is as child-friendly as can be and is right near the rug, where we have whole-group time, so it can be referenced easily. It is a non-negotiable, so it is displayed proudly in the room—but I respectfully find that it is a high-maintenance item that is of little value.

It is not as important to display a schedule as it is to help kindergarteners understand what each part of the day is about. Both help them feel the necessary consistency. This is done best by explaining to them what each component of the day is about and, of course, having them experience these components.

At some point, the students will have a reference point for what writing, reading, mathematics, and the rest entail. At that point, someone could consider posting a schedule, but what is the point? The students are less interested in knowing the sequence of activities than in knowing what each activity is going to be about, if they are not doing one of their routine activities, or if they are going to do a special activity. That is what I will go over in the morning. No posted schedule is necessary.

> **The students are less interested in knowing the sequence of activities than in knowing what each activity is going to be about.**

Another reason I don't go over the schedule posted in the room is that I don't want to lie to my students. I will explain later in this chapter that I don't plan out the day to match each subject to a period and do not teach the lessons in a certain sequence. Even if I have a general sequence worked out at the beginning of the day, it will usually not match the end result. Why tell them that something will occur in a certain way when it most certainly won't? Students don't learn on the clock. They don't care which subject comes first or second.

Every day, I know what I want to do, but I don't always know the sequence, or if I will get to everything. The day is like a checklist, in terms of the activities and the concepts I want to get across. My goal is to have all items checked off by the end of the day. How and when they get checked off is up to me and the particularities of that day. So, I don't always do mathematics during mathematics time, or reading during literacy time, according to the schedule posted on the wall. Sometimes I will do half of a mathematics lesson in the beginning of the day and the other half at the end of the day. Sometimes I will do the last half of the lesson the next day. Sometimes, I will do three mathematics lessons in one day and not do a reading or writing lesson. It all depends on what I want to accomplish, what the students are receptive to, and what I need to do to keep the learning flow constant. (You can complete the reproducible "Employing Interdisciplinary Teaching," page 137, as you teach specific skills in class, referring to it throughout the day, and see part 2, page 139, for more about teaching literacy and mathematics specifically.)

Perhaps you are thinking, "But students are mandated to have a specific number of minutes for each subject area for each day. Aren't you violating that rule?" No, for the following two reasons.

1. Sixty minutes of daily mathematics may be mandated, but that doesn't mean those minutes have to occur in one single chunk.

2. One always has to look for the purpose behind the rules (to be a thinking teacher).

Students are mandated to have sixty minutes of mathematics instruction a day on the assumption that if this occurs, they will master the mathematics standards for the year. Unfortunately, one doesn't follow the other. Only quality mathematics instruction will ensure that standards are mastered. You can mandate all the time you want, but time doesn't teach.

If you are mandated to provide sixty minutes of mathematics per day, that works out to five hours of mathematics per week. If you did a half hour of mathematics one day and four and a half hours of mathematics over the next four days, that would fulfill the requirement. I have not analyzed my teaching day or teaching week, but I am pretty sure that if I did, it would probably come close to the mandated amounts of time necessary for each subject.

When planning your class schedule, there is the long view and the short view to consider.

The Long View

You need a long view of your year so that you get to every standard in every subject by the end of the year. Manage your class time wisely and use it so that every second of the teaching day is filled with learning opportunities for your students, so that by the end of the year the students master every standard in every subject. This will happen more effectively if you are flexible with the schedule and responsible in your use of time. That said, know that the teaching year ends a few weeks before the students are let out for summer. This is because the last few weeks are usually spent on assessments, getting ready for graduation, and a host of other details.

It is so important for a teacher to know the following things.

- What the standards are
- What their students' abilities should look like by the end of the year
- How long it really takes to teach each concept and skill
- When you need to start teaching each one
- Which standards need a lot of spiraling, and which ones don't. *Spiraling* is constantly reinforcing concepts and skills learned in many different ways and contexts after you have taught them. I explain more about spiraling in chapter 9 (page 183).

The Short View

I look at the day as blocks of time. On Mondays, I may have a block of about an hour in the morning before students have gym, another hour before they have lunch, and then a block of two-and-a-half hours before dismissal. On Tuesdays, the blocks are spaced differently but add up to the same amount of time. I know that I have a little over four hours every day to teach reading, writing, mathematics (more on those in part 2, page 139), science, and social studies, and to have choice time.

Each day, I think of what I want to get done and figure out which blocks of time and which sequence would be best to do these things in. Unfortunately, I don't have the time to write this down, except for a few crib notes on an index card and on the dry-erase board in my room. Then I am flexible as to the flow of the day in terms of what is going on in the classroom, what direction the students want to go in, and what direction I want to take them.

As I mentioned about going through the curriculum and making it your own (page 27), I did not start out teaching this way. However, it was not long before I realized that it is important for students to learn skills and concepts, and that this was more important than the exact part of the day *when* they learned them. I found that flexibility and small segments of learning with a multidisciplinary approach accelerated and solidified learning. Earlier I advocated for being a thinking teacher and this is a concrete application of this. I know that some teachers thrive on the reassurance of documentation and specific blocks of time. Remember, however, that there is an alternate way that has many benefits, follows educational research, and in my experience works. If you want to take the plunge, the water is fine.

Lesson Plans

Former U.S. president Dwight D. Eisenhower put it in a nutshell when he said, "Plans are useless, but planning is indispensable" (as cited in Wheeler, 2017). Thinking about how you are going to teach something and finding the resources to do it are probably the most worthwhile things you can do as a teacher. Writing up lesson plans is probably the least—in my opinion. I never teach without planning. I may write up a mandated lesson plan, but I don't write up my real plans. If you need to write things out, do so. You might need hard copy or digital lesson plans written out. Do what works for you, but know the following as you think about what and how you will teach.

- Where your materials are
- Which students you are going to focus on
- How you are going to work with them
- What you are going to do if the plan doesn't work
- How you are going to motivate students

- What the sequence of the lesson is going to be
- How much time the lesson might take
- How you will figure out if students are learning what you are presenting

During the lesson, I am observing, assessing, and documenting what is going on. After the lesson, I am reflecting on the lesson.

Everything a teacher is expected to do regarding planning a lesson is being done in a very thorough manner. However, to write all this down would literally take me hours. So, the bottom line is, I am the lesson plan. In the morning, I take an index card on which I write a few key words about each lesson that I use as a reminder or cheat sheet during the day. I will write down the teaching point of each lesson, the resources I will use (including books, music, videos, and manipulatives), some targeted questions and names of students, along with what skill I think they need to work on that day. That's all the paper and writing that needs to be done for me regarding planning a lesson. Any *official* lesson plans I am mandated to do are quick and generic, as with the plan book.

One reason given for writing up lesson plans is so that the next year a teacher can go back to a prior lesson and learn from and improve it. Even when my plans were all written up and preserved, I would never go back to reference them. That is because every year is new. Teaching is not about going back; it is about going forward. Every year, you are building the house from the foundation up using a new blueprint. Last year is outdated, like the operating system on your old computer. Yet, in many of the schools I have taught in, full lesson plans were a requirement, even if it meant copying a full lesson with all its bells and whistles already written up in the prescribed curriculum onto a formatted lesson-plan page given to me by the school.

FLEXIBILITY: MY LESSON PLANS AND CHARTS

Any plans I write up—the official plan book—are as quick and generic as can be. If I am teaching a unit on three-dimensional shapes and introducing a different shape each day, I will write *sphere, cube, cone, pyramid,* and *cylinder* for each day's lesson. I teach this way every day except—you guessed it—the day I have my observation. On that day, the students get their usual full day of learning, but the time schedule is followed to a T, I write lesson plans and instructions for group work and follow them to a T, and I have my performer's hat on all day. I am not as efficient and dynamic

continued ▶

> as I could be, and the students don't learn to their potential, but that is what happens when form overrides function.
>
> Lastly, the reason I can be flexible with the schedule is that I have discovered that students learn just as well at the beginning of the day as at the end of the day. Yes, they do! There is a popular teacher myth that says that students can't learn, or don't learn as well, after lunch, so everything of importance must get done in the morning—don't bother in the afternoon. We know that children are ready, willing, and able to learn all day, every day.
>
> Sure, different parts of the day pose different challenges that can either be used as an excuse not to teach or turned on their head to motivate students to learn. It is also hard to predict the general attention level and motivation of the class. This is why I use the flexible schedule, precisely to overcome those issues. But overcome them I do, and there is as much learning going on in the afternoon as in the morning.

Monthly Calendar

I don't reference my mandated daily schedule with students often, but my monthly calendar is an important tool. I reference it a lot during whole-group time, using it to teach the words for the month, day and date, numbers, and the concept of scheduling. The calendar is a chart that students learn to read over time in a step-by-step manner.

At the beginning of every month, I post on the calendar anything important that is going on that month such as field trips, holidays, and birthdays. I make a little picture that relates to the event—a birthday cake for a birthday, for example, and a one- or two-word description on the bottom of the picture.

This gives me a whole month to help students learn about each event and when it will be coming. So, if we are taking a trip to the aquarium, I will have touched on it a little every day. By the time of the trip, the students know what an aquarium is, what animals are there, how we are getting there, how long it will take to get there, what we will be doing there, and so on.

Talking about events marked on the calendar also gives students a sense of the movement of time, as they see the event getting closer and closer as we move through the calendar. To a young child, *yesterday* means anything that happened in the past and *tomorrow* means anything that can happen in the future (Katesurfs, 2017). Through the calendar, students start to learn exactly what *yesterday* and *tomorrow* mean. After a few months, students will gather around the calendar when the events of the new month are posted and start figuring out for themselves and having discussions about what the events are and how long it will be until they happen.

Charts

The charts I have up and that we use a lot follow.

- A one hundreds chart
- A number line from 1 to 100
- Two alphabets
- Two identical word walls
- One monthly calendar
- Two one-hundred-days-of-school charts
- Each student's current independent reading levels, how high he or she can rote count to 100 by 1s, and how far he or she can write to 100, along with the date of each student's latest attempt
- Mathematics and literacy charts (which we refer to more near the end of the year; see part 2, page 139, for more about teaching these subjects)

All of these charts are valuable as references because they relate to what we are learning in class and therefore, the students can read and understand them.

I want to now talk about three other kinds of charts: (1) behavior, (2) job, and (3) class rules.

Behavior Chart

By now you can probably anticipate what I think about behavior charts—the charts designed to monitor and improve student behavior—but I will tell you anyway: I have seen them all. From the one that looks light a streetlight and has green for good, yellow for a warning, and red for "Uh oh, you're in trouble," to the movie theater one where you're watching the movie, you're in the lobby, or you're kicked out of the theater. As you now know, managing student behavior takes a lot of thought, planning, and preventive action—much more work and sophistication than a simple chart.

Behavior charts are high-preparation and high-maintenance items—the last thing streamlined, efficient teachers who want to maximize their observing, thinking, and teaching need. I have seen too many of them fall into disuse and disrepair within a few weeks of their introduction, remnants of another failed initiative, or thrown into the teacher junkyard—with no improvement to student behavior, of course. These kinds of charts "create more stress for all the children in the class who fear that they will see their status shift due to 'bad' behavior" (as cited in King, 2019). It is the teacher who teaches the skills, not the charts, and he or she does that through building relationships and communicating (King, 2019).

Once I had to submit a behavior plan to discuss what methods and charts I would use to manage the class. I wrote up one page of what they wanted to hear, but what I should have done was just march into the office and present myself. I give students the feedback they need—a smile, a scowl, a hand movement, a nod, a glare, a wave—this is usually all the feedback students need. When I do a read-aloud, I am trying to read the book, while simultaneously watching what each student is doing and how he or she is reacting to the book, while simultaneously communicating proper behavior to individuals via gestures and eye movements.

The closest I get to an actual behavior chart is a dry-erase board hung near the circle area. It is a small board that serves as a partner to the index card I keep in my back pocket. On it, I scrawl ideas I get during the day, or reminders for that particular day. One area of the board is usually left blank. It is not a chart at all. The only similarity it has to a traditional behavior chart is that it also uses the students' names, but in a way that does not create the stress a traditional one does.

If a student is persistently disruptive and all the subtle stuff doesn't work, and speaking directly to the student doesn't work, I will write a letter of the student's name on the board. I will add or deduct a letter accordingly, but I will not usually need to write more than a few letters of the name of the most difficult student. Of course, once the students know about this practice, I will look at a disruptive student and give a knowing glance to the dry-erase board. The student gets the message. If a student has some or all the letters of his or her name on the board, it means that he or she will be dealt with later, with a consequence I think is appropriate, perhaps to sit thirty seconds while the students are playing, and have a discussion as to what prompted the behavior and how it can be avoided in the future.

Job Chart

There is no job chart. This is another high-maintenance item of little value that takes up a lot of wall space and doesn't really serve its purpose, which is to have worthy members of the class help out with class chores and duties. To make a job chart that works, you would have to think of all the possible jobs your students can do, keep eliminating those that become obsolete, and add new ones that become available as the year goes on or that present themselves in certain situations. Then you have to make a card or stick with the name of each student in the class and assign him or her a job—which also means that there are only as many jobs as there are students in the class! Then you would have to rotate the jobs perfectly, so that everything is fair, and everyone has the opportunity to do every job. That's a lot of work for something that can be done much more simply and effectively.

Despite having no job chart, my room is filled with busy students performing all kinds of jobs, and everyone gets to do every job by the end of the year. The major jobs are putting supplies on the tables and collecting them at the end of an activity. These can include paper, writing implements, art supplies, and manipulatives. There are various room maintenance jobs that entail cleaning up and monitoring, such as monitoring the whiteboards and the computers.

Make no mistake—students are ready, willing, and capable of assisting with a lot of the day-to-day class operations. That is why I consider students my co-teachers. But before I pick someone to do a job, he or she must know what it is and how to do it. I roll out the jobs very slowly and add more complex jobs as the year goes on, so not every student has to do the same job every day.

I never give students a weekly job. They are hired on the spot and laid off if they can't do the job or don't merit the position. There is no job security. It is totally situational and purposeful. A job comes up, someone has to do it, I get someone to do it, it is done. Every job is always available, so every student feels as if he or she could get it. They also know that they will not get a job if they are not in my good graces. Since every job is available and everyone wants to do a job, the students watch and learn from a student who is doing a particular job, so when it is their turn, which they have the comfort of knowing will occur, they will be able to do it right.

> **Students are ready, willing, and capable of assisting with a lot of the day-to-day class operations. That is why I consider students my co-teachers.**

If a student pesters me to do a job, and my response is "If you pester me, you won't get the job." That works. I also avoid making the most obvious choice. So, for the most part, the students don't sit in anticipation of getting a job. They do whatever is being called for at the time, and I find the student I need for a particular job at the time. Some of the most popular jobs that teachers divvy up I don't do at all, such as line leader or table monitor. Instead, line leaders change every day and I split up the duties of the traditional table monitor and have different students do them each time the students go to the tables.

To keep everything fair, it is my responsibility to constantly think of what jobs must be done, who can do them, when they last did them, and so forth.

Class Rules Chart

The common rules—listen to the teacher, be quiet, raise your hand—wouldn't make sense to the students in my class. Rules are not so simplistic. They don't always have to listen to me. They don't always have to be quiet. And they don't always have to raise their hands to ask a question.

Actually, I have a list of class rules posted in the room because it is required. They are off to the side, but there for anyone to see, and as follows.

- **Rule 1:** Be ready to learn.
- **Rule 2:** Do your best.
- **Rule 3:** Be nice to the students.
- **Rule 4:** Be nice to the stuff in the class.

The students can't yet read these rules, and I don't formally go over the rules with them, but they know this is what I expect them to do every day because they live it in the classroom. The room's design, predictable, fair, and responsive management practices, and teacher modeling all contribute to them internalizing the rules without ever having to say them. If I must have rules posted in the class, I can live with those.

> **Rules are not so simplistic.**

Homework

I do give homework to my class. This is because homework is mandated. However, as you can probably guess, I make it work for the kindergarteners and myself.

I give things to do at home that I think benefit students—and they are all optional. I give them books on their level to read at home and access to educational computer games. I know these are effective in school, so they must work at home too. I make a homework packet of about twelve pages. I give it out on Monday and collect it on Friday. I only check if the homework was done, not if it was done correctly. This is because I can't tell who completed the homework—a big flaw in the whole idea of giving homework in the first place. Homework isn't, and shouldn't be, the place where you are teaching new things to the students. It shouldn't be the place where you are putting parents in the role of schoolteachers. Parents are your partners, but they are not schoolteachers.

I always give homework based on what I taught the week before and prior to that. In my first year, I spent a lot of time weeding through loads of worksheets that are available in books and online to find ones that were based on what I was teaching and were appropriate for the students. I designed it so the students could do their homework with the least amount of direction from parents and guardians.

I hoped and assumed that this nightly exercise reinforced what I was teaching in class but always wondered what it would be like if there were no homework at all. One year, the principal declared that there would be no more homework in kindergarten. In one sense I was relieved, but in another sense, I had become used to the routine and was kind of coming around to the idea that maybe homework was useful. Kindergarteners who had no homework did just as well as those who had homework. My current opinion about homework is that if it is given properly, it may help—a little. If it isn't given at all, it won't matter much. If it is given improperly, it will not help but subject the students to a lot of work that is a waste of time.

> **Kindergarteners who had no homework did just as well as those who had homework.**

Parent-Teacher Conferences

When do you start preparing for your parent-teacher conferences? The week before, a few days before, the night before? Nope. You start preparing for your parent-teacher conferences on the first day of school. If you teach the way you should (keep parents and guardians informed via handouts or emails, alert them to issues, and resolve any issues the parents or guardians have as they arise), no major issues will come up at the conference. The conference will be a celebration of the Super Child, the Super Parent or Guardian, and the Super Teacher—in that order.

Almost every parent-teacher conference I have attended for my own children has started with the report card. I take the attitude that the report card I have prepared accurately reflects how the student is doing. The purpose of the conference is not to go over it point by point. I keep the report card in a manila envelope. I use the time to do what I think the parent wants me to do: tell them about their child in plain language. It is not a sugarcoating, but I obviously keep it positive and am nonjudgmental if I bring up an issue. I avoid using teacher terms or acronyms when speaking to parents and guardians. Most parents don't know what *differentiation* is, and *F&P* sounds like an oil company. Terms like *objective*, *teaching point*, and *shared reading* are terms I use with other teachers.

I then usually give the parents a quick tour of the room to illustrate something I highlighted in the conference and inform the parents how they can help their child at home. I let the parents know from the get-go that any questions at any time are welcome, and I check again for questions near the end of the conference.

Right before the parents leave, I give them the report card and tell them that they can look it over at home and contact me if they have any questions about it. By this time, I usually have informed parents and guardians about their child's progress, so the report card itself becomes less of an evaluative tool for them. Occasionally a parent will take out the report card at the conference to read it. I tell them the same thing I tell the other parents: I have another parent coming and that they can read it at their leisure. I usually don't get any follow-ups on the report cards. The whole conference takes about ten minutes. See the reproducible "Preparing for Parent-Teacher Conferences" (page 138) for a checklist that will help you plan for these meetings in advance.

In a Nutshell

When thinking about plans, charts, and schedules, use the same principles that a thinking teacher applies to everything he or she does—make sure it is meaningful, purposeful, and adds to your practice and the students' learning. Make sure to take into consideration the demands and expectations of your school to work out a beneficial balance you are comfortable with. Easy to do? No—but as a thinking teacher you are up to it and know that the benefits to your classroom and your professional development are worth it.

Homework will always be a conundrum and its value debated. If you do give homework, remember that it should not be used for teaching new ideas, but for a review and reinforcement of concepts taught. If you create classroom environment that is child-friendly and communicate effectively with parents from the beginning of the year, you should be looking forward to parent-teacher conferences as a celebration of everyone involved in the teaching process.

Have You Mastered the Chapter?

Welcome to the formal assessment section of the book—a quiz to test your knowledge of the chapter. Please try the questions. The answers are provided after the questions section for a quick check. I explain the *why* after the quiz, and that is the most important part to consider.

According to this chapter:

1. Teachers should spend a lot of effort:
    a. Doing paperwork
    b. Streamlining their practice
    c. Cutting and pasting
    d. All of the above

2. Children learn best:
    a. In the morning
    b. After they have had a movement activity
    c. In the afternoon
    d. Any time of day

3. Writing up your lesson plan:
    a. Should be a lengthy and comprehensive process
    b. Gives you your script for your lesson
    c. Means that your lesson is well planned
    d. None of the above

4. What is most true about homework?
    a. It is still an unresolved issue in education.
    b. It is a waste of time.
    c. It usually accelerates the learning process.
    d. It should never be given.

5. Start planning for your parent–teacher conferences:
    a. Over the summer
    b. A week before the conferences
    c. On the first day of school
    d. At parent orientation night

Answers and Explanations

1. **b. (Streamlining their practice)** Paperwork and cutting and pasting are an unavoidable part of teaching and should not be routinely dismissed as counterproductive. However, they tend to multiply and eventually overwhelm unless the teacher makes sure that both activities are always done with purpose and efficiency.

2. **d. (Any time of day)** The common wisdom is that children are perky and fresh in the morning, and they are. They are also refreshed after a movement activity. I have found that kindergarteners are just as receptive to learning in the afternoon. Perhaps it is the teacher who is fatigued at that point.

3. **d. (None of the above)** Unfortunately, writing up a lesson is often a lengthy process that has little correlation with how well thought out it is, if resources were evaluated and prepared for the actual lesson, and whether the teacher is prepared to teach it effectively. That's not to say that lesson plans are not valuable (though scripted ones offer limited opportunities for adjustments, spontaneity, and teachable moments).

4. **a. (It is still an unresolved issue in education)** Waste of time? Better than sliced bread? A little of both? The endless controversy about this most perplexing issue rolls on.

5. **c. (On the first day of school)** If you want to start planning in the summer, kudos to you. But parents and guardians will be happy if they are informed and their children are happy, and that begins on the first day of school.

Employing Interdisciplinary Teaching

Use this chart to write some of the skills you are teaching during a week in each subject area. Examples follow.

- **Reading:** pointing, the sight word *and*, the letter *Mm*
- **Writing:** idea generation, rehearsing, labeling
- **Mathematics:** *long* versus *short*, counting on from 10, comparing volumes
- **Science:** *living* versus *nonliving*, parts of a plant, seasons
- **Social studies:** school community, members of a family, occupations

Keep this chart nearby as a reference to help you work on these objectives, skills, and concepts throughout the day in all subject areas.

Week of _____

Content Area	Skills
Reading	
Writing	
Mathematics	
Science	
Social Studies	

Preparing for Parent-Teacher Conferences

To ensure a happy parent coming into the conference, do the following from day one.

- ☐ Communicate frequently but not excessively with the parent or guardian. Have contact information within the first week of school. Remember that an informed parent is a happy parent.
- ☐ Keep students happy by engaging them to learn in a fun, safe environment. That's what it's all about, anyway! Remember that a happy child equals a happy parent.

Do the following during the conference.

- ☐ Keep the focus on the actual report card to a minimum.
- ☐ Keep the focus on the student's progress to a maximum.
- ☐ Celebrate the student.
- ☐ Show samples of the student's work—especially writing samples. They are guaranteed to melt hearts.
- ☐ Be open and truthful about the student's academic and behavioral progress, both positive and negative. If improvements are needed, say what steps you will take and the steps the parent can take to make this happen.
- ☐ Avoid pedagogical terms or acronyms. Use plain language to communicate educational terms. Remember kinderese? This is parentese.
- ☐ Make your room accessible to the parent. Give a quick tour and show where the child sits, where the cubby is, and so on.
- ☐ Do your best to be relaxed. A relaxed teacher equals a relaxed parent (most of the time).
- ☐ Remember that you can do all of this in the allotted time!

PART 2

Clarity in Literacy and Mathematics

In the following chapters, I am going to share with you the discoveries I have made on how kids learn literacy and mathematics, and the practices and methods I have developed to help them learn best. I use these techniques effectively in the real classroom every day. My methods were developed from taking what worked best from several curricula and adding the discoveries I have made along the way.

This section of the book is not a comprehensive, textbook-style substitute for your current curriculum and the many instructional books you may have read and can find about these subjects. However, there is a lot of valuable information that should give you a solid theoretical framework as well as viable techniques that should complement your curriculum and help you teach these subjects effectively.

For literacy, I have used and learned from the following.

- Fountas and Pinnell (www.fountasandpinnell.com)
- Fundations (https://wilsonlanguage.com/programs/fundations)
- Jolly Phonics (www.jollylearning.co.uk)
- Journeys (www.hmhco.com/programs/journeys)
- Read Well (www.voyagersopris.com/literacy/read-well/overview)

- Reading Mastery (www.nifdi.org/programs/reading/reading-mastery)
- Teachers College Reading and Writing Project (https://readingandwritingproject.org)
- Handwriting Without Tears (https://lwtears.com/hwt)

For mathematics, I have used and learned from the following.

- enVisionmath 2.0 (https://bit.ly/3hT5k51)
- Eureka/Engage NY Math (https://greatminds.org/math)
- Everyday Mathematics (https://everydaymath.uchicago.edu)
- Math in Focus (www.hmhco.com/programs/math-in-focus)
- Singapore Math (www.singaporemath.com)

CHAPTER 8

Teaching Literacy

A reader is always reading a book, always looking for that next exciting book to read, always visiting the library or bookstore or going online to get more books. Readers' houses are filled with books. They are members of book clubs. They cuddle up with books and read into the night. They love the way books feel and even the way they smell. They love holding a book and feeling the paper in their hands as they turn to the next page. I don't relate to any of this.

Although I don't think of myself as a reader, I do engage with print quite a lot. I spend a lot of my day reading online. I follow the news. I research anything from a particular period in history to the latest inventions to how to refinish a deck or buy the best computer printer. Come to think of it, though I am not a reader, I am reading all the time! In fact, if you compared the number of words that I process in a week to those a classically defined reader processes, we would probably be very close.

Anytime I describe the kind of reading I do in a workshop or class, I am suspect as a teacher because I am not a *true* reader. The idea is that, as a teacher, you are to teach students to love books, because reading and books go together. You are to teach students to learn to read, so they will want to read more books, and this will reinforce their love of books. While it's true that I don't love reading, I do love information. I love learning about new things, and analyzing and processing information. It doesn't matter how I get it—by print, picture, or sound.

However, to *get* information, I need to be a good reader. The better reader I am, the more information I can get and the easier it is for me to examine and process that information. Reading is a vitally important tool. A student in my class may turn out to love information too. Or turn out to prefer poetry. Or both. I am also sure that there will be a few classic readers that emerge from my class.

The way I approach reading in class is with a desire that my students develop a firm foundation in the fundamentals of reading with exposure to and fluency, for their age-level, in all the different genres, without bias to a particular one. So, my goal in teaching reading is not necessarily for students to develop a love of reading or of books, but to be able to read competently in all genres. The main reason for reading is to acquire information—to understand what you are reading. As they say, "Children first learn to read and then they read to learn" (Klemm, 2012).

At the beginning stages, the books are so easy to comprehend that comprehension is almost a given—and that is why I don't emphasize it in this chapter—but that doesn't mean that you don't work at comprehension at the beginning of the year using various means that students will later be able to bridge into their reading. I want to mention this now, as I have spent a lot of time on reading mechanics. In focusing on reading mechanics I am not at all minimizing the importance of picture and syntax cues in the reading process. This is not a comprehensive textbook. It is to provide you with helpful insights I have discovered and to help you through parts of the process that many find challenging.

This chapter explains why to assess for reading early on, the reading sequence, leveled books, self-leveled books, independent reading, teaching writing, and independent writing. It covers a lot of ground, so I suggest doing an initial skim of the whole thing and then reading again, digging deeper. As I mentioned in chapter 3 (page 39), your goal is to form a picture in your mind of how students go from knowing virtually no letters at the beginning of the year to being readers and writers by the end of the year and envisioning what that would look like. What skills and concepts would they need to acquire on this journey, and how are you shepherding them along the way, teaching the necessary skills and concepts and consistently assessing?

Early Assessment

Some students come into kindergarten with rudimentary reading skills. However, many students won't know how to identify even one letter when they start kindergarten. You will have students anywhere in between these extremes.

I will explain reading levels later in the chapter, but I have found that there is a progression of skills that students acquire before they attain the first reading level of A (Fountas & Pinnell, 2016). I created my own categories to compensate for that. The following categories help me target my instruction and group students more productively.

- **aaaa:** Very few letters (sounds), no sight words (I will explain all about sight words later in the chapter.)
- **aaa:** More than half letters (sounds), two or fewer sight words
- **aa:** Most or all letters (sounds), more than three sight words

You may have noticed that the categories are not very specific and that I use general terms such as *very few* as opposed to specific number ranges. When I use the term *letters*, I am not disclosing if this means letter-name recognition or letter-sound correspondences. I am not addressing capital versus lowercase letters. I have not given a specific sequence of letters to assess or addressed vowels and consonants. Remember: this book is about being a thinking teacher. Assessing a potential reader is more complicated than counting letters and putting a student in a category. Bear with me. After you have a fuller understanding of how English works and the reading progression that includes concepts of print, you should be able to come back to this section and use the categories as is or customize them. In terms of assessment materials, you will know at that point if you need a simple grid of letters and a sight word list, or if you want to assess verbally with or without ancillary documentation.

I figure out where each new student is by the first week of school and categorize each student's proficiency accordingly. Sometimes I have an *A* reader or higher right off the bat. The students who are *aa* are the best candidates to become *A* readers in a few weeks. Once I know where each student is, it's just a matter of moving him or her up the stages of reading, as I outlined.

I track the students' progress very easily. I have a clothespin for each student and a sentence strip that has the letters *A–G* on it. Each student's clothespin is by the letter that indicates his or her reading level, as shown in figure 8.1. I cluster the students who are not yet A level (aaaa, aaa, and aa) into a

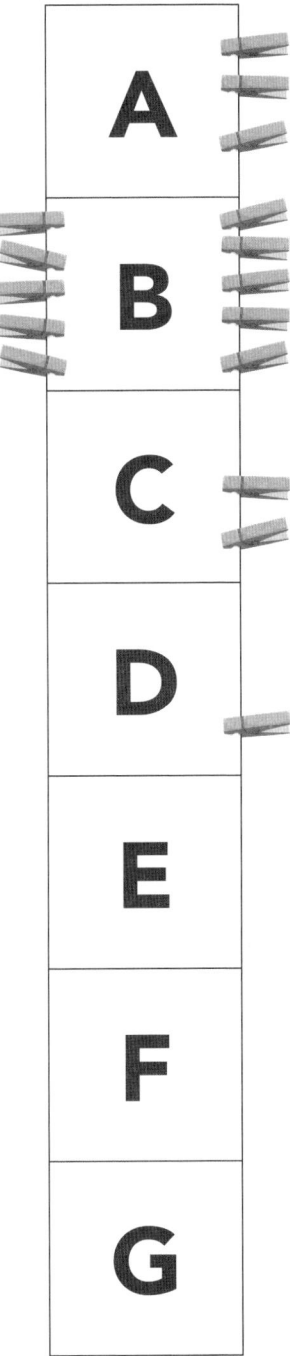

Figure 8.1: Reading levels indicated with clothespins.

pre-A category that is off to the side of the chart. This way I, and each student, can quickly see where everybody is at any time. This is not a focus of the class. It is off to the side, like a clock. You can look at it if you want to. The clock is telling time, but you don't have to watch it constantly.

Since students can see one another's level on the chart, you might think that students who are at lower levels feel bad about it and the high-level readers feel entitled, but this is not the case. I don't feel the same way about this kind of chart as I do a behavior chart (page 129). It's all how the classroom is managed and how students perceive the chart. Students see differences, but they don't pass judgment on them, unless someone has taught them to do so. So, a chart of reading levels is the same to them as a chart on height, weight, or birthdays. I have two other such charts—one for counting to 100 and one for writing numbers to 100. Although teachers routinely display graded student work in their rooms and throughout the school, I understand that posting charts of this sort might be challenging their comfort level. I find it to be an invaluable tool in my practice.

Teaching Reading

As you read this section, it may seem to be just about teaching reading, but it really is about teaching literacy. That is to say, when you teach a letter or do any balanced literacy component, you are doing so in the context of teaching students to both read *and* write. Literacy is the coin and reading and writing are but each side of it.

Prereading Skills

While *phonological awareness*, which is the awareness of sounds in language (such as rhyming, alliteration, and letter sounds), is a big asset when a student begins reading instruction, students don't need to know all their letters before learning to read. According to University of Oxford senior research officer Lynette Bradley and professor of psychology Peter Bryant (2010):

> Children become explicitly aware of the phonemic structure of words as a direct result of learning to read. They have to learn about letter-sound correspondences when they come to grips with the alphabet, and it seems quite likely that it is this experience that first makes them explicitly aware that words can be divided into the sounds that these letters represent. (p. 37)

What initially look only like symbols to students are letters that are revealed to the reader as they are learned. It's like those games where you slowly scratch off the gray material to reveal what is underneath. Of course, the symbols are English words and the sentences are made up of words people would say in a sentence. So, if you are familiar with these, you can pick up the blobs and attach them to other words and to sentence structures you already know. If not, you are lost—like many children who did not grow up with a strong language base or did not speak English as their first language. Strong language skills equal strong readers (Nation & Snowling, 2004). It's not about what the eye is seeing on the page as much as what the ear has heard and the mind understands about language.

Enhance language skills all the time. This equals good reading, among other things. Read aloud often, asking questions, prompting discussions, and allowing talk—even in the hallway (Oczkus, 2012). Yes, you can teach reading even when you are walking down the hallway with your class (page 97). Teachers should be showing videos, singing songs, and doing balanced literacy activities, such as shared reading. How to break down the reading progression throughout the school year is in the reproducible "Teaching the Reading Decoding Skills" (page 179).

> **Strong language skills equal strong readers.**

Reading Components

I have discovered many things about the effectiveness and limitations of certain reading components and will guide you through them so that your students can achieve reading competence by the end of the year. The following topics are covered: phonics, blending, long vowels, mantras, and sight words.

Phonics

Teachers should be teaching the letters to their students. Most people would call this *phonics*, and so would I. Phonics has limitations, and you will butt up against those as you teach letters.

Phonics Limitations

I will go into this a little further. Without a knowledge of phonics (simple phonics: *B* has a /b/ sound; more advanced: *gh* has an /f/ sound), students couldn't read. However, adults who have vocabularies of nearly 42,000 words (De Leon Huld, 2018) have probably learned every phonics rule and have earned advanced college degrees, cannot properly pronounce a word they don't know and have never heard before using phonics alone. The best they can do is guess.

Try it. Find a name or a word that you never heard before and try to read it correctly. How about *latrogenic*? Is it *lahtrojehnic, laytrojehnic, laytrojeenic, lahtrohgehnic, latroghenich*, or any combination thereof? It's like reading a word in a foreign language—because it is foreign to you. You might be able to figure out what it means from what you are reading, but you wouldn't know how to pronounce it unless you then realized that you have heard that word somewhere. How would you pronounce *Houston*, the street in Manhattan? Any self-respecting New Yorker knows that it is *Howstun*. What about the most famous phonics rule ever—*silent e*? How would you read the words *have*, *come* and *some* if you had never heard them before in conversation?

What do you do when you encounter a word you've never heard before? Consciously or unconsciously, you start comparing the word to other words that have the same letter sequences or features of this word and apply those pronunciations to this word. Unfortunately, letters and letter sequences can have different sounds in English, and every phonics rule has many exceptions, so you will end up guessing at what the word is. Overall, phonics instruction is bound by many limitations (Frank & Metcalf, 2014).

Phonics simply gives you a starting point to help you guess at a word. You will never know exactly how to read the word until you hear it from somebody else—reading is verbal. Then you'll either say, "Oh, I learned a new word and now know how to pronounce it," or you will say, "Wow, I've heard of this word before—so this is how you spell it!" Why does every phonics rule have many exceptions? This is because English is built on different languages that have different pronunciations and has acquired (and continues to acquire) words from other languages that have even more varied pronunciations (Harries, 2013). That is not a bad thing. It makes English a very expressive and cosmopolitan language. However, at the end of the day, the rules of phonics, like the pirate's code in *Pirates of the Caribbean* (Bruckheimer & Verbinski, 2003), are just suggestions and guidelines.

> **Phonics simply gives you a starting point to help you guess at a word.**

If phonics can only help an educated adult so much, then how far can it take a young student who is just learning how to read? Far, but not far enough. He or she looks at a word and is making guesses based on the phonics already known. This is one of the reasons early books have pictures. The picture is like someone standing next to the student asking, "Could your word be this, or maybe this, or maybe this?" Students do need something to latch onto to start dissecting the blobs, so phonics it is. Phonics is important. Very important. Super important. But it has its limitations and alone it will not produce competent readers. I look at phonics like the rocket boosters on the rocket. They launch you at the beginning, but at some point they fall to the side as the rocket goes into orbit.

Start phonics instruction with the individual letters (Oczkus, 2012). Teaching a letter *to mastery*—which is your goal—means that when a student sees either the upper- or lowercase form of the letter, he or she can say the corresponding sound automatically (*automaticity*); if the student hears that sound alone, he or she will be able to say which letter it is and write both cases of the letter properly without any outside prompts. This would be the first step to seeing the upper- or lowercase letter in a word, and sounding that letter out, as well as hearing a word, identifying a particular letter's sound and writing out that letter. See the reproducible "Teaching Each Letter to Mastery" (page 181) checklist to ensure each student shows proficiency with each letter.

Letters

Different curricula have different letter orders and tell you how long it takes to teach each letter and whether to teach the upper- or lowercase letters or both. They even tell you if you should teach the letter-sound only and not the letter name.

I will tell you what I learned about teaching the letters. The order you teach the letters need not be dogmatic. No matter what letter order a curriculum has research tested, it doesn't really matter. The students are going to need to know every letter. On the other hand, a developmentally appropriate order would work better than a random one. This is what you should keep in mind when you pick an order: the first letters you teach should be consonants that are used most frequently, have a consistent sound, and are easy to learn. So, *Z* is easy to learn and consistent (a *z* usually sounds like a *z*), but it is not used frequently. *G* is used frequently but is hard to learn and not consistent (sometimes it has a /j/ sound). *C* is easy to learn and is frequently used, but not consistent (it sometimes sounds like /s/). These letters can wait.

Others, including *B*, *D*, *F*, and *L* are frequently used, consistent, and easy to learn. These are the letters you are looking for. It doesn't really matter which of these you teach first. On the other hand, you can't go crazy with these rules, as *S* and *T* are not consistent (*S* and *T* combine with *H* to make different sounds, *S* on its own makes the /z/ sound and some others), but they are so ubiquitous and so easy to learn that they should be among the first letters you teach anyway.

You should teach at least one vowel early, maybe after the fourth or fifth letter you present. Teach an easy one like *A* first, although all the vowels are challenging and take a long time to learn. If they are not given the proper time, kindergarteners will confuse one vowel with another. Spend a lot of time on each vowel. Teach the short sound of the vowel first. The long sound will come later. It is important for students to get a vowel under their belts early because then you can start to teach blending.

Yes, blending can be taught immediately (more on that later). You don't have to wait until they learn all the letters.

Spend a lot of time on each letter and make sure that the students have learned a letter to your satisfaction before going on to the next one. I don't agree with programs that recommend teaching one letter per day or a few letters per week. What happens is that students spend the rest of the year relearning each letter. Go on to the next letter after the previous one is learned, but don't spend more than a week on each letter. As with anything else you teach, you will constantly assess. You will know who is struggling and be able to review and reinforce the letters through small-group and individual instruction.

At the beginning of the year it might take a week for most of the students to master each letter, but as you go forward, and the students get into the routine of learning how to learn letters, each letter takes less time to master. Then you can start doing two letters a week. It usually takes until February to learn all the letters to mastery.

So, teach a few consonants, then a vowel, a few more consonants, another vowel, and so on. Space out the vowels but have them done before you get to the infrequent letters—particularly those at the end of the alphabet. I guess they are there for a reason. My advice is to teach the letter *q* as |qu|. That is to say, pair them together like they are friends.

Some people recommend not teaching the names of the letters because they are confusing (Jolly, 2013). However, the classic technique of associating a child-friendly word whose first letter has the most common sound of the letter being learned (*goat* for *G*) works fine. A little extra effort and repetition may be expected for a letter like *G*, but it doesn't warrant not teaching letter names. Knowing the letter names gives a frame of reference for each sound in reading and in writing.

I think that you should teach the upper- and lowercase letters at the same time and here is why. Although the students will be writing and reading mostly lowercase letters, many kindergarteners come in knowing more of the uppercase letters. You can therefore reinforce their knowledge of the uppercase letters and at the same time use them as a gateway to the lowercase letters. Some letters will take longer to teach for this reason, as some lowercase letters look like smaller versions of their capitals and some look totally different. There are, however, programs that teach upper- and lowercase separately (including Wilson Language Training's Fundations).

Don't go crazy with the word that is going to teach the student the letter. "*A*, apple, /ah/" works, but so does "*A* avocado, /ah/" and "*A* antelope, /ah/." Whatever works, you can even use all three versions at the same time. The word is going to be dropped in due time anyway. What you are working toward is for the student to see the letter and automatically say the corresponding sound directly, omitting the intermediary word.

Phonics is a very imperfect system, but I feel strongly that each student needs to know each letter to mastery and that is the essence of phonics. At the beginning of the year, you will assess the students to see what letters they know already; however, it still pays for students who already know the letters to go through the whole introduction of each one, as they probably don't know each letter to mastery. If you do it right, it serves as a reinforcement of what they know, and it teaches them new things—especially blending. Few children enter kindergarten with that important skill. By February, when they have mastered all the letters, we have a letter party and parade. We have parties and parades for almost everything.

Blending

Along with all the other ways you teach students to use letters in reading and writing, you should work on blending as soon as you can. Blending is a very important but difficult skill, an essential bridge from pretending to read to actual reading. It is the magical moment when a student can smoothly combine the sounds of two or more letters together. You will have to spend a lot of time teaching it, so you have to start early.

Letter Automaticity

Blending starts with learning letters. You've read about steps 1 and 2, which is all prep work for step 3, when students actually start to blend letters.

1. Students have *letter automaticity* with a letter. That is, the student sees the letter and can automatically say its sound (not the name—forget the name for now). As you teach new letters, add them to the list so that a student must be able to read each letter automatically in any order presented.

2. You've added a vowel to the consonant letters already learned like it's just any other letter and wait until the student can read all the letters learned, including the vowel, automatically.

3. Now, start pairing the vowel with any of the letters already taught to mastery. The vowel can be the first letter or the last letter. You can do *na* or *an*. It doesn't matter. These are the *letter pairs*. Start by having the students read the letter pairs by reading each letter individually, and then modeling blending one letter sound into the other.

No magic technique enables a student to go from reading letters individually to blending them together. It requires a lot of modeling and repetition. I use the phrase *singing the letters* when I demonstrate blending. The students like this analogy and follow my voice as it first goes up as I start the blend and smooth the letters together and then drops back down near the end.

Match as many individual vowels as you can with different letters, so students are exposed to a lot of different letter pair combinations. Keep in mind that certain consonants are easier to blend with vowels. You will figure this out as you go along, and you will have to work on some blends a little harder than you do on others.

When the time is right, add another consonant to a letter so that the vowel is in the middle—the classic consonant-vowel-consonant (CVC) word. In the previous example, you can add *p* to the end of *na* to make *nap*, or *f* to the beginning of *an* to make *fan*. Notice that learning to blend started way before you introduced the CVC word. I call CVC words *sandwich words*. The vowel is sandwiched between the two consonants. I am teaching students to read sandwiches. As they learn more letters and vowels, keep working on letter automaticity, letter pairs, and CVC words.

You might assume that when students blend, they are blending the vowel into the first consonant and then adding the last consonant (*na* + *p*). However, they may be reading the first consonant and then adding that to a blend of the vowel and last consonant (*n* + *ap*). It's their choice, not yours, and they should have both skills.

When a student learns to blend, it's a great moment—like going from crawling to walking or learning how to ride a bicycle, or maybe even driving a car.

Consonant Blends, Digraphs, and Word Families

After mastering the individual letters of the alphabet, and doing well with blending CVC words, you can start teaching consonant blends and digraphs, (*sh*, *th*, *br*, *sl*, and so on). I call blends and digraphs *two-letter things* with students. To early kindergarteners, they are neither letters nor words, so the term *two-letter things* works. The idea is to have the students eventually process them in the way they do individual letters.

- A *consonant blend* is a common combination of two consonants that to the ear can almost be processed as a new sound—for instance, *st* or *cl*.
- A *digraph* is a combination of two consonants that make an entirely new sound—for instance, *ch* or *ph*.

Through observation and experience, I have come up with the idea that, in general, we, as humans, are good at blending up to what we perceive as three sounds at a time.

CVC words are made up of three letters, each with an individual sound, so that is a good start for kindergarteners. However, I am talking about three *sounds*. People can blend three sounds, or what they perceive as sounds. And a sound can be a consonant blend, digraph, or a syllable. In my experience, students will start treating a blend or digraph as one sound after they learn it. So, the word *shop* will not look like *s-h-o-p* but will start looking like *sh-o-p* after a student has learned the *sh* digraph.

Next, you can introduce word families (*at*, *ing*, *ack*, *est*), so that they will start seeing a word family as one sound. A *word family*, also known as a *phonogram*, is a spelling pattern that usually starts with a vowel, represents one syllable, and is seen at the ends of words. If you teach the word family *op*, now the word shop looks like *sh-op*. That is only two sounds, so you can add one more. Take a word like *crack*. It would be a two-sound word: *cr-ack* after you have taught the blend *cr* and the word family *ack*. You can add another word family, *ing*, and a kindergartener will see it as a CVC word, *cr-ack-ing*. You now have someone who, five months prior, could not read one letter reading a two-syllable word comprised of eight letters!

You can teach one consonant blend or digraph and one word family each week. The order doesn't really matter. Pick ones that you feel will most benefit the students.

Long Vowels

Around this time, maybe in March, you are really going to hammer down the concept of vowels. Vowels are special because they are in just about every word. You have to be absolutely sure that your students have mastered the short vowel sounds, because you are now going to teach them the long vowels. Yes, you are.

You can preteach a long vowel, such as *A*, by introducing a word family (*ake*, for instance) that already has a long vowel embedded.

Tell the students that each vowel has two sounds, the short sound that they know already and the one that says its name. Then work on *vowel automaticity* with long and short vowels and start introducing CVC words that have either one. You don't have to teach *silent e* because at this early point in their reading history, phonics will already be failing the kids. Too many words don't fit the rule, such as *have, love, come*, and so many others. Why teach a rule that will be broken immediately? Of course, at some point, you should make students aware of that rule, but that point is not now.

So how does a prereader know whether to read a vowel as long or short? They don't. As an adult reader, you may not either when you encounter a word you've never seen before. You would try one way, and if you had already heard that word and it made sense in the context of what you were reading, you would know you were right.

If not, you would try a different vowel sound. Early readers should do the same. I always say, "If one thing doesn't work, try another thing—you'll know when you are right." In a nutshell, I don't teach phonic rules, I teach phonic *options*.

Following this idea, I slowly introduce alternate sounds of letters, so that students will learn that *c* sometimes has the sound of /s/ and that the letter *s* sometimes has the sound of /z/ or even /sh/, and so on. If one sound doesn't work, try another!

Mantras

Around this time, I start teaching the students the reading mantras. These mantras are simple, general rules that they should keep in the backs of their minds when they are encounter difficult words. They encourage the students to problem solve the difficult words by using all of their accumulated knowledge and to think flexibly (reading is thinking; everything is thinking), creatively, and with confidence.

The basic mantras that I keep reinforcing follow.

- **"Look for the sandwich words in the big words."** You will find two sandwiches in the word *catfish*. (Hopefully, by this time, the students see *sh* as one sound.)

- **"Look for other little words in the big words."** If you encounter the word *another*, look for a word that you know. How about *the*? (Now you can blend *a* and *n* and use the letter *o* as a bridge to the word the, and you might be able to figure out this difficult word as a kindergartener.)

- **"If one sound doesn't work, try another."** If the /ch/ sound doesn't work, try the /c/ sound on its own. If the /s/ sound doesn't work, try the /z/ sound.

- **"Read what you know, and go from there."** If a word is simply too difficult to figure out even after trying decoding or using pictures, context, and syntax to figure it out, there is not a stop sign—but don't move ahead until you have exhausted all possibilities and make sure that you still understand what you are reading.

Of course, the student is using a multitude of approaches to read a word, as everyone does, all happening at the speed of light and all internally. So, these mantras are not exclusive. However, verbalizing these four mantras after someone has reached a certain reading level really helps.

Sight Words

What about sight words—those that students memorize? Where do they fit in as a student is learning to read?

First, let me clarify the difference between a sight word and a high-frequency word.

- A *sight word* is one that is technically unreadable, as it does not follow the general rules of phonics. To read a sight word, it has to be memorized (includes *the, of, no,* and *to*).
- A *high-frequency word* is a word that one sees over and over when they read.

Some sight words occur with high frequency, so they would be considered both sight words and high-frequency words. The words I just listed—*the, of, no,* and *to*—fit that category. You see them all the time in print. However, many high-frequency words are not sight words. In fact, most aren't. Words such as *am, can, in,* and *it* are examples of this. They are easily readable using basic phonic skills and are commonly seen in print.

But consider this: at the beginning stages, every word could be considered a sight word, because every word is unreadable except through memorization. However, I am not going to teach someone to memorize every word—only select ones that are very frequent. So, in terms of teaching reading, it is not of great concern to me if a word is technically a sight word or not. I am only interested in a sight word if it is a high-frequency word.

While decoding will be the primary way students will learn to read, it is beneficial to memorize some of these high-frequency words early on. Beginning readers are still learning letter-sound correspondences and negotiating text and, frankly, need all the help they can get. Knowing high-frequency words reduces the number of words they need to figure out when reading.

> **I am only interested in a sight word if it is a high-frequency word.**

Here is a testament to the power of high-frequency words:

> In the 100 Magic Words system, the words are divided into colors, and are learned in order from most commonly used to less commonly used. So, once learners know the 12 "Golden" words, they have already mastered the words which make up around one quarter of all text. If they are then able to learn the next 20 "Red" words, they have learned the words which make up one third of all text in total. (Vize, 2008)

There are many high-frequency word lists out there, the most famous being the *Dolch List* (Dolch, 1936), which has 220 words. *Teaching Basic, Advanced, and Academic Vocabulary: A Comprehensive Framework for Elementary Instruction* (Marzano, 2020) is another option.

Now that you know the difference between sight words and high-frequency words and why it is really the high-frequency words that are important, I have to reveal something. For some reason not known to me, all high-frequency words are referred to as *sight words* by many in the educational community. Yes, that means that whether you teach the students to memorize *the* or *can*, you are teaching them a sight word.

From here on, I am going to conform to the common parlance and refer to all high-frequency words as *sight words*. Why didn't I do so from the beginning? Because it's important to know the proper meaning of terms before you adhere to the quirks in the system. Now, I will talk about which sight words to teach, the word wall, teaching one word a week, and the sight-word fallacy.

Which Sight Words to Teach

Most teachers get a list of sight words to teach during the year. If I am given a list of sight words, I don't go down the list and teach the words in that order, just as I don't teach the letters starting from *A*. If there is a word on the bottom of the list that I see in a lot of the books we are reading, or if I think that it would benefit their writing, I teach it and then check it off the list. By the end of the year, the class will know all the words on the list, so I try to teach the sight words in an order that will be most beneficial to their reading development. I also know from experience that with everything else I am teaching them and with their brain power ability at that age, they can learn, memorize, and retain about one sight word a week. I don't teach more than that.

The Word Wall

Every time the students learn a sight word, digraph or blend, or word family, I put it on the word wall. I have a different color code for each, so all sight words might be in red and all digraphs or blends might be in green. I use a very large font, so students can see them clearly from across the room. When it comes to the word wall, the first thing you need to do is to teach the students to access it a lot. Then you have to teach them not to access it a lot. You teach them that the best word wall is the one in their brains. That way they can use it anywhere, especially when they are outside of school.

My word wall starts out very humbly at the beginning of the year. If you looked at my word wall in October, you might think that my class was not learning anything. But by May, my word wall is almost at capacity. Figure 8.2 is an example of the word wall displaying a sight word, blend, and word family.

Figure 8.2: Word wall.

One Word a Week

Teaching one sight word a week means about forty words per school year—this is in accordance with every reading curriculum I have ever looked into. But watch what happens. By the time March rolls around, many words on the official list become readable to the students, as they now know how to blend. Examples would be words such as, *it*, *in*, *if*, *up*, *him*, *get*, *can*, and so many more. This means that a student will be able to read loads of the sight words (you know that they are really readable high-frequency words) that I have not taken the time to officially teach.

When I had to give a sight-word assessment to my students at the end of one year, the average score was about one hundred sight words on their own, quite easily. That is because even though I officially taught them about forty sight words over the course of the year, I also taught them how to read.

The Sight-Word Fallacy

It makes sense to teach sight words as part of the reading curriculum. It is a great shortcut and aid to competent reading. On the other hand, as with any good thing, too much of it proves detrimental. I think of sight words as another kind of rocket booster for reading. Essential at first, not so much afterward. If they are not taught properly, sight words can actually inhibit the ability to read, both in the short and long term.

The faulty logic goes that if memorizing thirty-two words is like magic for reading, then memorizing sixty-four words is doubly magic, and memorizing 128 words is more magic than anyone could handle. This is not the case. Sight words are powerful tools but need to be taught in moderation. And so it was with a high-level supervisor who was a literacy *expert* my first year of teaching kindergarten. She demanded that the students memorize one-hundred sight words by Thanksgiving. Where she came up with that number, I will never know, but this administrator was not one to be questioned.

As I mentioned, a kindergartener is good for memorizing about one sight word per week, so I knew that my kids would know about ten by Thanksgiving, if they were lucky. So, I didn't even try to follow what she said. Of course, I could have gotten in trouble for this, but I knew that one hundred words couldn't and shouldn't be attempted. You also know by now my attitude about getting into good trouble, anyway. Around March or April, the supervisor followed up on her demand. Without the teachers' knowledge, she picked random sight-words and had an assessor choose a few kids from each class to test secretly. It turned out that the students in my class did really well on the assessment, and the other classes did very poorly. The teachers were teaching the one hundred words, but the students weren't learning them. It was above their capability level. More importantly, the other students weren't learning to read because so much instructional time was being dedicated to memorization. This supervisor's policy did lasting damage to the school, and it was confirmed the next year. Those students ended up being below-grade readers because the curriculum of the year before was too sight-word heavy.

> ### HOW WE READ ENGLISH
> I would like to take a little detour to talk about how people read English in the first place. I couldn't have done this until we'd gone over phonics, digraphs or blends, and word families, but now that we have, we can explore a little more.

Let's start with European languages. Many European languages have a "transparent alphabet code, a nearly perfect one-to-one correspondence between each individual sound (phoneme) in the language and a visual symbol—a letter or letter pair" (McGuinness, 2006, p. 2). This means that in these languages, each letter has one particular sound and that's it. This makes those languages supposedly easier to read and write.

English, on the other hand, is a very inexact language whose spelling "system suffers from both afflictions, multiple spellings for the same phoneme, and multiple ways to decode letters and letter sequences" (McGuinness, 2006, p. 3). This means that you never know exactly what sound a letter should make when you are reading, and you never know exactly what letter to write for a particular sound when you are in the process of writing a word. This suggests that English is a very difficult and confusing language to learn.

On its face value, English seems to be an exclusively alphabetic language. That is to say that we read it by decoding the letters. Not all languages work on the system of decoding letters. McGuinness (2006) describes early languages that used *pictograms* (a picture that represents a thing or concept) and present-day languages that use *logograms* (abstract symbols that represent words) and other present-day languages that use symbols to represent syllables. These have to be memorized. Since human memory for abstract symbols overloads at about two thousand, systems were developed to keep the number of symbols within that range.

I have not found any authority on language systems that make the following point, but it's one that I've observed in the classroom. I believe that English is not simply an alphabetic language. If it were, it would be a difficult and frustrating language to read and write. But you are reading this now. It may be quite easy for you. I discovered that English has aspects of all three types of language systems. There is definitely the decoding of letters in English, but there is also the memorization of words and syllabic word parts, like word families, that you can use to combine to figure out new words. There is probably a lot more memorization that goes on in reading English than is acknowledged. It stands to reason that if people have a capacity to memorize two thousand symbols, they will use that capability, even if they are confined to twenty-six letters.

I think that reading English follows this process: when you read, you are using an inscrutable combination of phonics, memorization, word analysis and synthesis, sentence structure, and prior knowledge. And everyone does it a little bit differently. That is why it is important to learn letters as well as digraphs, blends, word families, and sight words. It is equally important to have a huge warehouse of vocabulary and prior knowledge because you can only read words you already know—that is, that you have heard already.

The more you read, the stronger and sharper your reading skills become. So many of the skills are internalized that you can't really break down and

continued ▶

> describe when and how each skill is being used. If a student is reading well, let him or her just do it. Don't bog students down with having to describe and name the strategy they just used. They probably didn't use just one, and it would be too complicated for them to unravel the process, just as would it be for you if you had to break down and explain all the reading strategies you just used to read this sentence.

Leveled Books

I look at each reading level as a different stage in learning how to ride a bike. The hardest thing to do is get on the bike and start. Along the way we teach students how to balance, brake, make turns, get on and off the bike by themselves, and do all that on a controlled course. Finally, we take them to the playground, give them the bike, and say, "Go ahead and take a ride!"

In leveled reading programs like Irene Fountas and Gay Su Pinnell (2016), students go from easy books to harder books throughout elementary school. They will start as an *A* reader in kindergarten and finish as a *Z* reader in the upper grades. A kindergartener will usually get to level *D* by the end of the year, but this varies greatly. The books increase slightly in difficulty, like tiers in a video game, so the students have to apply all they already know on the new level plus master new things. Then it's on to the next one.

Leveling Up

From what I have observed, even with all of this instruction, most students for most of the year are not reading in kindergarten. At least not the way we usually think of as reading. That doesn't mean that they cannot negotiate a book, or even get all of the words right and demonstrate comprehension of the text. But are they truly reading it? By the end of the year most are on the threshold of what would be considered proper reading. Some have even crossed that threshold.

Of course, none of this makes sense until I define what I consider conventional reading to be and the stages students go through to get to that point. It is important to understand this, especially for those who use leveled reading programs such as that by Fountas and Pinnell (2016). There are other leveled reading programs, but since these are widely used, I will use their terminology here.

I define *conventional reading* as being able to look at a sentence and see all the letters of each word as they are and using a variety of techniques to decode the letters and say the words, for the most part, correctly. Of course, the ultimate purpose of being able to read is comprehension, but right now I am now focusing on decoding words. And now, here is a good guideline that shows how reading skills usually correlate to reading levels in a leveled reading system such as Fountas and Pinnell (2016).

- A student does not need to know all the letters or how to blend to get to *A* or *B* level.
- A *C*-level reader needs to know most, or all, of the letters but need not be able to blend.
- A *D*-level reader needs to know all the letters, the basic digraphs, blends, and some word families. They don't need to know how to blend or about the long vowels, but it helps a lot.
- Once the blending kicks in—and it does take time—and the long and short vowels kick in, the student is ready for *E* level.

In books up to level *E*, students use a combination of memorizing, anticipating what comes next, looking at the picture, and the dawning understanding that letters stand for sounds (Reading A–Z, n.d.). They see words as blobs of varying lengths, then as blobs with letters they know sticking out of the front, then the back, and then the middle. Finally, they are able to see all the letters. In fancy terms, they are going from logographic to orthographic reading. Every student is different, but if I had to describe the reading progress of a generic student (and no student is generic), I would say that he or she would become an *A* reader in October or November, a *B* reader by the end of December, a *C* reader in February or March, and a *D* reader in late April or May. The student has a good chance of becoming an *E* reader or higher by the end of the school year—that would mean he or she would be reading, by my definition, at that time.

Figuring out something that looks like a blob is a commendable skill, but it is not the same as reading a word. The blobs don't go away until the end of *D* level, which is why I consider an *E*-level reader to be a true reader. They are certainly not fluent readers yet, but they have cracked the code. It is useful to know that students can't read at the earlier levels, because then you know what to expect from them. If an *A* reader sees the sentence *I can eat some cheese*, I know he or she can't read it independently. If that were possible, that person would automatically be designated as a *C* reader, at the very least. Looking at that sentence—*I can eat some cheese*—a *C* reader would do better, but not know that *ch* has its own sound, that two *e*s together make a long /e/ sound. This reader wouldn't know about silent *e* and that the letter *s* sometimes makes a /z/ sound. But this kindergartener could still get the words right, which is something an *A* reader couldn't do. A *C*-level reader has advanced guessing skills that an *A* reader doesn't yet have. (Actually, reading never stops being a guessing game. As you become a better reader you become a more educated and accurate guesser. That is why you could argue that an *A* reader is reading, and I won't dispute that. But at the same time, I look at reading as being able to guess accurately at words one is actually seeing and being able to read a whole book without any outside help.)

Back to the sentence the *A* reader can't read: *I can eat some cheese.* He or she can't read it the first time he or she sees it but can the second time. This reader will even be able to guess what the next sentence will be, assuming the next one follows some rules you have taught about *A* books already, such as that the sentence pattern repeats on every page. The same with *B* books and *C* books. By *D* books, the training wheels are almost off, and by *E* level this reader is riding a two-wheeler on his or her own, although there is still a lot to learn and the teacher must make a big effort to reconfirm that the reader is understanding what he or she is reading. My point is that at the early reading levels, kindergarteners by definition, need outside assistance in reading their books, at least at first. One can't expect kindergarteners to pick up books they have never seen before and read them on their own, without support. It is beyond their capability. If it turns out someone can read the books independently, you then have yourself a student who is higher than that particular level.

Ensuring Accurate Leveling Labels

It's important to know how to categorize books into their proper reading level for two reasons.

1. **Many books are labeled incorrectly:** It doesn't make sense to me, either, but I am an observer. I know what I see. Book publishers get it wrong; websites get it wrong; and—even more often— teachers get it wrong. And I'm not talking hairline differences between levels. I'm talking *D* books being labeled as *A* books and beginning-chapter books labeled as *A* books, and everything in between.

2. **A student on a certain level has to be reading books on exactly that level and challenged with appropriate books from the next level:** If they get books at too far below their level, they will not be challenged or learn anything, and if they are given books too high above their level, they will be too challenged and still not learning anything. As with most things in teaching, it all revolves around psychologist Lev S. Vygotsky's (1978) theory of the zone of proximal development, or what is more commonly known as *scaffolding*. This would be teaching to the level just above what the

student can do independently (Cherry, 2020). Good readers are really the sum of all the keys or tools they have, like the carpenter with a toolbox or the custodian with the keys. On each level, you teach kindergarteners and they develop new reading skills and learn how to apply the skills they have mastered in new ways or in combination to unlock the print they are seeing.

What do I mean by an *A* book, anyway? Most teachers know it's an *A* book because there is a big *A* on the front or back of it. The *A* was put there either by the publisher or by another teacher. You can also look up the level of a book online. The first thing I do when I start teaching in a new room is to make sure all the books are leveled and labeled correctly (page 158). This is very tedious work, but it has to be done

In my estimation, if you are using leveled books, the main things to learn are the capabilities and lack of capabilities each student presents on each level. When students are reading a book to me, I can usually predict what words they will be able to read, what words will give them trouble

> **Good readers are really the sum of all the keys or tools they have.**

and why, and what words they won't be able to read. This is because I know, at this point, which keys they possess, which ones are still developing, and which ones are beyond their reach. Once you learn to develop a profile of the skills each student possesses at varying levels, you can predict and anticipate where the student will succeed and be challenged within the text. In this way, you can focus on helping develop that next skill that would make the challenging words in the text less so and slowly move him or her to develop the attributes of the profile of the next level.

Self-Leveled Books

Here are my unofficial rules about how to level. These rules should enable you to categorize a book very quickly and accurately. The criteria I have developed are from reading and comparing many leveled books over the years. I categorize by letter, from A to E books, and discuss fiction versus nonfiction in this section.

A Books

These books will have one sentence on each page. The next page will have the same sentence with one word changed—usually the last word. If the last word is not changed but a different one is, it would make it a hard *A* book. A kindergartener should not be able to read the first sentence solo. If he or she can, then that student's reading level is much higher than an *A* reader.

So, if the first sentence is, *I played in the park*, the student might guess at what the sentence is but not be able to read it. Once the student hears the sentence read correctly, he or she can then go to the next page, see a picture of a house, remember the sentence from the prior page, and read the sentence that says, *I played in the house.* But a student might also read the sentence as *I played in the home*, since they can't actually read words. They may even look at the garden in the picture instead of the house and say, *I played in the garden.* This is OK too, because the student does not know letters yet. The fact that the word *house* starts with the letter *h* does not clue him or her to the fact that the word starts with an /h/ sound.

B Books

Like *A* books, these books will have one sentence on each page, but the sentence will take up two lines. The sentence will repeat throughout the book, but one word will change on every page. Sometimes the last word of the initial sentence, and sometimes a word in the middle of the sentence, will change. In addition, sometimes an easy sight word will change as well, so there would be two changes per sentence. For instance, *I played with the ball in the park.* Next page: *I played with the ball in my house.*

By this time, the students should be familiar with a few sight words and show that they are starting to break through the blob and start to see words that they know. They still may not know all their letters. As with an *A* book, students still need someone to start the book.

The *B* book also usually has a surprise ending that does not follow the pattern of any of the previous sentences. The book I was referring to might end with the sentence *I love to play*. Students are not really responsible for being able to read this on their own. The purpose of including this sentence in the book is to get them to think that there is more to a book than just a simple repeating sentence pattern. If a student is able to read the surprise ending consistently, he or she is showing readiness for the next level.

C Books

These books will have one or more sentences on a page. If there are two sentences on a page, each sentence will have a different pattern. Instead of one word and possibly a sight word changing every time the sentence repeats, two words and possibly a sight word will change. So, if this is a one-sentence-per-page book and the first sentence is, *I can go to the park and play*, the sentence on the next page might be, *I can go to the field and run* or, *I can go to a field and run.* Sometimes the book will introduce a new pattern in the middle of the book: *Do you like to play in the park?*

By this time, students should know all the letters of the alphabet. But they still can't read words, so if the word is *park* and they say *playground*, that is OK. They should know that *p* has the /p/ sound. If the word is *park* and they say *field*, it is not acceptable at this point. Teachers usually need to start off when students are working on *C* books. Some teachers say that students should be able to start a *C* book solo. I disagree, because they still cannot yet read.

At some point along the way, students will have read enough books, know enough sight words, and may even have some rudimentary blending skills so that they can start a *C* book on their own. That is when I know they are ready for *D* books. They are still seeing blobs, but the blobs have letters at the beginning and the end.

D Books

D-level books always sound to me like those *Fun With Dick and Jane* (Gray, 1946) books. They are repetitive, but there is no obvious pattern. So, for instance, they might go like this: *I like to play. Do you like to play? Let's go play in the park. I like to play in the park. The park is so much fun to play in.*

A lot of words with consonant blends and digraphs are introduced in *D* books. Words such as *fish* or *chop*. There are also many words with word families, such as *bake* or *back* and the addition of inflected endings, such as *ing, s,* and *ed*. Read: *backs, backed, backing*. You should be teaching these things at this time of the year—around March or April (assuming you start school in August or September). A student who is developing blending skills and knows about long vowels has a big advantage in reading *D* books, as this is the final stage before real reading, the *E* book.

A student who has mastered the letters, digraphs, blends, word families, and blending, who has a good and developmentally appropriate mastery of language and sentence variations, has been exposed to appropriately leveled books for the whole year, and is showing good comprehension, is knocking on the *E*-level door and will probably get in by the end of the year. Not only that, but in May or June you will get to see the explosion that happens when students start assembling all the skills and techniques they have learned and realize that the sum is way more than its parts. It's like creating a monster—a powerful reading monster that can go to levels much higher than *E* by the end of the year.

E Books

The *E* book is the easiest book to read in which there is no obvious pattern or anything related to one. That doesn't mean the books don't have repetitive words or features, but they lack the stiffness in style of the prior levels and seem to have crossed the threshold into what one would consider authentic texts.

By the time they are *E* readers, students know all their letters and a lot of consonant blends, digraphs, and sight words. They can blend the sandwiches (CVC words), know their phonic options, know about short and long vowels, read what they know, and figure out what they don't know. They see all the letters in each word and can figure out the reading puzzle. They are readers!

Independent Reading

How do students incorporate what you are teaching about reading? One of the main ways is through independent reading. This is when they have the time, space, and opportunity to try out their skills. It's similar to teaching them to play basketball or teaching them how to play chess. You can spend all day teaching students how a pawn, knight, or queen moves, and they may learn this, but if they are not applying it to the game of chess constantly, they will not learn how to play. This is what independent reading is all about. But there is just one problem. Students can't read independently in kindergarten. In fact, they can't read at all! They can't even start a book on their own. How then can they do independent reading? It must be some kind of joke.

Well, it's not a joke to administrators who expect to see little kindergarteners sitting on their own and reading while the teacher sits with a small group on the side catering to their reading needs—sometimes as early as September! I don't know how this model started, and I don't know why this model has ever been applied to kindergarten. I do know that it is unrealistic, and that even if it could be accomplished with kindergarteners, it's not the best way to spend the independent reading time.

Some teachers will insist on making this unrealistic model work, so they try to teach a small group, leaving the rest of the class to their own devices. This leaves twenty students not reading at all and five trying to learn from the teacher in a very distracting environment. Some teachers have the students read the same book over and over, so they don't need help starting new books, but you don't want students to associate reading with something boring and repetitive.

My goal during independent reading is to have all students reading all the time. But what I am really expecting is for everyone to be attempting to read. Since they generally cannot read without assistance until later in the academic year, what does independent reading look like before then? At the beginning of the year, I constantly encourage the students to be reading, whatever that is to them. It's the same way I would encourage five-year-olds to try to get a basketball in a hoop ten feet high. I know they can't do it, but if I make them think they can do it, at least they will try. Remember, *do your best* is one of my class rules. I put out a bin on each table that has a range of books that I think will appeal to students and don't focus on reading levels at this time.

At some point, students are familiar with books and incorporate enough of the skills I have been teaching (including concepts of print, sight words, sentence patterns, and so forth) that I can put out bins of *A* books on the tables in addition to the unleveled books that are already out, and students seamlessly transition to *A* books—each student at his or her own pace.

Now, I am running around the room like a juggler again, trying to keep twenty plates spinning on poles at the same time, but this time I am trying to get each student started with the leveled books. This usually consists of simply reading the first sentence of the book so that the student is aware of the sentence pattern. With this simple prompt, kindergarteners can usually work out the rest. Some catch on right away and some need more reinforcement. I work with everyone every day. I call this *speed conferencing* (page 166), which I explain in the next section. By the end of a week, most can start these books on their own and read them all the way through. You will see a range of capabilities and become aware of who can go to the next level and who needs additional help.

Now the bins of unleveled books gradually come off the tables and we are reading leveled books until the end of the year. It's all a slow build, everything subtle and scaffolded, and you know where you are heading. Now it's time to introduce students to book bags, so they can start taking leveled books home. I scaffold from me choosing a few books for them, to me choosing more books for them, to them choosing a few of the books on their own, and to them choosing all the books on their own. How many books do they take home? As a thinking teacher, you decide. Remember—no spoon-feeding. There is no magic number of books. There's no magic anything. It's all about thinking, experimenting, and problem solving. (If you must know, I do like the number five.)

Every week the students start off with new books, so the process repeats itself. However, every week they are also learning more about letters, sight words, and other reading skills to incorporate into their reading. They start doing more of the reading on their own. When they master a book, they go to the next level, where they are again more dependent on my assistance. We go through the same juggler process again. Over time, they are more independent on their new level. However, I don't see these fruits of my labor until the last few months of school. At this point I will have a class of students reading on their own, and I can tone down my frantic juggler pace and focus for an extended period on one or more students.

Reading Proficiency Help Methods

I use a variety of methods to move each student forward in reading (and writing) competence. Speed conferencing and tutoring individual students are the most effective. I will explain why I am skeptical about small-group work as an instructional focus for early readers who are challenged by the curriculum. The reason you are meeting with the group is, most likely, that they didn't get what you were teaching to the whole class. In most cases, a small group to a struggling student is really just a smaller whole group. That is to say, if students didn't get it in the whole group, they are unlikely to get it in the small group. In order not to waste anyone's time, I go right to the individual conference—tutoring, when you get right down to it.

Speed Conferences

I don't do individual conferences in the traditional sense, spending time focused on watching one student read, magically figuring out the one thing that I can show him or her that will unlock the inner reader, teach it, watch him or her transform, and then float to the next needy reader and spread more fairy dust (and document all this while I'm doing it). This would work well in an idealized world, where each and every student were actively engaged, time were limitless, and I had four hands.

So instead, I use speed conferencing to keep students reading and give them what they need to get to the next level. I check on everyone during every independent reading session, see where they are, give them what they need to maintain or improve, and then on to the next. I am not the fairy; I am *The Flash*.

As outlined in the section on independent reading (page 164), at the beginning of the year conferences might last for a few seconds at a time. I might cycle through the whole class two or three times during a thirty-minute independent reading session. As competence and reading stamina advance, the amount of time per student increases and the number of times I cycle through the class decreases, but I always monitor every reader's progress. It is only near the end of the year that I am afforded the time to do individual conferences with select students during one period.

I do use the more traditional conferencing model and meet with each student for an extended period, so I can figure out how I can help (see the following section on tutoring). The only way to really dig down deep and get to the core of how to help a reader is this way.

Tutoring

I tutor each student, some more and some less. I meet with every student individually for an intensive analysis to see exactly where he or she is and to understand his or her reading process. It is really not much different than the idealized individual conference that I said is virtually unattainable in a classroom setting.

To do this, I have to be totally focused, and so does the student. How does this work within the context of the classroom? It doesn't. I do this on my prep period. Prep time is not limitless, so I have to be smart as to how often I see each student. Using prep time for tutoring is an imperfect system, so I meet with students on an as-needed basis. That is to say, I am not able to create a formal schedule to ensure that every student is seen with a particular frequency. Each conference need not take up a lot of time, so I can get to quite a few students in one period. It is the quality and focus of the conference that really moves the student forward.

I get my cues about who to meet and what to work on by taking notes during my speed conferencing. (You know by now that they are mental notes or quick jots on an index card in my back pocket.) However, using a system such as a grid or a dedicated app will work as well. When mandated, I am able to convert my findings into conference notes. I also keep track who I am meeting with to ensure that every student is accounted for and moving ahead. I sometimes have a specific skill, such as teaching punctuation, that I am going for. Other times I let the student read and figure out what I think would be helpful to for him or her to learn. I also do all of my reading assessments and running records this way.

How long to meet with each reader? That's one of those magic numbers again. I meet with each student according to immediate needs, so it varies. However, I can give you a workable range of about ten or fifteen minutes for each student.

I use my preps to assess, teach, and plan. That's what you are supposed to be using them for anyway. I just have a rotation of my students involved in it. This may not be the most common way to use a prep period, but I find that this method is essential to the student's progress, not only in reading but in the other subjects. I use this system to fill a need that is not being fully addressed by current curricula. Perhaps a distinction will someday be made between individual conferences that can be done in the classroom (speed conferencing) and true individual conferences that can be done in a more appropriate setting so that this can be accommodated into the teaching model.

The Writing Progression

The writing progression starts with writing that usually consists of a scrambled picture and a (potentially recognizable) letter or two on the paper. As students develop the concept of what a story is—by teachers reading stories, by acting out stories together, by teachers going through the thinking process and mechanics of writing a story—they start trying to write a whole story on one page, usually using pictures alone. Then they will learn to spread out the story over a few pages. As they do this, they will learn to label items in the pictures that they draw. As they learn more letters, the labels will develop from one letter to a few letters. Students usually hear the most salient sound of a word, usually the first letter, then they hear the last letter, and then the letters in the middle (Teachers College Reading and Writing Project, 2011). You will see the labels follow that progression.

When the labels become readable, and students know enough sight words and their independent reading exposes them to simple sentences, you start moving them away from writing labels to writing sentences. Labels are training wheels. Drop them once the sentence-writing starts. Students can label important things if they like and as a writing device, such as in informational books, but not as a requirement.

If you teach students to write independently and assimilate the literacy skills they have been learning, by the end of the year they will be writing a sequence of well-structured and original sentences. They will be writing long and sophisticated sentences that progress from baby sentences like, *I have a ball* to longer sentences like, *I will play with you when I get a big ball*. By the end of the year, they will start writing anything they think up and want to express, whether they can spell the words correctly or not. They don't have to write every word correctly. Actually, they can't unless you taught them the word or the letter, digraph, consonant blend, or word family.

When I look at the bulletin boards of a kindergarten class in October and students are able to write sentences such as *I went to the train station*, I can ascertain what probably happened. The teacher wrote the sentence starter *I went to the* on the board and then wrote a menu of words and phrases next to it—- one of which was *train station*. The best a kindergartener who is writing independently should be able to do by the end of the year is probably, *I went to the trayn stayshun*. It is very tempting to teach students how to be menu writers. Unfortunately, it has the same effect as teaching students to read using sight words alone (page 156). Without the menu, the student is lost. The goal of teaching writing is for the student to be able to write independently. We do provide temporary tools for writing, such as the alphabet chart and a few sight words, but as in reading, those are tools. It is the difference between giving one student a blank canvas to paint on and another student a paint-by-number kit. I totally understand why some teachers use sentence starters and word lists to help their students write. That is because a scrambled picture with a letter on it does not look like much on the bulletin board or in a student's portfolio. But it is really like giving a baby crutches because you want him or her to walk. And that is writing in a nutshell. If you couple these tips along with a good writing curriculum that introduces the students to the different writing genres, you are well on your way to developing strong writers.

What about resources? The paper you provide to write on will go from having a big space for a picture and maybe one line to one with a small space for a picture and many lines for sentences. I don't use blank booklets to write in. It simply confines students to write a book of that length. I teach them to number their pages. That way they can make a book with as many pages as they like. It is also a practical way to reinforce the learning and writing of numbers. Provide color in the form of crayons, markers, and pens at the beginning of the year. They are mostly drawing pictures, so why not go for it? At some point, usually November, the crayons and markers go away, and the pens stay. The color will come back when the students pick one of their stories to publish. This way they can draw and color to their hearts' content and have a real picture book.

Notice that I didn't use the word *pencils*. I don't use pencils for a number of reasons. First of all, they are downright dangerous with their sharp points. Also, they have to constantly be sharpened, which is a tedious daily job. Students love writing and then erasing, which will make holes in their paper. And they love to simply play with the erasers themselves. The erasers don't last very long, so then you have useless pencils or you have to provide big erasers. But the main reason I don't use pencils is that I want to see everything the students have written. If they write something and then erase it, I don't have any data to evaluate, whereas I would have otherwise.

Independent Writing

For writing instruction, students simply apply the literacy skills you have been teaching around particular genres and adding to that particularities of writing, such as capitalization and punctuation. When students successfully apply these skills in another context, that is *transfer* (Gardner, 1999). Not so simple a task, but this means that as the student moves up the ladder of literacy, to the side of each rung is often the student's reading and writing level. When students are reading, they are learning how to write. They are analyzing something written. When students are writing, they are learning how to read because they need to incorporate those skills to put readable words on the page.

In the section on reading, I did not focus much on comprehension, although it is an essential goal, and therefore you should not minimize your focus on it in the classroom. The section was not designed as a comprehensive textbook. In the same manner, I am not going to focus on structure, elaboration, meaning, or craft in this section, although they are at the core of good writing and need to be taught from the get-go. As in the section on reading, I will simply give you a few tips and insights I would like to share that should be beneficial in the overall understanding of the writing process that you can incorporate into your curriculum.

The main thing to remember is that students can only write up to the level of their literacy development. So, if they don't yet know letters, they can't write words or parts of words independently. If they don't yet know *sh*, they won't be able to write *ship* independently. Don't expect them to and don't stress if their writing does not reflect those elements at this point. I use the word *independently* repeatedly because independent writing is the only kind of writing that has any meaning when assessing their written work.

What Independent Writing Looks Like

Since the goal is to write independently, part of what students need to do is get their own paper, choose their own writing implement, access their own prior writing, make their own books, and then put everything away themselves. The way this is accomplished is very similar to the way I described teaching the students how to unpack when they come to school and how to clean up after an activity (page 116). The following process takes a few weeks.

1. At first, I do everything for them and slowly give everything over. At the beginning of the year, I take out the markers and papers, and I clean up. I get another piece of paper if someone needs it.

2. I slowly teach the students to self-check what they need to do before they can ask me for another paper. When a student starts to consistently ask me if he or she can get a new paper and says, "I really need one," I say, "You can get it yourself."

3. I then start upping the number of papers a student can get at a time, maxing out at three. I add more complex paper as an additional paper choice.

I do the same form of speed conferencing that I do during independent reading and I staple the students' work for them.

I notice that a lot of classrooms have writing folders for each student to save their works in progress. I do too. However, I notice that a lot of these folders are overstuffed with papers. I will tell you how I avoid this.

1. When independent writing time is over, I stagger the cleanup. I go from table to table and tell each student to "Stop and drop." That means that they stop writing and put down their pens. Kindergarteners don't mind doing this because they know they will be able to start off the next day where they left off today—if they want to, and if they remember what they were doing.

2. Then I tell them to pack up their writing folders and leave the folders open on the table. At the start of the year I help; later in the year I expect students to be able to put their stories back into their folders neatly. When I see a table that has all their folders ready, I tell them to put the folders away and go to the rug. Of course, I set up something interesting there, so they are not just waiting around for the others.

I used to have students put their works in progress on one dedicated side of the folder and their finished work on the other, until I realized this was unnecessary. They know their work. It's just a matter of their getting the pieces into the folders and putting the folders away.

I always teach the students that writing is thinking. Always remember that writing is about expressing one's thoughts on paper. Everything else is secondary, including spelling, sentence structure, word spacing, penmanship, and punctuation. That is why I have the students write on simple lined paper, not penmanship paper. I am concerned more about letter formation than pretty letters at this point; see the Penmanship section (page 172).

Another thing to take into consideration is that students need to have something to write about before taking the pen in hand. That is to say that before they sit down and try to write a story, for example, they should have that story pretty much outlined in their minds. If they can express it, they can write it, no matter how rudimentarily it comes out on paper. That means that a lot of work should go into developing the skills of idea generation and rehearsal with the class. This part of the writing process is often left out, as in many classrooms the students are let loose to write immediately after the minilesson is over with the idea that the teaching point is fresh in their minds. What often happens is that they pick up pens and commence writing. This looks educationally sound, but when the teacher analyzes the new writing, the lack of thought that went into it is very evident.

If you had started two or three separate stories over the past few days and I gave you some time to either work on one of them, or begin a new one, you would probably have a mental picture of all three in your mind and would be exploring new story ideas as you were walking away from me and accessing your folder. By the time you got to the table, you would probably have a pretty solid idea of what you were going to do that day, or you would spend time to review everything before you picked up your pen. At this stage of the game, young children don't know to do this, and even if they are aware of this process, they have not yet developed the working memory and conceptual skills needed to perform these tasks as quickly as you can (Dewar, 2019).

Writing starts in the brain and travels down the arm and into the hand and then onto the paper. I remind students of this, and then after a lesson, students go to their writing folders. I withhold writing implements for a few minutes. This is the time for them to reread their previous works, figure out if they want to revise an existing page, add a page to their story, or think of a great new idea and rehearse it. It sounds like a sophisticated process for a kindergartener to master, because it is. At the beginning of the year they are approximating it, but over time they measure and compare each writing piece and devise a mental plan as to the next steps they will take that day. I track their progress the same way I do in all subject areas by observing and assessing.

Penmanship

Penmanship often falls between the cracks of literacy programs; however, it is an important skill (Chassiakos, 2017) and you should spend a lot of time teaching how to write the letters properly in kindergarten. The focus is not on classic penmanship per se, but on letter formation—the methodology of how to write each letter. The students usually get one chance to learn how to write a letter correctly, maybe for their lifetime, and this is it.

When do you focus on this? When you are teaching the individual letter. It is part of letter mastery. Think of this component of letter mastery as equally important to learning letter sound correspondences and you will have a class of students who form their letters properly. Once students learn how to write a letter a certain way, it is very difficult for them to unlearn (Grisold, Kaiser, & Hafner, 2017), for better or for worse. You can use a writing curriculum to teach letter writing, but don't get bogged down on teaching the specific direction of each line or go crazy about a certain kind of writing paper or paper with *cloud* lines or *worm* lines.

Writing programs I have used, such as Handwriting Without Tears (by Learning Without Tears at https://lwtears.com) and Fundations (by Wilson Language Training at https://wilsonlanguage.com/programs/fundations), teach a *methodology*, or specific instructions, for writing each letter. That's a lot of methodologies for the students to remember. I noticed that most incorporate one of two basic rules and sometimes both of the rules together, so I dispensed with the methodologies and stuck to the following two rules.

1. Start from the top and go down (for most letters, like *b*, *l*, and *z*).
2. For letters that are circle based (like *o*, *c*, and *a*), start at the top and then go to the left. You can teach *go to the left* even before you teach *left* and *right* by continually demonstrating it.

These two rules, along with a lot of demonstration, giving the students opportunities to write the letters, and checking that they are doing the letters correctly will reap huge dividends when their fine motor skills enable them to write with good penmanship.

When it comes to writing upper and lowercase letters, the students just have to know the sizes of the upper and lowercase letters relative to each other. It would be like an adult and child standing next to each other—they would need to remember how high the child goes on the adult. There are not that many variations—some letters are half as tall as the uppercase letters, some letters are as tall, and some are half as tall and have a tail.

You can demonstrate and teach how to write the letters on specially formatted paper, but have the students write the letters on simple lined paper to see if they really understand the relationships. The specially formatted paper is like training wheels on a bike. You want to get rid of it as soon as you can. When students can write a letter on regular paper properly and consistently, by George, they've got it! Don't drill them on whether the letter starts on the *cloud* line or the *airplane* line and don't even give them the special paper anymore. They are past that stage and can now write on their own on standard paper.

Fiction Versus Nonfiction

I couldn't finish a section on literacy without clarifying the distinction between these two sometimes confusing categories. This is a very important distinction to understand. It forms the foundation of how we categorize genres for reading and writing. I was always taught different definitions of these terms, so I was always perplexed. A lot of students are probably bewildered about them.

Some educators explain to students that fiction is a book that will entertain you, while a nonfiction book is one that wants to teach you something. Well, a lot of fiction books teach me things and a lot of nonfiction books are very entertaining. Students point this out all the time. Fiction and nonfiction are really very simple concepts. I would say that fiction is something made up, even if it is based on facts. Nonfiction is something completely factual. The way I explain it in kinderese is that fiction is a *pretend* or *fake* book and nonfiction is a *real* book. End of the story. They get that. I reinforce this by saying "Fiction is fake. F-f-f-fiction, f-f-f-fake."

People associate fiction with stories and narratives and nonfiction with lists and instruction or reference books. What if you had a story about a real event? Would that be fiction or nonfiction? What if you had an instructional book on how to train a dragon. Would that be fiction or nonfiction?

The students are able to figure this out as they learn the five kinds of writing that are usually taught in kindergarten (Teachers College Reading and Writing Project, 2011).

1. **Stories:** Also known as *narratives*, they have a beginning, middle, end, plot, problem, and so on
2. **Instructional book:** A how-to book
3. **Informational book:** An all-about-something book
4. **Persuasive:** A book that gives an opinion, reviews something, tries to convince someone to do something, or complains about something (and students relate to complaining the most)
5. **Poem:** Yes, just a poem

The beautiful thing is that a book that fits any of these categories can either be fiction or nonfiction. Use the reproducible "Classifying Fiction Versus Nonfiction" (page 182) chart to do that for the books in your classroom before the school year begins. You can have a fiction story about dragons or a nonfiction story about lizards. You can have a fiction instructional book about how to plant a magic seed or a nonfiction instructional book about planting. You can have a fiction informational book about wizards or a nonfiction informational book about doctors. You can have a fiction persuasive book about why invisible beans are the best food ever or a nonfiction persuasive book about why pizza is the best food ever. Finally, you can have a fiction poem about talking trees or a nonfiction poem about autumn. Ta da! Now students can categorize any book. First

> **First figure out the category a book fits in, then figure out if it is fiction or nonfiction.**

figure out the category a book fits in, then figure out if it is fiction or nonfiction. Or do it the other way; it doesn't matter.

At the beginning of the year I reinforce the idea of fiction versus nonfiction, real versus fake, until the students are able to do that consistently and confidently with any book they encounter. As they start being exposed to different kinds of books and especially as we start to write in genres that go along the five categories, they learn how to tell the difference between a story, a how-to book, an all-about-something book, a complaining book, and a poem. Then I just put the two ideas together and they get it. So, if they write a story about themselves, they will know that it is a nonfiction story. If they read a book about talking penguins, they will know that this is a fiction story. If they read a book about how to brush teeth, they will know that it is a nonfiction how-to book. If they read a book all about trolls, they will know it is a fiction all-about-something book. This sets them up for the rest of their academic career. So, when they learn the terms *realistic fiction*, *historical fiction*, and *literary nonfiction* they easily understand them because they are simply scaffolding on concepts they already have mastered.

Even at the kindergarten level, students will pick up on the different aspects of a book and this is a great topic of conversation. They do this especially with books that flow from nonfiction to fiction, such as in a book that has a dream sequence in the middle. We just call this a *nonfiction, fiction, nonfiction sandwich*. There are sandwiches everywhere!

In a Nutshell

It is helpful to always keep in mind that when you are teaching any component of literacy you are teaching both reading and writing simultaneously. So, if you are doing a read-aloud, you are teaching writing as well; when you are engaging in independent writing, you are also teaching reading. In teaching reading and writing, you are developing thinkers (like yourself) who have to juggle the many different methods they have at their disposal to make intelligent and efficient decisions when problem solving and creating text.

Be aware of the strengths and limitations of the many classic pathways to reading, such as phonics and sight word instruction and realize that English is an imperfect but adaptable, open-ended and still developing language that requires flexible and dynamic thinkers to truly unlock its beauty.

Have You Mastered the Chapter?

Welcome to the formal assessment section of the book—a quiz to test your knowledge of the chapter. Please try the questions. The answers are provided after the questions section for a quick check. I explain the *why* after the quiz, and that is the most important part to consider.

According to this chapter:

1. Letters need to be taught:
    a. In a specific order
    b. Uppercase first, lowercase second
    c. Only based on their sounds, not their names
    d. To mastery

2. Blending should be taught:
    a. Immediately after a student has mastered one consonant
    b. Immediately after a student has mastered one consonant and one vowel
    c. Not until all vowels and consonants have been mastered
    d. None of the above

3. By a strict definition of the terms, the word *the* is a:
    a. Sight word
    b. High-frequency word
    c. Both
    d. Neither

4. During speed conferencing, the circus performer you most resemble is:
    a. The ringmaster
    b. The trapeze artist
    c. The juggler
    d. The clown

5. Phonics:

   a. Is the most important component of reading

   b. Is a limited tool for reading

   c. Needs to be mastered before reading begins

   d. Is consistent and predictable in the English language

6. The following is true about sight words:

   a. Students should memorize as many as possible

   b. You should teach three sight words a week

   c. They are one of the many tools that promote good reading

   d. All of the above are true

7. Assess your students' reading and writing skills:

   a. Right away

   b. After the first week of school

   c. After you have taught a few letters

   d. Based on your assessment calendar

8. Writing, like teaching, is all about:

   a. Planning

   b. Being organized

   c. Thinking

   d. Being motivated

Answers and Explanations

1. ***d. (To mastery)*** Do you remember in what order you were taught your letters? While there are different theories as to the best approach and order (and they should be considered thoroughly on their merits), the main goal is for students to achieve letter-sound correspondence. That should always be the prime consideration whatever method you eventually settle on.

2. ***b. (Immediately after a student has mastered one consonant and one vowel)*** Don't delay teaching blending; it takes a long time for students to master. You need a vowel and a consonant to begin and it doesn't matter if the vowel is blended into the consonant or the consonant is blended into the vowel. When learning to read, students will have the opportunity to blend in both ways.

3. ***c. (Both)*** A sight word is not easily readable using general phonics rules. A high frequency word is found in print often. *The* qualifies as both.

4. ***c. (The juggler)*** During speed conferencing you will have the excitement of walking on a high wire, feeling like you are surrounded by talented performers, and using your sense of humor to engage students, but during this period, you will be multitasking to the maximum and therefore mostly resembling a juggler who keeps all balls in motion at the same time.

5. ***b. (Is a limited tool for reading)*** It would be great if phonics were consistent and predictable, but English is too complex for that. As phonics is not the only skill needed for reading, students can start developing those other reading skills before you begin phonics instruction. Thinking and problem solving are the most important components of reading, as with all other subjects.

6. ***c. (They are one of the many tools that promote good reading)*** I have found that teaching about one sight word a week, which would be between forty and fifty a school year, is digestible to kindergarten-aged students, and it frees up opportunities for them to master important decoding skills such as blending.

7. ***a. (Right away)*** As soon as possible. Don't delay! The more you know what they know, the better you can teach them what they need to know.

8. ***c. (Thinking)*** If you have gotten this far in the book, you should know that this is the correct answer.

Teaching the Reading Decoding Skills

Use this graphic organizer to help you determine what sequence to teach reading decoding skills. The development of decoding skills works in conjunction with other literacy acquisition activities such as language development, read-alouds, phonological awareness, comprehension, and so on.

Month	What to Teach									
September	1	2								
October	1	2	3	4						
November	1	2	3	4						
December	1	2	3	4	5	6				
January	1	2	3	4	5	6				
Early February	1	2	3	4	5	6				
Late February		2		4	5	6	7	8		
March		2			5	6	7	8	9	10
April		2			5	6	7	8	9	10
May		2				6	7	8	9	10
June		2				6	7	8		10

Each number corresponds to the step to take in that time.

1. Teach each letter to mastery, with the goal of letter automaticity. It should take a full week at the beginning of the year for each letter. As students learn how to learn a letter, you should be able to teach three letters over two weeks (1.5 per week), or even two letters per week. Even so, certain letters will take more time. Don't rush it: teach to mastery.

2. Teach one sight word a week. You can use a list but be opportunistic and teach words that would have immediate benefits for reading and writing.

3. Introduce a vowel early in the sequence and introduce the next vowel when the prior vowel is fully mastered. This takes time. Don't push it, but also don't delay. I recommend the regular sequence of Aa, Ee, Ii, Oo, Uu.

4. Teach two-letter blending (vowel-consonant and consonant-vowel).
5. Focus on identifying letters at the end and later, in the middle of words.
6. Teach the CVC (consonant-letter-consonant) blend—the threshold of real reading!
7. Teach one consonant blend or digraph per week. Exhaust the digraphs before you begin the blends.
8. Teach one word family (phonogram) per week.
9. Introduce one long vowel sound per week. Order is teacher's choice! Keep reinforcing afterward and contrast the sounds with short vowels.
10. Teach and reinforce the four reading mantras.
    a. Look for the sandwich words in the big words.
    b. Look for other little words in the big words.
    c. If one sound doesn't work, try another.
    d. Read what you know and go from there.

Teaching Each Letter to Mastery

Use this checklist to ensure that each student has a foundational understanding of each letter. Check off each box as applicable.

Student's name: _____

What letter you are teaching: _____

Student can:

- ☐ Identify the uppercase letter on sight by name.
- ☐ Identify the lowercase letter on sight by name.
- ☐ Recite the learning sequence forward and backward (for instance, "A, apple, /a/", "/a/, apple, A").
- ☐ Say the most common sound of the uppercase letter on sight.
- ☐ Say the most common sound of the lowercase letter on sight.
- ☐ On hearing the name of the letter, write the uppercase letter with proper letter formation.
- ☐ On hearing the name of the letter, write the lowercase letter with proper letter formation.
- ☐ On hearing the sound of the letter, write the uppercase letter with proper letter formation.
- ☐ On hearing the sound of the letter, write the lowercase letter with proper letter formation.
- ☐ Orally produce words that begin with that letter independently.
- ☐ Identify the name of the letter on hearing a word that begins with it.
- ☐ Say the most common sound of the uppercase letter on sight with automaticity (reading!).
- ☐ Say the most common sound of the lowercase letter on sight with automaticity (reading!).

Classifying Fiction Versus Nonfiction

Use this chart to help you classify the books in your classroom into fiction and nonfiction across all genres. First classify the book by genre, and then determine whether it fits the description of fiction or nonfiction.

Book Title	Genre (Story, narrative, how-to book, informational book, persuasive book, or poem)	Fiction (Pretend or fake)	Nonfiction (Real world)

Genres follow.

1. **Stories:** Also known as *narratives*, have a beginning, middle, end, plot, problem, and so on
2. **Instructional book:** A how-to book
3. **Informational book:** An all-about-something book
4. **Persuasive book:** A book that gives an opinion, reviews something, tries to convince someone to do something, or complains about something
5. **Poem:** Yes, just a poem

CHAPTER 9

Teaching Mathematics

I overcame my mathematics phobia by working hard to understand the mathematics concepts that were presented to me in obtuse ways when I was a student. I then realized that I might not have had the phobia if I had learned these concepts properly in the first place. For example, I learned about *pi* in eighth grade. I did not understand what it was, nor did I understand the Pythagorean theorem, logarithms, sine, cosine, and other mathematics concepts I was taught. I did well on the tests because I was able to fake an understanding of these ideas by cataloging the problems our teachers gave us in class and comparing them to the problems we had on the tests, and by memorizing all the formulas. It was pretty taxing on my brain and a much more complex thought process than simply learning the concepts. When I encountered test questions that varied greatly from those we learned in class or that asked for original and creative thought in applying a concept, I was lost.

I have a very persistent mind and don't like not understanding what I am learning. So, I have a part of my brain that stores all the things I have yet to figure out, and in that compartment, I put all those mathematics concepts. I guess my mind churns away at them subconsciously, and sometimes it has an epiphany. In about my sophomore year of high school, I was walking down the street and the concept of pi just popped into my brain, as clear as could be. In a movie-like flashback, I could hear my teachers doing their lessons and, armed with this new power, I understood everything they had been saying. Though, I at last understood pi, I wish my teacher had spent time showing me what it is, before bombarding us with terms like *circumference*, *ratio*, and *irrational number*.

Years later, when my graduate school mathematics professor was reviewing pi, most students knew the term but not what it meant. So, I told one of my friends that I was going to show her what pi is, and that it wouldn't take more than five minutes. She was dubious but consented. I found a piece of string, gave it to her, and said,

"Make a circle with the string." She did. I gave her another piece of string and said, "Put that string on the circle so that it looks like you are cutting the circle in half." She did that as well. I then said, "Now take that string you just put on the circle in your hand, and then put it on top of the string you made the circle out of, so it covers it. I then asked, "How many of those strings would you need to go all the way around the circle?"

She picked up the string and laid it two more times around the circle and said, "Three."

I said, "That's pi."

She said, "That's it?!"

I answered, "Yes, that's it!"

And that is how you teach mathematics.

I never used the word *diameter*, or told her that *circumference* = $pi \times d$, that the string really goes around the circle not three but 3.14 times, or that pi is an irrational number that goes on infinitely. But my teacher did, all before teaching me what pi is.

We don't teach pi formally in kindergarten, but we do teach counting, measurement, 2-D and 3-D shapes, and addition and subtraction. These are heavy-duty ideas, but they are easy to teach if you understand them (Dixon et al., 2016). Once you understand them, you break them down into lessons and translate them from adult language to kinderese (page 45). Then you let the students play around with the new idea or skill during group and independent practice so they can translate what you taught them into their own personal language and check to see if they can apply the idea or skill. If they can't do this with the assessment you give them, you find ways to tap into students' own personal language (*differentiate*), until they do get it.

In all subject areas, you often preteach concepts, content, and skill long before you teach the lessons they pertain to. You then build one understanding on another and keep scaffolding them. As you do this, you have to *spiral*, or keep reinforcing the concepts with students to make sure they retain them. This is especially true for mathematics. It is really important for teachers to gain an understanding of the amount of effort they need to put into each mathematics standard and how much "glue" they need to apply so that the students keep the concept. I cannot understate the importance and power of preteaching and spiraling when it comes to teaching, reinforcing, and expanding on mathematical concepts. See the reproducible "Preteaching and Spiraling" (page 203) to best prepare for both necessities.

Some concepts adhere like super glue, some adhere like glue sticks, and some adhere like sticky notes. See the different ways the following concepts adhere.

- You must put in a lot of effort to teach counting (to 100), but students retain it pretty well. Counting adheres like super glue.
- It takes a lot of effort to teach the concepts associated with more and less and a lot of effort to help them retain the concepts. The concepts of *more* and *less* adhere like sticky notes.
- It's easy to teach the concepts of *same* and *different*, but very difficult to teach how to compare objects that are different from one another and see how they are similar. This is sticky note territory.
- It is pretty easy to teach measurement and students will retain what they learn. Measurement adheres like super glue.
- It is difficult to teach the concept of the relational words *left* and *right* and for students to retain the difference between the two. Sticky notes all around on this one.
- It is easy to teach 3-D shapes, but you have to put in a lot of effort for students to retain what they learn. Shapes adhere like glue sticks.

Also keep in mind the rule of seven. The rule, one of the oldest concepts in marketing, says that the prospective buyer usually needs to have a clear and consistent marketing message at least seven times before they will buy a product from you (TutorialsPoint, n.d.). When you are marketing your concepts to little minds, the same should apply, as this illustrates that repetition and persistence pay off.

The easiest mathematics (and other) standards take the least amount of preteaching, lessons, and spiraling, and the hardest standards need the most preteaching, lessons, and spiraling. Teaching mathematics in kinderese, following the mathematics progression I outline (with the help of manipulatives and other teaching), will get students where they need to go.

I will not go over every mathematical concept you may be expected to teach—my space and focus limit that. Also, there may be concepts I cover that you are not required to teach or are not part of your standards. Please focus on what is pertinent to your needs. My goal is to give you an overview of what I think is the best methodology to use in teaching mathematical concepts to kindergarteners, the conceptual challenges I have found that exist in specific topics, and a pathway to teaching these concepts effectively.

Mathematics in Kinderese

There is a lot of emphasis on students using the right mathematics terms (Dunston & Tyminski, 2013). There is also a lot of focus on having students answer mathematics questions that use language similar to that found on standardized tests (Bennett, 2018). This makes sense because in mathematics there are standardized terms that students need to be fluent in. The students will be taking standardized tests in mathematics in the future, some as early as kindergarten. However, this doesn't mean that you should teach mathematics concepts initially using the standard terms, nor should you teach mathematics using the phraseology of standardized tests, which vary anyway. You must teach mathematics in the kindergartener language—kinderese (page 45). When I am teaching mathematics, I basically use any language that is necessary to get the concept across. I forego proper word order and syntax and even make up new words and phrases, if I have to, to get the point across. As far as I am concerned, one of the biggest problems in how we teach mathematics is the language we use to communicate the concepts. Kindergarteners can understand mathematics concepts quite easily; they just might benefit from alternate explanations and terminology as well.

Children are capable of learning complex, multisyllabic words. My eldest daughter, like many other children, loved dinosaurs when she was in kindergarten and could rattle off their names as well as the ages they lived in, without a hitch. But these words were names of dinosaurs, not concept words like *greater* and *fewer*. Children can learn to say these words, but for them to grasp their underlying concepts, everything has to be translated into a language they can understand.

The importance of ensuring that students have the prior background knowledge in mathematical concepts that are requisite for mastering new ones cannot be understated. Teachers should verbalize their thinking process and give students opportunities, through discussion and presentations, to outline their mathematical thinking as well (Clarke, Doabler, Nelson, & Shanley, 2015). Linking concepts to real-world applications and using alternative language that also introduces vocabulary that students will build on is also effective (Dixon et al., 2016).

> **Kindergarteners can understand mathematics concepts quite easily; they just might benefit from alternate explanations and terminology as well.**

A term that represents a concept should reveal or remind the students about that concept, at least at first. It shouldn't be a complex word that a kindergartener has to memorize. Sometimes the accepted term simply does not work. This is why I call the vertex or point of a shape, an *ouchie*. Kindergarteners don't understand the word *vertex* and that the word *point* can have many meanings, but they understand when you hold up a triangle, touch each point, say *ouch*, and call it an *ouchie*. From there, you can start distinguishing between shapes with three ouchies or four ouchies. By the time you introduce the proper mathematics terms *vertex* and *point*, students will have incorporated the word *ouchie* and used it as the bridge to the new terminology while retaining the original concept.

I mentioned how preteaching and spiraling are essential tools in properly scaffolding mathematical concepts. Be aware that there is something called *underscaffolding* (taking so large a conceptual jump that you leave students intellectually stranded) and *overscaffolding* (when stops are so incremental that students are not challenged; Johnson, 2019). In scaffolding, you are engaging in the pedagogy of apprenticeship with students (Daniels & Westerlund, 2018).

Always look for new opportunities to make sure you are addressing prior knowledge, communicating concepts through understandable language, and scaffolding effectively.

Foundational Concepts

Whatever mathematics curriculum I am given, I always cover the following topics first, whether or not the curriculum emphasizes them and whether or not the curriculum lists them as early units.

- Sorting
- Patterning
- Categorization
- Relational words

These topics are foundational, as many concepts in mathematics assume an understanding of these topics. When one of my daughters had to take the Otis-Lennon School Ability Test (OLSAT; TestPrep-Online, n.d.) for admission into a gifted program, I looked at the sample questions. They were mostly logic questions. Practically every question was a variation of sorting, patterning, or categorization. Mathematics, of course, is an exercise in logic.

While I am teaching sorting, patterning, and categorization, I also work on teaching counting, both rote counting and knowing the quantity each number represents. I teach it almost the same way that I teach the alphabet. Although I know a lot of students come into a kindergarten class counting to the mid-teens or 20, I introduce each number, starting from one and working my way up to 20. By the time we're done, the students are already getting a grasp of place value and are beginning to understand the pattern that will ultimately get them to 100, and beyond. They also learn how to write each number properly, just as they learn to write the letters properly.

In most curricula, there will be a unit focusing on the numbers 1–10 and then maybe 10–20. A few units later, there is a unit for numbers 20–100. It takes a few months of dedicated work to get most students to count to 100 by ones. I start at the beginning of the year and time it so they get there by the time of the actual unit. If I relied only on the unit to do the work for me, it would not work—as with most mathematics units. Along with my chart of reading levels, I have two charts that go from 1 to 100, with a clothespin for each student. The first one is a chart of rote counting and the second one is a chart of writing the numbers. The reproducible "Ensuring Mathematics Concept Readiness" (page 204) can help you prepare for teaching mathematics by ensuring readiness.

How can some of the major skills and concepts we teach in kindergarten be taught in a way that gives students a strong foundation? Let's start with counting.

Teaching Counting

In our number system, we always count in groups of 10 (Russell, 2020). We don't even have a number for 10 itself—it is just a 1 and a 0. That zero means nothing, but it also means that you have completed one group of ten. That is why the word *teen* in 14 stands for *10*, so it would be more proper to call 14 *ten and four*. You could even call it *tenty four*.

I spend a lot of time teaching the students how to rote count. This is a stepping stone to number sense in the same way that learning the alphabet is a stepping stone to learning to read. While I am drumming in counting by ones, I constantly tell students that we count in groups of ten. I start teaching place value from the first day, by tying it in with counting the 100 Days of School. I use craft sticks and make groups of ten with them as we move along the days of school.

Kindergarteners commonly find it difficult to master the teens (Kawas, 2010), and they come quite early in the counting sequence. I have observed over and over that students frequently skip some of the teen numbers when counting. It's possible that this is because the teen numbers sound very arbitrary. The numbers 1–10 are arbitrary also, but students pick them up quite easily. You have to use a lot of repetition, reinforcement, and memorization techniques to help students through the teen numbers. However, it also helps to explain to the students what exactly is going on with the teen numbers. So, capitalizing on their budding understanding of place value, I call eleven *one-teen* and twelve *two-teen*. I call thirteen *three-teen*, fourteen *four-teen*, and fifteen *five-teen*. The students then see a sequence based on the numbers 1 to 9. They use that understanding to count from 20 to 100, but the understanding begins with the teens.

I simply say the following, starting with the number 11.

11: "This is *one-teen*, but we call it *eleven*."

12: "This is *two-teen*, but we call it *twelve*."

13: "This is *three-teen*, but we call it *thirteen*."

14: "This is *four-teen* and we call it *fourteen*."

15: "This is *five-teen* and we call it *fifteen*."

16 to 19: "This is *six-teen* and we call it *sixteen* . . ."

This makes a lot of sense to kindergarten students and it helps them learn the teens without skipping any of them while laying the foundation of place value. As I am doing this, I teach how to count by tens, which they pick up very quickly. Once students understand the repetition of 1 to 9 and can count by tens to one hundred, it's only a matter of time before they link the two and can count to one hundred by ones very quickly and accurately. Next, it's time to start teaching the students to count the following sequences.

- By fives (5, 10, 15, 20 . . .) to 100
- By twos (2, 4, 6, 8, 10 . . .) to 30
- Backward by ones from 20 to 0

There is a lot more to teaching counting and developing number sense, but I have given you an overview of the key conceptual issues that kindergarteners have with it.

Teaching *More* and *Less*

If I showed you five red balls and lined them up to three green balls and asked you to tell me if there were more red balls than green balls, you would say there are more red balls. If I asked a kindergartener the same thing, he or she would get the answer right. If not, I could easily teach the concept of *more* and they would get it very quickly. If I asked you to tell me which balls were *less*, you would answer green. If I asked a kindergarten-aged student the same thing, he or she would probably not be familiar with the term *less* but would be able to learn it and apply it in no time.

Consider the approach to teaching more and less, but before you do, please note this about terminology: a lot of curricula are so particular about proper terminology that they want kindergarteners to use the terms *more* and *greater* and *less* and *fewer* correctly. This is a distinction that even few adults know, as these words are used interchangeably in common language. The terms *greater* and *fewer* technically refer to a given number of discrete objects, and *more* and *less* refer to non-discrete things, like water or emotions. I use the terms interchangeably, as the concept, in this case, has to come before the terminology. This is kindergarten—subsequent teachers will, hopefully, clarify the terms when the students are developmentally ready.

More

In this same scenario, if I asked you to tell me *how many more* red balls there are than green balls, you would say two without even thinking about it. A kindergartener would be lost with this question and probably answer five, because there are five red balls and they are more than the green balls. Kindergarteners are perfectly capable of seeing that there are two more red balls—they just don't understand what you are asking them. Children are very logical. They heard you use *more* in the first question and then heard *more* in the second question. The phrase *how many more* in the second question does not make sense to them at that point. If pressed for an answer, they will give the answer "five" because they reason that the red balls are more than the green balls and there are five red balls. But that is not the answer that you are looking for. The fault is not with the student, it is in your question.

What you really want to ask might go something like this: "Look at the two lines of balls. Look at the point where they are equal. How many *extra* balls are there after the equal?" This sounds like a very convoluted way of asking a simple question, but a child will understand this and give you the right answer. You just have to teach them what *equal* means first. When you teach equal, you can even use the word *equal*. The students will get the concept and the terminology. And I don't use kinderese unless I have to, so I keep pruning that convoluted sentence. You can scaffold it to, "How many extra red balls are there?" I am using a new word, *extra*, to contrast it with the word *more*, so students will be alerted not to think in the *more* mode—yet. You shouldn't

> **You shouldn't use the same term to cover two different concepts—at first.**

use the same term to cover two different concepts—at first. I use as many terms I can think of to illustrate the more-or-less concepts. The more alternative terms I can eventually expose students to, the better they will be able to answer questions regarding the underlying concept, whether it is on a standardized test or in real life.

Over the course of the year and using many different examples, I slowly morph the word *extra* into the word *more* and finally ask, "How many more red balls are there than green balls?" The students will give me the answer "two" without a hitch, because now they understand the underlying concepts. I can now line up ten red balls and two green balls, and a student will be able to figure out that there are eight more red balls. A lot of curricula spend a week on lessons about how to teach one more and then another week on how to teach two more, as if it makes a big difference to a student to see one or two more balls. It doesn't. It's the concept that counts. Once a student has it, he or she can figure out how many more balls there are based on how high he or she can count at the time.

One of the ways I morph the word *extra* into the word *more* is by using the word *more* in contexts that do not confuse students. If I make a line of three balls and tell a student to put one more, he or she will do just that. I know that I am using *more* in a different context, but students can pick this up very easily. I don't see their brainwaves. I can see what they can do and understand and work with that—and this is consistent across almost all students, so it's valuable to know. Now they will also be able to hear almost any variation of the question "How many more red balls are there?" as asked on a standardized test and be able to translate that as well. If not right away, then with a little reinforcement.

The two big problems with the child's understanding of the simple question, "How many more red balls are there?" are (1) using the adult shorthand version of the question, and (2) using the same term for two different concepts. This happens a lot.

Less

You can also teach "How many less green balls are there?" It is a little more difficult, because the concept of *less* is not as common as *more* and it is also a harder concept. However, you would have taught *more* and *extra* and *equal* first, and that prior knowledge will help. Additional preteaching is required for the concept *less*, as in, "Which line of balls is less?" You can start using the term *take away* for *less* as you did *extra* in relation to *more*, and you can, after having students show you their fingers, say, "one less" so that they take away one finger.

In the case of five red balls and three green balls, you would ask, "Which is the one where it used to be equal and they took two away?" Then you would ask, "It used to be equal. How many did they take away? What color balls did they take them away from?" These are the convoluted questions that would end up being "How many *less* green balls are there?"

Teaching *Same* and *Different*

This situation is similar to more and less. The concepts are accessible to kindergarteners, but the language is not. The way *same and different* is taught usually goes like this. They are taught what *same* means and they pick up that pretty quickly. Then they learn *different*, or *not the same*, and they do well with that. Then you show them two things and ask, "How are these the same and different?" The students are paralyzed, because to them, *same* is an oppositional concept to *different*. Children are logical. They think, "How can two things be the same and be different at the same time? It doesn't make sense!" And they are right—it doesn't. This is yet another question that has underlying assumptions the students know nothing about and is an adult shorthand version of a more appropriate question.

I teach the students that *same* means exactly the same. So, two boys are not the same, a big dog and a little dog are not the same, and a red car and a blue car are not the same—even if they are the same model. If a student sees two squares, they would only be the same if they were the same size and color. The mathematics term for this is *congruent*—but I don't teach them this term yet. Anything that is not exactly the same as what you are given is therefore different, or not the same. Most things are different from each other. Very few things are the same.

Now comes the benefit of all the work that you did in teaching sorting. When you teach sorting, you group things together—by color, size, and so on. The students have already, at this point, learned to sort by color, shape, size, and other attributes, so they can see two different objects and list the multiple ways they can be grouped together. But they never lose sight of the fact that the two objects are different from each other. You make the point when you are teaching sorting, that many items you sort are *different* from each other, yet you can *group them together*. That is to say, for example, that two triangles may be different in color, but you can sort them together if you are sorting by shape. A triangle and a circle are different, but you can group them together if you are sorting by size and they are both small. You can also group them together if they are the same color and you are sorting by color. Students intuitively understand that they are finding things that both items have in common.

When you see a boy and a girl who have green eyes and say that they are the same because of this, what you are really doing is theoretically pulling out (or *abstracting*) the eyes from both of them and seeing that the *eyes* are exactly the same as each other. You can do this for one or more attribute.

Now I introduce the term *similar*, to mean that I am finding things that are the same (yes, you can start scaffolding this in) between two different things. So, students learn three terms: *same*, *different*, and *similar*. I don't think that we should ever phrase a question as, "How are these things the same and different?" Similarly, I don't like the term *compare and contrast* that is used in the upper grades. I know what the question wants you to do, but the words used that way don't make sense to me. When we want to ask, "How are these two things the same and different?" we should teach students what similar means and ask, "How are these two things similar to each other and how are they different from each other?"

Teaching Shapes

You already know about the term *ouchie*, but that is not what is most important about teaching students about two dimensional shapes. The thing about 2-D shapes is that they are very tricky—even for adults. For example, any polygon that has three sides is a triangle. However, there are many different types of triangles—*equilateral*, *right*, *isosceles*, *scalene*, and so on. But unless we are in trigonometry class, we still call all of them *triangles*. On the other hand, any shape that has four sides is a quadrilateral. If we call all three-sided shapes triangles, then we should be calling all four-sided shapes quadrilaterals—but we don't.

It goes as follows.

- A quadrilateral that has all sides parallel to each other is called a *parallelogram*.
- A quadrilateral in which not all sides are parallel is called a *trapezoid*.
- A quadrilateral in which all sides are equal is called a *rhombus*.
- A quadrilateral that is a parallelogram in which all sides are at right angles is called a *rectangle*.
- A quadrilateral that is a parallelogram, a rhombus, and rectangle is called a *square*.

No one expects kindergarteners to learn all these distinctions and terminology at this time. So, the way to teach the quadrilaterals, or four-sided polygons, is to teach each shape as a separate entity, as if one had nothing in common with the other.

I teach the following quadrilaterals.

- Square
- Rectangle
- Rhombus (diamond)
- Trapezoid

Once students have learned these shapes, as well as the other 2-D shapes that I teach (such as triangle, pentagon, and hexagon), I start going a little deeper. I will usually follow this order but seize any moment to teach and reinforce these concepts.

- **Triangles:** I start showing the students different (remember *same* and *different*?) types of triangles and tell them that they are all different from each other, but we still call them *triangles*. They are similar in that they all have three sides. Now the students are set up for learning the names of the different triangles when they are older.

- **Quadrilaterals:** Now we proceed to the four-sided shapes. I show them the shapes and note that they are indeed different from each other and go by different names. However, they are similar in that they all have four sides. The students now understand that there are different kinds of triangles as well as quadrilaterals, although they are not familiar with the term quadrilateral—yet. Inevitably, a student will ask why different four-sided shapes have different names and why different three-sided shapes (triangles) have the same name. I simply respond, "That's just the way it is," with a wink. He or she accepts that. I know this student is well on his or her way to becoming a great mathematics learner and will easily master the different kinds of triangles encountered in trigonometry class!

- **Other shapes:** I now show the students that there are many different kinds of pentagons and hexagons, but each different one doesn't have a special name. I explain that these shapes are similar to the triangle, as you can draw a shape that has three sides in many different ways, and it is still called a *triangle*. You can draw a shape that has five sides many different ways and it is still called a *pentagon*. You can draw a shape that has six sides many different ways and it is still called a *hexagon*.

Teaching *Left* and *Right*

One of the most popular methods to teach students left and right is to have them make an *L* with the thumb and index finger to remind them that "L is for left." Great idea on paper, and I would have liked it if this actually worked, as I am a lefty and would take great pride in knowing that this hand was taught before the right hand. However, students of this age don't always see an *L* the way we write it. They can also see a backward *L*, or what we call a *reversal*. Students do this all the time in kindergarten, with letters and numbers (Watson, 2019). They will see an *L* with the thumb and index finger of either hand, so this method is not going to work for teaching left and right. In my experience, teaching left and right through songs like the *Hokey Pokey* or the *Cha-Cha Slide* doesn't work either.

Remember the morning quiz (page 97)? On some mornings, I ask each student to shake my hand, looking for which hand is extended. I then extend my right hand, to either reinforce or teach students that there is a particular hand for shaking. I then find opportunities for shaking hands until everyone knows which hand you extend for shaking hands. I then scaffold the term *right hand* to *the hand you use for shaking*, and the students get it. Now is the time I start doing the *Hokey Pokey* and those kinds of games with the students.

Once the right hand is established, it's time to focus on the other hand—the hand that you don't shake with. This gets scaffolded into the left hand. I put up a sign that says *left* on the left side of the SMART Board and one that says *right* on the right sight of the SMART Board. Then, as a reminder, I try to find as many practical applications for the terms during the day, and that's about it.

I found a great many opportunities to teach this concept when the students are lined up. A good example is when I discussed how the class walks up the stairs (page 95) and announce which side I am walking up. Another way is when my students are in the line and encounter two doors in front of them. I instruct the leaders to go through the left or right door. The floors in my school are tiled, so I can, for instance, give the following instructions: "Walk five tiles forward, now face left and go forward three more tiles. Now face left and walk four tiles more. Now face right and go six tiles forward." Over time, I start giving the instructions all at once, so they can follow a sequence of multiple instructions. This is my way of introducing them to the concept of coding. This also helps explain why I don't have permanent line leaders in my class and why, when it is time to line up, I choose randomly.

Another easy way I can reinforce the concept of left and right is when I have an opportunity to hand over an object, be it a manipulative, paper, or writing implement. I ask the student to hold out either the left or right hand for it. As part of the morning quiz (page 97), I might ask a student to walk to the left side or the right side of the cubbies before starting to unpack things.

Conceptual Thinking

The last thing I want to say about mathematics is that there is a misconception that young students primarily think in concrete terms. This is true in a few ways and not so true in others. Kindergarteners obviously don't think in sophisticated conceptual terms yet (McLeod, 2018). They usually need manipulatives and hands-on activities to help them learn. However, my experience is that kindergarteners are much more conceptual than we give them credit for.

Many curricula couch concepts in stories and objects that students can relate to in concrete terms. For instance, in teaching *more* and *less*, a curriculum might introduce two children who buy ice cream, with one child having more scoops than the other. But the story often diverts the students from thinking about the underlying mathematics concepts. My students tend to get caught up in the story and ask questions such as, "Why were they buying ice cream?" "Who was buying it for them?" "Where did they get the money?" "Did they have strawberry?" and dozens of others.

> **My experience is that kindergarteners are much more conceptual than we give them credit for.**

After students have learned a concept, I apply it to a concrete situation. That is one of the main reasons for teaching mathematics in the first place—to figure out real-world applications. Until then, I will usually use simple shapes, such as circles and squares, to teach more and less, addition and subtraction, and a host of other mathematics topics. No stories—just the concept I want to get across. The students are able to abstract the concepts because they have fewer distractions and because they can think logically and conceptually at a pretty high level.

Manipulatives and Other Teaching Tools

As conceptual as children are, they still benefit from the use of manipulatives when they are learning mathematics concepts. There are tons of manipulatives out there, and the administration is always supplying more; however, my favorites follow and appear in figure 9.1.

- Interlocking cubes (such as Unifix Cubes)

- Magnetic ten frames
- Attribute blocks (especially for sorting)
- A good set of 3-D shapes
- Double-sided counters (red on one side and yellow on the other)

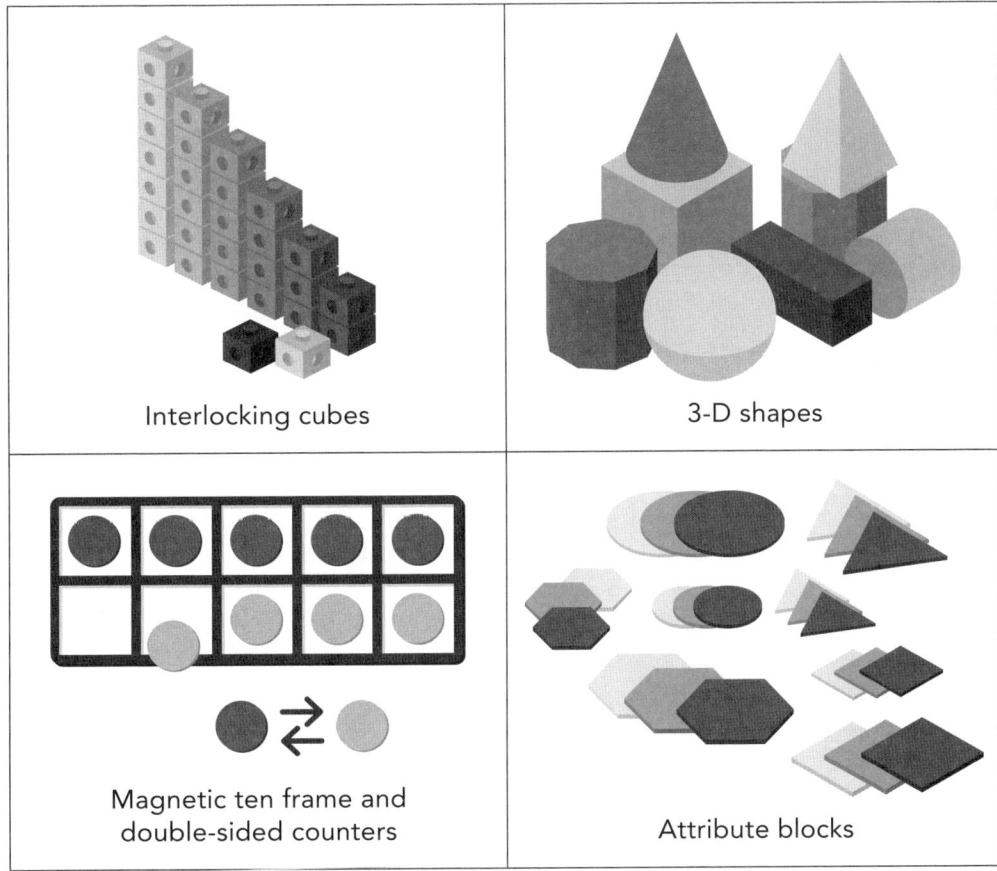

Figure 9.1: Mathematics manipulatives.

There are others that I have not mentioned, but these manipulatives are my tried and true mathematics co-teachers!

My favorite and the most effective teaching aid I have ever used is the simple whiteboard with a dry-erase marker and eraser. (I used to use socks as erasers until I got some real ones.) I know a lot of teachers have access to whiteboards, but I just want to reiterate how important and effective they are—for all subjects! Whiteboards are versatile, and you can use them as you teach, but most importantly to assess, in a very fun way, what students have learned. You simply look at what they are writing on their boards in response to your questions—instant assessments.

SCIENCE AND SOCIAL STUDIES: THE FORGOTTEN SUBJECTS

The fact is that many teachers teach science and social studies peripherally or not at all (Tallman, 2016). Sometimes they are open about this, and other times they keep it under wraps. But it is all too common an occurrence. There are many reasons the focus of teaching in school is on literacy and mathematics. One is that teachers are more accountable for these subjects than those of science and social studies. Standardized tests are based in literacy and mathematics. People will prioritize what they are accountable for over what they are not accountable for, and teachers are no different.

Science and social studies instruction should never be compromised in favor of other subjects. Of course, they don't need to be taught in perfectly crafted time boxes, but the standards in those subject areas are equally important to those of other areas. These worthwhile subjects improve your class and contribute to better reading skills. No matter how exciting and interesting your literacy and mathematics instruction, your class will grind to a halt if you don't infuse it with the content and mental challenges of science and social studies. These two subjects supplement and complement literacy and mathematics and serve as a purpose to learn those two subjects. It is also a part of the curriculum in which it is very easy to involve parents.

In my social studies curriculum, some of the topics we cover are *me*, *family*, and *community*. At various times of the year, I have parents and guardians work with the students to make books and presentations about each individual child, the child's family, and the family members' occupations. Each student gets the opportunity to present his or her book to the class. If we are learning about plants in science, I can send home seeds and explain to parents and guardians how to do a science experiment designed to compare how a seed grows in a sunny environment versus a dark one.

Another important thing: prior knowledge and vocabulary are more important in reading, which is a comprehension exercise, than the decoding skills and fluency we usually associate with good readers. According to literacy expert Daniel Willingham (as cited in Sedita, 2018), "Whether or not readers understand a text depends far more on how much background knowledge and vocabulary they have relating to the topic than on how much they've practiced comprehension skills." What are the best subjects for providing students with content and vocabulary? Science and social studies.

> I realize the irony of stating that these two subjects are neglected and then only giving them short mention. This does not minimize their importance. However, curricula and standards vary more widely for these subjects than for mathematics and literacy, so it would be difficult to encompass all of that within the scope of this book. With the knowledge you have acquired regarding curriculum development and as a thinking teacher, you will know how to read through the science and social studies curricula and adapt them best for your students.

In a Nutshell

Mathematics concepts, even sophisticated ones, are not beyond the intellectual reach of most kindergarteners if they are presented in a clear, logical, and digestible manner, using language kindergarteners understand. Bone up on your kinderese and use any language that is relatable to kindergarteners to get concepts across—you can scaffold up to the proper terminology later. Always make sure that the first person who understands the concepts thoroughly is you! Mathematics is the subject where the techniques of preteaching and spiraling are indispensable, so find ways to use them daily.

Have You Mastered the Chapter?

Welcome to the formal assessment section of the book—a quiz to test your knowledge of the chapter. Please try the questions. The answers are provided after the questions section for a quick check. I explain the *why* after the quiz, and that is the most important part to consider.

According to this chapter:

1. Mathematics instruction lends itself to a lot of:
    a. Preteaching and spiraling
    b. Intimidating terminology
    c. Memorization
    d. Post-teaching and frisbeeing

2. A valuable asset in teaching mathematics concepts would be your fluency in:
   a. Motherese
   b. Kinderese
   c. Latin
   d. Numerology

3. A foundational mathematics concept is:
   a. Addition
   b. Shapes
   c. Measurement
   d. Sorting

4. A recommended way to help students conceptualize the number eleven is to call it:
   a. Ten and one
   b. One-teen
   c. Eleventy
   d. Equals standing up

5. A little circle compared to a big circle is:
   a. The same
   b. Similar
   c. Congruent
   d. Equal

6. A square is:
   a. A rectangle
   b. A rhombus
   c. A quadrilateral
   d. All of the above

7. Don't you:

    a. Forget about me

    b. Come a-knocking at my door

    c. Dare

    d. Forget about science and social studies

Answers and Explanations

1. ***a. (Preteaching and spiraling)*** There is surely a lot of intimidating technology and memorization in mathematics. However, there are ways to ease the complex concepts into the students' awaiting minds. That would be by giving repeated glimpses of the concept in many different configurations before formally teaching it (preteaching) and constantly reinforcing the concept thereafter (spiraling). Never did figure out what frisbeeing was.

2. ***b. (Kinderese)*** The knowledge of Latin is useful in so many ways, even for mathematics, but the ability to speak to young students in a variation of English that they can relate to is key to conveying new concepts to them. By this time in their lives, children have outgrown *motherese* (commonly called *baby talk*) and unfortunately, numerology is not considered part of mathematics.

3. ***d. (Sorting)*** The knowledge and understanding of addition, shapes, and measurement are all foundational, however, they sit on a prior foundation of learned skills, one of which is sorting.

4. ***b. (One-teen)*** The number eleven can certainly be called *Ten and one* and should be shown in that configuration using manipulatives. It also looks like an equals symbol standing up, and students should be aware that small changes in figure orientation make a big difference in our interpretation. *Eleventy* is certainly a cool name for eleven but we don't use it. However, to achieve conceptual consistency between the word *eleven* (which seems arbitrary) and later teen numbers that follow the format *number-teen* (fourteen, fifteen, sixteen, and so on), you can explain that it makes sense to call *eleven one-teen*, to call *twelve two-teen*, and to scaffold the term *one-teen* to the accepted word *eleven*.

5. ***b. (Similar)*** In mathematics, the word *congruent* has the meaning *exactly the same*. The word *equal* means equivalent, and is usually used when comparing numbers. A little circle is not exactly the same as a big circle but has a blatant similarity to it in that it is also a circle. That is why the word *similar* should be used when comparing them. Kindergarteners can understand this and should be taught these terms when learning *same* and *different*.

6. ***d. (All of the above)*** It's definitely hip to be a square because it has the attributes of a quadrilateral (four-sided closed figure), a rhombus (four-sided closed figure with equal sides) and a rectangle (a four-sided figure that has right angles with not necessarily equal sides). When you teach shapes, it would be too complex for kindergarteners to understand these differences, so just teach a square the way it is commonly understood. They will pick up the fine distinctions of four-sided shapes in the upper grades.

7. ***d. (Forget about science and social studies)*** It's up to you if you want to follow the advice of the first three answers, but giving short shrift to the subjects of science and social studies would be sad and short-sighted. What is the purpose of learning to read, write, and do mathematics if they can't be applied to the storehouse of human knowledge and experimentation we call *science* and to the functions of how we operate as humans, which we call *social studies*?

Preteaching and Spiraling

Use this chart to make a list of the mathematics concepts you will be teaching during the year. Each time you begin a new unit, look at the upcoming unit to identify skills and concepts you will preteach during that unit. After the unit is over, look back and see which concepts you need to spiral with your students for reinforcement.

	Units		
Skills and Concepts			

Ensuring Mathematics Concept Readiness

Before you teach a mathematics concept, even one that looks relatively simple, you need to first understand it thoroughly. As a supplement to your curriculum, use this checklist to make sure that you have mastered the concept.

Mathematics concept: _____

- ☐ I can explain the concept to an adult.
- ☐ I can relate the concept in kinderese.
- ☐ I can demonstrate the concept two different ways.
- ☐ I can give two examples of the concept.
- ☐ I have developed a sequential method for students to practice the skills associated with the concept.

CONCLUSION

A lot of research has gone into trying to find out how students learn and how best to teach them. But in the final analysis, teaching is about people and human nature, so it is either too complex for science to figure out or perhaps people are not rational and predictable in a way that suits a scientific model. Teaching, to me, is a soft science, like sociology or anthropology. It is a social science, which is kind of an oxymoron. Scientific research and analysis are of great benefit to the teaching profession, but teaching is also an art. In this way, teaching is like music—another passion of mine. Science can be beneficial to musicians and listeners in cataloging songs, recording and preserving music, coming up with music programs, and a host of other applications, but it will never be able to write catchy songs or play an instrument as movingly as a human being can.

To use the rice and beans analogy, science is the bed of rice on which the savory beans, the art, sits. You need both to be a balanced teacher. Students will be open-minded and inquisitive if the teacher is like that already. A thinking teacher yields thinking students. I have heard countless educators say that they want to teach students to ask questions, to be risk takers, to think in new ways, to find their own solutions, and to be problem solvers. The only way for students to end up that way is to be led and taught by people who are like that already. Make sense? An open-minded teacher leads to open-minded students. Yet, when teachers exhibit those qualities in their work, they are sometimes hammered down, like the proverbial nail that's sticking out of the board.

> **An open-minded teacher leads to open-minded students.**

Teachers are the resilient rubber nails that will always pop up again. Teachers are magicians, they are jugglers, they are performers, and they are artists. They are masters of their craft, can manage twenty-five-plus students without breaking a sweat, work productively with colleagues and administration, keep parents involved and updated about the class, and help each student reach his or her full potential in the cognitive, motor, and social-emotional spheres.

I hope that after you have *killed the Buddha*, you will develop a classroom that has *wa, controlled chaos*, and the *hum*, and where everything is taught in kinderese.

If the sentence you just read made sense to you, I know that you are on your way to becoming an effective and happy kindergarten teacher.

REFERENCES AND RESOURCES

Adler, B. (Producer), & Logan, J. (Director). (1958). *South Pacific* [Motion picture]. United States: Twentieth Century Fox.

Alber, R. (2010, December 17). *Doing it differently: Tips for teaching vocabulary* [Blog post]. Accessed at www.edutopia.org/blog/vocabulary-instruction-teaching-tips-rebecca-alber on September 1, 2020.

Alford, K., & Griffin, T. (2019). *Unleashing the power of examples.* Accessed at www.facultyfocus.com/articles/effective-teaching-strategies/unleashing-the-power-of-examples on August 3, 2020.

Alison. (2020, February 17). *Four popular parenting tips that could be causing your child's bad behavior* [Blog post]. Accessed at https://pintsizedtreasures.com/four-popular-parenting-tips-causing-your-childs-bad-behavior on March 5, 2020.

Alkaboody, M. (2010). *Vocabulary knowledge and reading comprehension: A mutual relationship.* Accessed at www.academia.edu/3888032/Vocabulary_Knowledge_and_Reading_Comprehension_A_Mutual_Relationship_Mastoor on March 5, 2020.

Allen, R., & Boelter, L. A. (2016). Using natural and logical consequences. *University of Minnesota Extension.* Accessed at https://extension.umn.edu/encouraging-respectful-behavior/using-natural-and-logical-consequences#selecting-effective-logical-consequences-511961 on March 6, 2020.

American Montessori Society. (2019). *Maria Montessori quotes.* Accessed at https://amshq.org/About-Montessori/History-of-Montessori/Who-Was-Maria-Montessori/Maria-Montessori-Quotes on March 5, 2020.

American Psychiatric Association (2013). *Diagnostic and Statistical Manual of Mental Disorders* (5th ed.). Washington, DC: Author.

Archer, M. (n.d.). *Parents—The most important teachers.* Accessed at www.drmarlo.com/?page_id=133 on March 5, 2020.

Avery, T., & Givens, B. (Creators). (1938–present). *Bugs Bunny* [Cartoon short]. United States: Warner Brothers.

Ayers, B. (2009). *Teachers are now 'glorified clerks' imparting predigested wisdom.* Accessed at www.tes.com/news/teachers-are-now-glorified-clerks-imparting-predigested-wisdom on March 5, 2020.

Bandura, A. (2004). Observational learning. In J. H. Byrne (Ed.), *Learning and Memory* (2nd ed., pp. 482–484). New York, NY: Macmillan Reference.

Barker, J. E., Semenov, A. D., Michaelson, L., Provan, L. S., Snyder, H. R., & Munakata, Y. (2014). *Less-structured time in children's lives predicts self-directed executive functioning.* Accessed at www.frontiersin.org/articles/10.3389/fpsyg.2014.00593/full on June 19, 2020.

Barnas, M. (2000). "Parenting" students: Applying developmental psychology to the college classroom. *Teaching of Psychology, 27*(4), 276–277.

Bastien, C. E., & Jacobs, L. (Directors). (2012). *The magic school bus: The complete series* [DVD]. United States: New Video Group.

Baumrind, D. (1971). Current patterns of parental authority. *Developmental Psychology, 4*(1), 1–103.

Bennett, C. (2018, August 27). *10 test questions terms and what they ask students to do* [Blog post]. Accessed at www.thoughtco.com/test-question-terms-4126767 on March 5, 2020.

Bernstein, D. A. (2013). *Parenting and teaching: What's the connection in our classrooms?* Accessed at www.apa.org/ed/precollege/ptn/2013/09/parenting-teaching on June 29, 2020.

Bouzereau, L. (Director). (2000). *All about* The Birds [Motion picture]. Universal City, CA: Universal Studios Home Video.

Bradley, L., & Bryant, P. (2010). Phonological skills before and after learning to read. In S. A. Brady & D. P. Shankweiler (Eds.), *Phonological processes in literacy: A tribute to Isabelle Y. Liberman* (pp. 37–46). New York: Routledge.

Bruckheimer, J. (Producer), & Verbinski, G. (Director). (2003). *Pirates of the Caribbean: The curse of the black pearl* [Motion picture]. United States: Jerry Bruckheimer Films.

Buffum, A., Mattos, M., & Malone, J. (2018). *Taking action: A handbook for RTI at Work.* Bloomington, IN: Solution Tree Press.

Carver, C. S., & Johnson, S. L. (2018). Impulsive reactivity to emotion and vulnerability to psychopathology. *American Psychologist, 73*(9), 1067–1078.

Callahan, A. (2015). The power of play in child development. *Urban Child Institute.* Accessed at www.urbanchildinstitute.org/articles/features/the-power-of-play-in-child-development on September 11, 2020.

Center on the Developing Child at Harvard University. (2017). *Three principles to improve outcomes for children and families.* Accessed at https://developingchild.harvard.edu/resources/three-early-childhood-development-principles-improve-child-family-outcomes on August 3, 2020.

Chassiakos, Y. R. (2017). *The importance of handwriting in the digital age.* Accessed at www.healthychildren.org/English/family-life/Media/Pages/The-Importance-of-Handwriting-in-the-Digital-Age.aspx on August 3, 2020.

Chen, M. (2013). *Yogi Berra's famous quotes: 'Baseball is 90 percent mental. The other half is physical'.* Accessed at www.theglobeandmail.com/news/world/yogi-berras-famous-quotes-baseball-is-90-per-cent-mental-the-other-half-is-physical/article26494911 on March 5, 2020.

Cherry, K. (2020). *The zone of proximal development as defined by Vygotsky.* Accessed at www.verywellmind.com/what-is-the-zone-of-proximal-development-2796034 on March 5, 2020.

Chetty, R., Friedman, J. N., Hilger, N., Saez, E., Schanzenbach, D. W., & Yagan, D. (2010). *How does your kindergarten classroom affect your earnings? Evidence from Project STAR.* NBER Working Paper No. 16381.

Clarke, B., Doabler, C. T., Nelson, N. J., & Shanley, C. (2015). *Effective instructional strategies for kindergarten and first grade students at risk in mathematics.* Accessed at www.researchgate.net/publication/268742967_Effective_Instructional_Strategies_for_Kindergarten_and_First_Grade_Students_At-Risk_in_Mathematics on August 3, 2020.

Clifton, P., & Massot, J. (Directors). (1976). *The song remains the same* [Motion picture]. United States: Warner Brothers.

Colbert, J. (2008). *Circle time: A tool for supporting children's development.* Accessed at www.earlychildhoodnews.com/earlychildhood/article_view.aspx?ArticleID=514 on March 5, 2020.

Coulson, J. (2016). *The negative effects of time-out on children.* Accessed at https://ifstudies.org/blog/the-negative-effects-of-time-out-on-children on March 5, 2020.

Csikszentmihalyi, M. (2008). *Flow: The psychology of optimal experience.* New York: Harper Perennial.

Daniels, J., & Westerlund, R. (2018). *Scaffolding learning for multilingual students in math.* Accessed at https://wida.wisc.edu/sites/default/files/resource/FocusOn-Scaffolding.pdf on August 3, 2020.

Darier, E., & Schüle, R. (1999). Think globally, act locally? Climate change and public participation in Manchester and Frankfurt. *Local Environment, 4*(3), 317–329.

De Leon Huld, N. (2018). How many words does the average person know? [Blog post]. *Word Counter.* Accessed at https://wordcounter.io/blog/how-many-words-does-the-average-person-know on March 5, 2020.

de Paiva, A. (2018). Neuroscience for architecture: How building design can influence behaviors and performance. *Journal of Civil Engineering and Architecture, 12*(2), 132–138.

Dewar, G. (2019). *Working memory in children: What you need to know.* Accessed at www.parentingscience.com/working-memory.html on August 3, 2020.

Dewey, J. (1902). *The child and the curriculum.* Chicago: University of Chicago Press.

Discipline. (n.d.). In *Online Etymology Dictionary.* Accessed at www.etymonline.com/word/discipline on March 5, 2020.

Dixon, J. K., Nolan, E. C., Adams, T. L., Brooks, L. A., & Howse, T. D. (2016). *Making sense of mathematics for teaching grades K–2.* Bloomington, IN: Solution Tree Press.

Dolan, E. W. (2019). *Listening to the music you love will make your brain release more dopamine, study finds.* Accessed at www.psypost.org/2019/02/listening-to-the-music-you-love-will-make-your-brain-release-more-dopamine-study-finds-53059 on March 5, 2020.

Dolch, E. W. (1936). A basic sight vocabulary. *Elementary School Journal, 36*(6), 456–460.

Dr. Seuss. (1960). *Green eggs and ham.* New York: Random House.

Dr. Seuss. (1961). *The sneetches and other stories.* New York: Random House.

Dunston, P. J., & Tyminski, A. M. (2013). What's the big deal about vocabulary? *Mathematics Teaching in the Middle School, 19*(1), 38–45.

Elkind, D. (2008). *The power of play: Learning what comes naturally.* Accessed at www.journalofplay.org/sites/www.journalofplay.org/files/pdf-articles/1-1-article-elkind-the-power-of-play.pdf on March 5, 2020.

Erwin, C. (n.d.). *Follow through.* Accessed at www.positivediscipline.com/articles/follow-through on August 3, 2020.

Everyday Health. (2018). *At what age are children expected to achieve bladder control?* Accessed at www.everydayhealth.com/kidshealth/experts-what-age-do-children-control-bladder.aspx on March 6, 2020.

First Things First. (2020). *Brain development.* Accessed at www.firstthingsfirst.org/early-childhood-matters/brain-development/#:~:text=At%20birth%2C%20the%20average%20baby's,center%20of%20the%20human%20body on August 3, 2020.

Fisher, D., & Frey, N. (2008). *Better learning through structured teaching: A framework for the gradual release of responsibility.* Alexandria, VA: Association for Supervision and Curriculum Development.

Forman, G., & Hall, E. (2005). *Wondering with children: The importance of observation in early education.* Accessed at https://ecrp.illinois.edu/v7n2/forman.html on March 6, 2020.

Fountas, I., & Pinnell, G. S. (2016). *Guided reading* (2nd ed.). Portsmouth, New Hampshire: Heinemann.

Frank, K., & Metcalf, B. (2014). *Limitations of phonics.* Accessed at https://prezi.com/ctjnpkjv6g9b/limitations-of-phonics on August 3, 2020.

Fulghum, R. (1988). *All I really need to know I learned in kindergarten*. New York: Villard Books.

Funt, A. (Producer). (1948–1992). *Candid camera* [Television show]. United States: Allen Funt Productions.

Gardner, H. (1999). *The disciplined mind: What all students should understand*. New York: Simon & Schuster.

Geller, L. G. (1985). *Wordplay and language learning for children*. Urbana, IL: National Council of Teachers of English.

Gjersoe, N. (2018). *How young children can develop racial biases—and what that means.* Accessed at https://theconversation.com/how-young-children-can-develop-racial-biases-and-what-that-means-93150 on August 3, 2020.

Gladstein, R. (Producer), & Hallström, L. (Director). (1999). *The cider house rules* [Motion picture]. United States: Miramax Films.

Golding, W. (1954). *Lord of the flies*. New York: Perigee.

Goodreads. (2019). *Jean Piaget quotes*. Accessed at www.goodreads.com/author/quotes/12064.Jean_Piaget on March 6, 2020.

Gordon, L., Gordon C., (Producers), & Robinson, P. A. (Director). (1989). *Field of dreams* [Motion picture]. United States: Universal Pictures.

Grassian, S. (2006). *Psychiatric effects of solitary confinement*. Accessed at https://openscholarship.wustl.edu/cgi/viewcontent.cgi?article=1362&context=law_journal_law_policy on March 6, 2020.

Gray, W. (1946). *Fun with Dick and Jane*. Chicago: Scott, Foresman.

Grisold, T., Kaiser, A., & Hafner, J. (2017). *Unlearning before creating new knowledge: A cognitive process*. Accessed at https://core.ac.uk/download/pdf/77240027.pdf on August 3, 2020.

Groening, M. (Creator). (1989–present). *The Simpsons* [Television show]. United States: Twentieth Century Fox Television.

Hannel, G. I. (2014). *A pedagogy of questioning*. Phoenix, AZ: apoq.org.

Harries, E. (2013). How English has been shaped by French and other languages. *Language Update, 9*(4), 23.

Harris, S. (2006). *Killing the Buddha*. Accessed at https://samharris.org/killing-the-buddha on August 3, 2020.

Hayes, E. (2002). *Encouraging better behavior: A practical guide to positive parenting*. London: National Society for the Prevention of Cruelty to Children.

Hein, G. E. (1991). *Constructivist learning theory*. Accessed at www.exploratorium.edu/education/ifi/constructivist-learning on March 6, 2020.

Herrmann, E. (2014). *The importance of guided practice in the classroom.* Accessed at http://exclusive.multibriefs.com/content/the-importance-of-guided-practice-in-the-classroom/education on March 6, 2020.

Jackson, A. (2015). *New York's hottest public elementary school is harder to get into than Harvard.* Accessed at www.businessinsider.com/hunter-elementary-school-is-insanely-hard-to-get-into-2015-6 on March 6, 2020.

Johns Hopkins Medicine. (n.d.). *Oppositional defiant disorder (ODD) in children.* Accessed at www.hopkinsmedicine.org/health/conditions-and-diseases/oppositional-defiant-disorder#:~:text=ODD%20in%20children-,Oppositional%20defiant%20disorder%20(ODD)%20is%20a%20type%20of%20behavior%20disorder,teachers%2C%20and%20other%20authority%20figures. on September 24, 2020.

Johnson, E. M. (2019). *Choosing and using interactional scaffolds: How teachers' moment-to-moment supports can generate and sustain emergent bilinguals' engagement with challenging English texts.* Accessed at https://pdfs.semanticscholar.org/37cd/ee5d34ba6e00e5535ab05f76c9096b69a9e7.pdf on August 21, 2020.

Johnson, N. (2019, October 18). *Here's why you shouldn't force your kid to be friends with someone* [Blog post]. Accessed at www.parents.com/parenting/better-parenting/advice/heres-why-you-shouldnt-force-your-kid-to-be-friends-with-someone on August 3, 2020.

Jolly, C. (2013). *'Let's stop teaching letter names and start with letter sounds'.* Accessed at www.tes.com/news/lets-stop-teaching-letter-names-and-start-with-letter-sounds on March 6, 2020.

Katesurfs. (2017). *Children under 7 have no concept of time: Helping kids understand 'time'.* Accessed at www.katesurfs.com/2017/10/27/children-7-no-concept-time-helping-kids-understand-time on March 6, 2020.

Kaufman, D. (2016). *The importance of routine in childhood.* Accessed at www.melbournechildpsychology.com.au/blog/the-importance-of-routine-in-childhood on August 3, 2020.

Kawas, T. (2010). *Featured topic: Teen numbers.* Accessed at www.mathwire.com/strategies/teen.html on March 6, 2020.

King, E. W. (2019). *Why classroom clip charts do more harm than good.* Accessed at www.parents.com/kids/education/kindergarten/why-classroom-clip-charts-do-more-harm-than-good on August 3, 2020.

Kirkham, J. R. (n.d.). Long term benefits of positive reinforcement. *Trans4Mind.* Accessed at https://trans4mind.com/counterpoint/index-leadership/kirkham.shtml on March 6, 2020.

Klemm, Y. (2012). *First we learn to read, then we read to learn.* Accessed at www.dailyrepublic.com/all-dr-news/solano-news/local-features/local-lifestyle-columns/first-we-learn-to-read-then-we-read-to-learn on March 6, 2020.

Le Watergate. (1985, September 25). *New York Times.* Accessed at https://nytimes.com/1985/09/25/opinion/le-watergate.html on September 7, 2020.

Leach, S. (Creator). (1992–2009) *Barney & friends* [Television show]. United States: Lyrick Studios.

Leonhardt, D. (2010, July 27). The case for $320,000 kindergarten teachers. *New York Times*. Accessed at www.nytimes.com/2010/07/28/business/economy/28leonhardt.html on March 6, 2020.

Lin, X., Yanbin, L., Shousen, X., Ding, W., Zhou, Q., Hongfei, D., et al. (2019). Family risk factors associated with oppositional defiant disorder symptoms, depressive symptoms, and aggressive behaviors among Chinese children with oppositional defiant disorder. *Frontiers in Psychology*. Accessed at https://ncbi.nlm.nih.gov/pmc/articles/PMC6769082 on September 10, 2020.

Linkletter, A. (Producer). (1945–1969). *Art Linkletter's house party* [Television show]. United States: John Guedel Productions.

Martin, E., & May, L. (2020). *Reading and writing instruction for preK through first-grade classrooms in a PLC at Work* (M. Onuscheck & J. Spiller, Eds.). Bloomington, IN: Solution Tree Press.

Marzano, R. J. (2009). *Teaching basic and advanced vocabulary: A framework for direct instruction*. Alexandria, VA: Association for Supervision and Curriculum Development.

Marzano, R. J. (2020). *Teaching basic, advanced, and academic vocabulary: A comprehensive framework for elementary instruction*. Bloomington, IN: Marzano Resources.

Mayo Clinic. (n.d.). *Oppositional defiant disorder (ODD)*. Accessed at www.mayoclinic.org/diseases-conditions/oppositional-defiant-disorder/symptoms-causes/syc-20375831 on April 9, 2020.

McGuinness, D. (2005). *Language development and learning to read: The scientific study of how language development affects reading skill*. Cambridge, MA: MIT Press.

McGuinness, D. (2006). *Early reading instruction: What science really tells us about how to teach reading*. Cambridge, MA: MIT Press.

McLeod, S. (2018). *Jean Piaget's theory of cognitive development*. Accessed at www.simplypsychology.org/piaget.html on March 6, 2020.

Melbourne Child Psychology & School Psychology Services. (n.d.). *The importance of routine in childhood* [Blog post]. Accessed at www.melbournechildpsychology.com.au/blog/the-importance-of-routine-in-childhood on September 8, 2020.

Mishra, A., Garg, S. P., & Desai, S. N. (2014). Prevalence of oppositional defiant disorder and conduct disorder in primary school children. *Journal of Indian Academy of Forensic Medicine, 36*(3), 246–250. Accessed at https://researchgate.net/publication/286338207_Prevalence_of_oppositional_defiant_disorder_and_conduct_disorder_in_primary_school_children on September 8, 2020.

Moats, L. C. (2020). *Teaching reading is rocket science: What expert teachers of reading should know and be able to do.* Accessed at www.aft.org/ae/summer2020/moats on August 3, 2020.

Morin, A. (2019). *10 surprising reasons why kids misbehave (and how to respond).* Accessed at www.verywellfamily.com/surprising-reasons-why-kids-misbehave-1094946 on March 6, 2020.

Muelle, C. M. (2013). *The history of kindergarten: From Germany to the United States.* Accessed at https://digitalcommons.fiu.edu/cgi/viewcontent.cgi?referer=https: //www.google.com/&httpsredir=1&article=1110&context=sferc on March 6, 2020.

Mulgrew, M., & Carranza, R. (2019). *A clarification on lesson plans.* Accessed at www.uft.org/news/clarification-lesson-plans on March 6, 2020.

Nation, K., & Snowling, M. J. (2004). Beyond phonological skills: Broader language skills contribute to the development of reading. *Journal of Research in Reading, 27*(4), 342–356.

Nation, P., & Waring, R. (1997). Vocabulary size, text coverage and word lists. In N. Schmitt & M. McCarthy (Eds.), *Vocabulary: Description, acquisition and pedagogy* (pp. 6–19). Cambridge, UK: Cambridge University Press.

Nelson, D. G. K., Hirsh-Pasek, K., Jusczyk, P. W., & Cassidy, K. W. (1989). How the prosodic cues in motherese might assist language learning. *Journal of Child Language, 16*(1), 55–68.

Neville, H. F. (2007). *Is this a phase? Child development and parent strategies, birth to 6 years.* Seattle: Parenting Press.

Oczkus, L. D. (2012). *Best ever literacy survival tips: 72 lessons you can't teach without.* Newark, DE: International Reading Association.

Ohio State University. (2019). *A 'million word gap' for children who aren't read to at home.* Accessed at www.sciencedaily.com/releases/2019/04/190404074947.htm on March 6, 2020.

Parker, N. (2013, July 9). The angel in the marble: Modern life lessons from history's greatest sculptor [Blog post]. *Medium.* Accessed at https://medium.com/@nilsaparker/the-angel-in-the-marble-f7aa43f333dc on March 6, 2020.

Parten, M. B. (1932). Social participation among pre-school children. *Journal of Abnormal and Social Psychology, 27*(3), 243–269.

Pearson, P. D., & Gallagher, M. C. (1983). The instruction of reading comprehension. *Contemporary Educational Psychology, 8*(3), 317–344.

Penfield, W., & Roberts, L. (1959). *Speech and brain mechanisms.* Princeton, NJ: Princeton University Press.

Piazza, E. A., Iordan, M. C., & Lew-Williams, C. (2017). *Mothers consistently alter their unique vocal fingerprints when communicating with infants.* Accessed at www.cell.com/current-biology/fulltext/S0960-9822(17)31114-4?xid=PS_smithsonian on August 3, 2020.

Postal, K. (2011, November 11). How structure improves your child's brain: Teaching self-regulation without overstepping your bounds [Blog post]. *Psychology Today.* Accessed at www.psychologytoday.com/us/blog/think-better/201111/how-structure-improves-your-childs-brain on August 3, 2020.

Presseisen, B. Z., & Kozulin, A. (1992, April). *Mediated learning—The contributions of Vygotsky and Feuerstein in theory and practice.* Paper presented at the annual meeting of the American Educational Research Association, San Francisco. Accessed at https://files.eric.ed.gov/fulltext/ED347202.pdf on March 6, 2020.

Provine, R. R., Krosnowski, K. A., & Brocato, N. W. (2009). *Tearing: Breakthrough in human emotional signaling.* Accessed at https://journals.sagepub.com/doi/10.1177/147470490900700107 on June 29, 2020.

Reading A–Z. (n.d.). *Stages of development.* Accessed at www.readinga-z.com/learninga-z-levels/stages-of-development on March 6, 2020.

Rifkin, R. (2019) *Here's what works way better than forcing your kid to say sorry.* Accessed at www.todaysparent.com/family/parenting/heres-what-works-way-better-than-forcing-your-kid-to-say-sorry on March 6, 2020.

Rivera, D. (2015, October 28). *Let the child cry: How tears support social and emotional development* [Blog post]. Accessed at www.edutopia.org/blog/tears-support-social-emotional-development-diana-rivera on June 29, 2020.

Rudin, S. (Producer), & Linklater, R. (Director). (2003). *School of rock* [Motion picture]. United States: Scott Rudin Productions.

Russell, D. (2020). *What is the base-10 number system?* Accessed at www.thoughtco.com/definition-of-base-10-2312365 on May 28, 2020.

Ryan, R. M., & Deci, E. L. (2000). Self-determination theory and the facilitation of intrinsic motivation, social development, and well-being. *American Psychologist, 55*(1), 68–78.

Sabine, G. H., & Thorson, T. L. (1993). *A history of political theory* (4th ed.). Fort Worth, TX: Harcourt Brace.

Schaal, S. (n.d.). *Learning from demonstration.* Accessed at http://papers.nips.cc/paper/1224-learning-from-demonstration.pdf on March 6, 2020.

Schimmer, T. (2011, April 8). *Classroom management is about "predictability"* [Blog post]. Accessed at http://edupln.ning.com/profiles/blogs/classroom-management-is-about on September 14, 2020.

Scull, J., Paatsch, L., & Raban, B. (2013). Young learners: Teachers' questions and prompts as opportunities for children's language development. *Asia-Pacific Journal of Research in Early Childhood Education, 7*(1), 69–91.

Sedita, J. (2018, May 22). *Background knowledge and reading comprehension* [Blog post]. Accessed at https://keystoliteracy.com/blog/background-knowledge-and-reading-comprehension on August 3, 2020.

Segal, A., & Martin-Chang , S. (2019). *Fun with rhymes and word play helps children learn to read.* Accessed at https://theconversation.com/fun-with-rhymes-and-word-play-helps-children-learn-to-read-125119 on August 3, 2020.

Sendak, M. (1984). *Where the wild things are.* New York: Harper & Row.

Shay, A. (2017). *Mediated learning experience: Choosing cognitive modifiability.* Accessed at https://juniperpublishers.com/pbsij/pdf/PBSIJ.MS.ID.555583.pdf on March 6, 2020.

Siegel, D. J., & Bryson, T. P. (2014). *No-drama discipline: The whole-brain way to calm the chaos and nurture your child's developing mind.* New York: Bantam Books.

Siegler, R., DeLoache, J., & Eisenberg, N. (2006). *How children develop* (2nd. ed.). New York: Worth.

Silver, D. (n.d.). *Revisiting rewards: The downside to extrinsic motivation.* Accessed at http://nutsandboltssymposiums.com/wp-content/uploads/2016/04/Revisiting-Rewards-for-Nuts-Bolts.pdf on March 6, 2020.

Simpson, D. J., & Jackson, M. J. B. (2003). John Dewey's view of the curriculum in *The Child and the Curriculum. Education and Culture, 19*(2), 23–27.

Sosteric, M. (2012). *The emotional abuse of our children: Teachers, schools, and the sanctioned violence of our modern institutions.* Accessed at www.sociology.org/the-emotional-abuse-of-our-children-teachers-schools-and-the-sanctioned-violence-of-our-modern-institutions on March 6, 2020.

Sparks, S. D. (2019). *Students learn more from inquiry-based teaching, international study finds.* Accessed at www.edweek.org/ew/articles/2019/10/09/students-learn-more-from-inquiry-based-teaching-international.html#:~:text=New%20research%20suggests%20students%20can,even%20in%20very%20early%20grades.&text=Students%20learn%20both%20to%20seek,to%20develop%20theories%20and%20explanations on September 8, 2020.

Sperling, J. (2020, May 22). *How to respond to tantrums* [Blog post]. Accessed at https://health.harvard.edu/blog/how-to-respond-to-tantrums-2020051919845 on September 10, 2020.

Stanford Children's Health. (n.d.). *Temper tantrums.* Accessed at www.stanfordchildrens.org/en/topic/default?id=temper-tantrums-90-P02295 on March 6, 2020.

Stein, D. J., Hollander, E., & Liebowitz, M. R. (1993). Neurobiology of impulsivity and the impulse control disorders. *Journal of Neuropsychiatry and Clinical Neurosciences, 5*(1), 9–17.

Stephens, K. (2007). *Reliable and predictable discipline: Tips for enforcing consequences.* Accessed at www.easternflorida.edu/community-resources/child-development-centers/parent-resource-library/documents/reliable-and-predictable-discipline.pdf on March 6, 2020.

Stevens, K. C. (1980). The effect of background knowledge on the reading comprehension of ninth graders. *Journal of Reading Behavior, 12*(2), 151–154.

Streep, P. (2016, November 14). The enduring pain of childhood verbal abuse [Blog post]. *Psychology Today.* Accessed at www.psychologytoday.com/us/blog/tech-support/201611/the-enduring-pain-childhood-verbal-abuse on August 3, 2020.

Suchman, J. R. (1965). Learning through inquiry. *Childhood Education, 41*(6), 289–291.

Suskind, D. (2016, January 26). Teacher as researcher: The ultimate professional development [Blog post]. *Edutopia.* Accessed at www.edutopia.org/blog/reacher-researcher-ultimate-professional-development-dorothy-suskind on March 6, 2020.

Tallman, A. (2016, June 1). Making time for science and social studies [Blog post]. *EDU.* Accessed at http://edublog.scholastic.com/post/making-time-science-and-social-studies on March 6, 2020.

Taylor, J. (2009, September 3). Parenting: Don't praise your children! [Blog post]. *Psychology Today.* Accessed at www.psychologytoday.com/us/blog/the-power-prime/200909/parenting-dont-praise-your-children on March 6, 2020.

Teachers College Reading and Writing Project. (2011, August). *Teachers College Reading and Writing Workshop.* Presented at the meeting of Teachers College Reading and Writing Workshop, New York.

Teaching Tolerance. (2016). *Reframing classroom management: A toolkit for educators.* Accessed at www.tolerance.org/sites/default/files/TT_Reframing_Classroom_Managment_Handouts.pdf on August 3, 2020.

TES Professional. (2015). *Stop bad behaviour by refusing to reward it.* Accessed at www.tes.com/news/stop-bad-behaviour-refusing-reward-it on March 6, 2020.

TestPrep-Online. (n.d.). *What is the OLSAT test?* Accessed at www.testprep-online.com/what-is-olsat on March 6, 2020.

Thomas, W. P., & Collier, V. P. (2003). The multiple benefits of dual language. *Educational Leadership, 61*(2), 61–64.

Tolstoy, L. (1968). *War and peace.* New York: Signet Classic. (Original work published 1869)

Toor, R. (2016). *'Sweetie talk': Unthinking endearment that's meant to comfort instead can feel demeaning.* Accessed at www.spokesman.com/stories/2016/nov/20/sweetie-talk-unthinking-endearment-thats-meant-to- on March 6, 2020.

TutorialsPoint. (n.d.). *The rule of seven.* Accessed at www.tutorialspoint.com/management_concepts/the_rule_of_seven.htm on March 6, 2020.

U.S. Department of Education. (2012). *Restraint and seclusion: Resource document.* Washington, DC: Author. Accessed at www2.ed.gov/policy/seclusion/restraints-and-seclusion-resources.pdf on March 6, 2020.

Varlas, L. (2018). *ELLs count on language support in math.* Accessed at www.ascd.org/publications/newsletters/education-update/apr18/vol60/num04/ELLs-Count-on-Language-Support-in-Math.aspx on October 7, 2018.

Veltri, M. (2016, October 18). 和 Wa—Harmony [Blog post]. *Michael Veltri.* Accessed at https://michaelveltri.com/blog/wa-harmony-mushin on March 6, 2020.

Vize, A. (2008, November 24). *Magic 100 words: Why are English language learners so in love with M100W sight words?* Accessed at www.brighthubeducation.com/esl-lesson-plans/16793-magic-100-golden-words on March 6, 2020.

Vygotsky, L. S. (1978). *Mind in society: The development of higher psychological processes.* Cambridge, MA: Harvard University Press.

Wallace, M. (2018, January 7). Teaching children self-control [Blog post]. *Psychology Today.* Accessed at www.psychologytoday.com/us/blog/how-raise-happy-cooperative-child/201801/teaching-children-self-control on March 6, 2020.

Watson, S. (2019, October 18). *Letter reversals and what it means in children.* Accessed at www.thoughtco.com/students-letter-reversals-3111350 on March 6, 2020.

Watson, T. S., Watson, T., & Gebhardt, S. (2010). *Temper tantrums: Guidelines for parents and teachers.* Helping Children at Home and School III, pp. S4H33–1–S4H33–4.

Weber, C. L., Johnson, L., & Tripp, S., (2013). Implementing differentiation: A school's journey. *Gifted Child Today, 36*(3), 179–186.

Wells, R. B. (2016). *The consent of the governed.* Accessed at www.mrc.uidaho.edu/~rwells/techdocs/The%20Consent%20of%20the%20Governed.pdf on August 3, 2020.

Wheeler, D. S. (2017, August 9). *". . . plans are useless, but planning is indispensable"* [Blog post]. Accessed at http://leadershipreverie.blogspot.com/2017/08/plans-are-useless-but-planning-is.html on March 6, 2020.

Wiggins, G., & McTighe, J. (2011). *The Understanding by Design guide to creating high-quality units.* Alexandria, VA: Association for Supervision and Curriculum Development.

Yale University. (2019). *Classroom seating arrangements.* Accessed at https://poorvucenter.yale.edu/ClassroomSeatingArrangements on March 6, 2020.

Young, S. N. (2007). How to increase serotonin in the human brain without drugs. *Journal of Psychiatry and Neuroscience, 32*(6), 394–399.

INDEX

#
3-year rule, 34
4 ways of teaching, 34–35, 38
5-second rule, 41
55/40/5 rule, 33–34

a
ABCYa, 114
acceptance, 17–18
activities
    first day of school and, 40
    transitions and, 100–101
administration, working with, 25–27. *See also* working with administration and making curriculum work for you
All I Really Need to Know I Learned in Kindergarten (Fulghum), 1
assessments in reading, 142–144
attention, getting the class's, 98–100
authoritarian approach
    authoritative approach and, 66
    bathroom breaks and, 102
    classroom management and, 64–66
authoritative approach
    bathroom breaks and, 102
    classroom management and, 64, 66–67
    getting the class's attention and, 99
    reproducibles for, 86
autonomy, fostering, 89–91
Ayers, B., 18

b
backward design, 29
bathroom breaks, 101–103
Baumrind, D., 63
behavior. *See also* classroom management
    behavior charts, 129–130
    environment and, 40
    seven rules for the teacher and, 73–74
    strategies for managing specific behavior issues, 74–81
    strategies for minimizing misbehavior, 57–59
    why kindergarteners misbehave, 55–57
Berra, Y., 13
bias
    and differences in the classroom, 17–18
    gender and, 93–94
blending/blends
    digraphs and word families and, 150–151
    letter automaticity and, 149–150
Bradley, L., 144
Bryant, P., 144
"but—!" scenario, 76

c
Candid Camera (Funt), 45
categorization, concept of, 187
characteristics of an effective teacher. *See also* classroom management
    mindset and, 18–21
    observation skills and, 15–16
    thinking and, 16–17
charts
    about, 129
    behavior charts, 129–130
    class rules charts, 132
    job charts, 130–132
    reading level charts, 143–144
Chetty, R., 6

Chi, L., 4
children. *See also* kindergarteners/kindergarten
    and differences in the classroom, 17–18
    learning and, 3
choice time. *See also* managing whole-group and choice time; play
    about, 112–113
    cleanup and, 117–118
    fostering independence and, 90–91
    how not to do choice time, 114–115
    importance of, 107
    reproducibles for, 121
    rules and, 115–116
    start and end times for, 116–117
    station numbers and options for, 113–115
Cider House Rules, The (Irving), 33
circle time. *See* whole-group time
clarity in literacy and mathematics
    about, 139–140
    teaching literacy. *See* teaching literacy
    teaching mathematics. *See* teaching mathematics
clarity in the classroom
    about, 11
    employing practical classroom management. *See* classroom management
    knowing that teaching starts in the mind. *See* teaching starts in the mind, knowing that
    making schedules, charts, and plans. *See* making schedules, charts, and plans
    managing whole-group and choice time. *See* managing whole-group and choice time
    planning routines. *See* routines, planning
    preparing your classroom and yourself. *See* preparing your classroom and yourself
    working with administration and making curriculum work for you. *See* working with administration and making curriculum work for you
class schedules. *See also* making schedules, charts, and plans
    about, 123–125
    flexibility in, 127–128
    long view of, 125
    monthly calendar and, 128–129
    short view of, 125–126

classroom design
    disciplinary tools and, 68
    five-second rule and, 41
    preparing your classroom, 40–41
    psycho room scenario, 42
    rug arrangements and, 110–111
    tables and, 42–43
classroom management. *See also* characteristics of an effective teacher; managing whole-group and choice time
    about, 55
    chapter assessment and answers, 82–85
    disciplinary tools and, 67–72
    end goal of, 59–62
    in a nutshell, 81
    reproducibles for, 86–87
    seven rules for the teacher and, 72–74
    social-emotional learning and, 63–67
    social learning and discipline and, 62–63
    strategies for managing specific behavior issues and, 74–81
    strategies for minimizing misbehavior and, 57–59
    whole-group time and, 111
    why kindergarteners misbehave, 55–57
classroom rules
    choice time and, 115–116
    class rules charts, 132
    why kindergarteners misbehave, 56
cleanup
    choice time and, 117–118
    transitions and, 100–101
clerking mindset, 18–19
Colbert, J., 107
computers, use of in choice time, 114
conferences
    parent-teacher conferences, 132–134, 138
    speed conferences, 165, 166
consent of the governed, 66
consequences. *See also* classroom management
    disciplinary tools and, 67, 69
    seven rules for the teacher and, 72–73, 74
    tantrums and, 79
consonant blends. *See* blending/blends
consonants
    blending/blends, 149–151
    teaching letters and, 147–148
consonant-vowel-consonant (CVC) words, 150

Constructive Playthings, 113
controlled chaos, 59–62
conventional reading, defined, 158
Coulson, J., 70
counting
    foundational concepts and, 187–188
    student retention of, 185
    teaching counting, 188–189
creativity and choice time, 114
critical thinking
    about experts and thinking critically, 3–5
    mindset of an effective teacher and, 18
crying, 77
curriculum. *See also* working with administration and making curriculum work for you
    55/40/5 rule and, 33–34
    about, 27–29
    first day of school and, 39–40
    my path through, 29–32
    packaged curriculum, 28
    three-year rule and, 34

d

decoding
    high-frequency words and, 153
    how we read English, 157
    reproducibles for, 179
demonstrations, use of, 25, 35
de Paiva, A., 40
Dewey, J., 28
different and same, teaching concept of, 185, 192–193
differentiated lessons
    strategies for minimizing misbehavior and, 58
    teaching mathematics and, 184
    whole-group time and, 108–109
digraphs, 150–151
discipline/disciplinary tools. *See also* behavior; classroom management
    about, 67–68
    physical escorts and, 71
    positive reinforcement and, 67
    restraint and, 71
    sharp tongue and, 68–69
    social-emotional learning and, 62–63
    time away and, 70–71
    time-outs and, 69–70

Dolch, E., 154
Dolch List (Dolch), 154

e

Eisenhower, D., 126
Elkind, D., 112
employing practical classroom management. *See* classroom management
environment, 40. *See also* classroom design
examples, use of, 25, 35

f

families. *See* parents/guardians
farms (toy), use of, 113–114
feng shui for the classroom, 40
fiction versus nonfiction, 173–175, 182
first day of school, getting ready for
    classroom design and, 40–43
    curriculum and, 39–40
    parents'/guardians' contact information and, 44–45
    reproducibles for, 50
    students' names and, 43–44
five-second rule, 41
Forman, G., 15
Fountas, I., 158
Fountas and Pinnell, 158
four ways of teaching, 34–35, 38
friendships, "they don't want to be my friend!" scenario, 76–77
Fulghum, R., 1
Fundations, 172
Funt, A., 45

g

garages (toy), use of, 113–114
gender, lining up and, 93–94
getting ready for the first day of school. *See* first day of school, getting ready for
goals
    first day of school and, 40
    standards and, 19
Golding, W., 65
gradual release of responsibility model, 35, 66
Grassian, S., 70
guided practice, use of, 25, 35

h

Hall, E., 15
Hammerstein, O., 18
Hannel, G., 14
harmony, 60–62. *See also* wa
high-frequency words, 153–154. See also sight words
homework, 132–133
hum and controlled chaos, 60–62

i

I do it, we do it, you do it together, you do it alone, 35
impulsivity, 57
independence, fostering, 89–91
inner child, 3
inquiry, use of, 25, 35
interventions, 33
introduction
    about, 1–2
    about experts and thinking critically, 3–5
    about teaching, 2–3
    about this book, 6–9
    about this crucial grade level, 5–6

j

Jackson, M., 27
job charts, 130–132

k

Kids Say the Darndest Things (Linkletter), 45
kinderese. *See also* language development
    mathematics in kinderese, 186–187
    reproducibles for, 51–53
    speaking to kindergarteners, 46–48
kindergarteners/kindergarten
    about this crucial grade level, 5–6
    speaking to kindergarteners, 45–48
    why kindergarteners misbehave, 55–57
knowing that teaching starts in the mind. *See* teaching starts in the mind, knowing that
Kumbaya seating plan, 110

l

Lakeshore Learning, 113
language development. *See also* kinderese
    motherese, 45, 46
    prereading skills and, 145
    speaking to kindergarteners, 45–48
    wordplay and, 44
Language Development and Learning to Read: The Scientific Study of How Language Development Affects Reading Skill (McGuinness), 28
left and right, teaching concept of, 185, 195–196
less and more, teaching concept of, 185, 191–192
lesson plans, 126–128
letter pairs, 149
letters
    assessments and, 143
    blending/blends, 149–150
    how we read English, 156–158
    letter automaticity, 147, 149–150
    long vowels, 151–152
    penmanship and, 172–173
    phonics and, 147–149
    reproducibles for, 181
leveled books
    about, 158
    accuracy and, 160–161
    leveling up, 158–160
    self-leveled books, 161–164
Lewin, K., 40
line awareness, 92
lining up
    about, 91
    how to line up, 93–95
    stairs and, 95–96
    talking in line, 97
    why to line up, 92
Linkletter, A., 45
listening skills
    observation skills and, 15–16
    tantrums and, 78
literacy. *See* teaching literacy
logograms, 157
Lord of the Flies (Golding), 65

m

Magic School Bus, The (Bastien and Jacobs), 14
making schedules, charts, and plans
    about, 123
    chapter assessment and answers, 134–136

charts, 129–132
class schedules, 123–126
flexibility in, 127–128
homework, 132–133
lesson plans, 126–128
monthly calendar, 128–129
in a nutshell, 134
parent-teacher conferences, 132–134
reproducibles for, 137–138
managing whole-group and choice time. *See also* classroom management
about, 107
chapter assessment and answers, 119–120
choice time and, 112–118
in a nutshell, 118–119
reproducibles for, 121
whole-group time and, 107–112
manipulatives
station numbers and options and, 113
teaching mathematics and, 196–198
materials, mindset of an effective teacher and, 20
mathematics. *See* teaching mathematics
McGuinness, D., 28–29, 157
McTighe, J., 29
measurements, concept of, 185
mediated learning experiences (MLE), 14
mindset. *See also* teaching starts in the mind, knowing that
characteristics of an effective teacher and, 17
mental attitudes and, 13
mindset of an effective teacher, 18–21
Moats, L., 33
Montessori, M., 89
more and less, teaching concept of, 185, 190–191
morning quizzes
fostering independence and, 91
routines, planning and, 97–98
motherese, 45, 46. *See also* kinderese
motivation
disciplinary tools and, 68
transitions and, 100–101
movement
strategies for minimizing misbehavior and, 57
whole-group time and, 109–110

n

neuroarchitecture, 40
nonfiction versus fiction, 173–175, 182

o

observation skills, 15–16
oppositional defiance disorder (ODD)
restraint and, 71
strategies for managing specific behavior issues and, 79–81
ouchies/vertices, 187

p

packaged curriculum, 28
parallel play, 17
parents/guardians
contact information for, 44–45
homework and, 132–133
social-emotional learning and, 63
parent-teacher conferences, 132–134, 138
partner assignment, 77, 93, 95
patterning, concept of, 187
Pedagogy of Questioning, A, (Hannel), 14
pencils, use of, 169
penmanship, 172–173
permissive approach
classroom management and, 63, 64–66
going to the bathroom and, 101–102
phonics
letters and, 147–149
limitations of, 145–147
phonograms, 151
phonological awareness, 144
physical escorts, 71
pictograms, 157
Pinnell, G. S., 158
planning routines. *See* routines, planning
Plant, R., 3
play. *See also* choice time
importance of, 107, 112–113
parallel play, 17
and strategies for minimizing misbehavior, 57–58
playhouses, use of, 113–114
positive reinforcement, 67
Postal, K., 58
predictability
controlled chaos and, 59–60
seven rules for the teacher and, 72
prejudice
and differences in the classroom, 17–18

gender and, 93–94
preparing your classroom and yourself
    about, 39
    chapter assessment and answers, 48–49
    first day of school, getting ready for, 39–45
    in a nutshell, 48
    reproducibles for, 50–53
    speaking to kindergarteners, 45–48
prereading skills, 144–145
preteaching, 184

q

quizzes, 91, 97–98

r

Raz-Kids, 114
reading. *See also* teaching literacy
    assessments and, 142–144
    blending/blends and, 149–151
    conventional reading, defined, 158
    how we read English, 156–158
    independent reading, 164–165
    long vowels and, 151–152
    mantras and, 152
    my path through the curriculum and, 30–31
    phonics and, 145–149
    prereading skills, 144–145
    reading proficiency help methods, 166–167
    reproducibles for, 179–180
    sight words and, 153–156
reading comprehension, 5
reading programs, 158
relational words, concept of, 187
relationships, "they don't want to be my friend!" scenario, 76–77
remediation, 33
reproducibles
    being an authoritative teacher, 86
    classifying fiction versus nonfiction, 182
    employing interdisciplinary teaching, 137
    ensuring mathematics concept readiness, 204
    four ways to teach a skill, 38
    handling transitions, 106
    managing conflicts, 87
    practicing kinderese, 51–53
    preparing for choice time, 121
    preparing for parent-teacher conferences, 138
    preparing for the first day of school, 50
    preteaching and spiraling, 203
    skills for the effective teacher, 23
    teaching each letter to mastery, 181
    teaching the reading decoding skills, 179–180
restraint, use of, 71–72
rewards, use of, 67
right and left, teaching concept of, 185, 195–196
Rogers, F., 107
Rodgers, R., 18
rope, lining up on, 94
routines, planning
    about, 89
    attention, getting the class's, 98–100
    bathroom breaks and, 101–103
    chapter assessment and answers, 104–105
    independence and, 89–91
    lining up and, 91–97
    morning quiz and, 97–98
    in a nutshell, 103
    reproducibles for, 106
    transitions and, 100–101
rug arrangements, 110–111
rules
    55/40/5 rule, 33–34
    choice time and, 115–116
    class rules chart, 132
    five-second rule, 41
    rule of seven, 185
    seven rules for the teacher, 72–74
    three-year rule, 34
    why kindergarteners misbehave, 56

s

same and different, teaching concept of, 185, 192–193
sand tables, use of, 113
sandwich words, 150
scaffolding, 160, 187
schedules
    about, 123–125
    flexibility in, 127–128
    long view of, 125
    monthly calendar and, 128–129
    short view of, 125–126
science, 198–199
self-control, 59

shapes, teaching concept of, 185, 193–194
sharp tongue, use of, 68–69, 73
sight words
    about, 153–154
    assessments and, 143
    sight-word fallacy, 156
    which sight words to teach, 154
    words per week, 155
    word walls, 154–155
Simpson, D., 27
singing the letters, 150
SMART Boards, use of in choice time, 114
social-emotional learning (SEL)
    authoritative approach and, 66–67
    discipline and, 62–63
    permissive and authoritarian approaches and, 64–66
social studies, 198–199
socioeconomic status and learning, 2, 14
sorting, concept of, 187
Sosteric, M., 69
speed conferences, 165, 166
Sperling, J., 78
spiraling, 125, 184
standards, mindset of an effective teacher and, 19
station numbers and options, 113–114. *See also* choice time
students' names, memorizing, 43–44
supplies, mindset of an effective teacher and, 20
Suskind, D., 19

t

tables and classroom design, 42–43
tantrums, 77–81
teachers/teaching
    about, 205
    about experts and thinking critically, 3–5
    about teaching, 2–3
    characteristics of an effective teacher, 15–17
    four ways of teaching, 34–35
    how to spend your time, 32–33
    mindset of an effective teacher, 18–19
    reproducibles for, 38, 137
    seven rules for, 72–74
Teaching Basic, Advanced, and Academic Vocabulary: A Comprehensive Framework for Elementary Instruction (Marzano), 154

teaching literacy
    about, 141–142
    assessment and, 142–144
    chapter assessment and answers, 176–178
    fiction versus nonfiction and, 173–175
    how we read English and, 156–158
    independent reading and, 164–165
    independent writing and, 169–173
    leveled books and, 158–164
    in a nutshell, 175
    reading, teaching, 144–145
    reading components and, 145–156
    reading proficiency help methods and, 166–167
    reproducibles for, 179–182
    writing progression and, 167–169
teaching mathematics
    about, 183–185
    chapter assessment and answers, 199–202
    conceptual thinking and, 196
    counting, concept of, 188–189
    foundational concepts and, 187–188
    left and right, concept of, 195–196
    manipulatives and other teaching tools and, 196–198
    mathematics in kinderese and, 186–187
    more and less, concept of, 189–192
    in a nutshell, 199
    reproducibles for, 203–204
    same and different, concept of, 192–193
    shapes, concept of, 193–194
Teaching Reading Is Rocket Science (Moats), 33
teaching starts in the mind, knowing that
    about, 13
    bus drivers and, 14
    chapter assessment and answers, 21–22
    characteristics of an effective teacher and, 15–17
    mindset of an effective teacher and, 18–21
    in a nutshell, 21
    reproducibles for, 23
"they don't want to be my friend!" scenario, 76–77
"they hit me first" scenario, 75–76
thinking
    about experts and thinking critically, 3–5
    characteristics of an effective teacher and, 16–17
    mindset of an effective teacher and, 18–19

three-year rule, 34
time away
    disciplinary tools and, 70–71
    seven rules for the teacher and, 73
    whole-group time and, 111
time-outs, 69–70
toileting, 101–103
transitions
    handling, 100–101
    reproducibles for, 106
tutoring, reading proficiency help, 166–167
two-letter things, 150. *See also* blending; digraphs

U

U.S. Department of Education, 71

V

vocabulary. *See also* teaching literacy
    reading comprehension and, 5
    socioeconomic status and, 14
vowels
letter automaticity and, 149–150
    long vowels, 151–152
    teaching letters and, 147–148
Vygotsky, L. S., 160

W

wa, 60–62. *See also* harmony
water tables, use of, 113

whole-group time. *See also* managing whole-group and choice time
    about, 107–108
    dance breaks and, 109–110
    differentiation and, 108–109
    monthly calendar and, 128
    questions and discussions and, 111–112
    rug arrangements and, 110–111
    time for, 108
Wiggins, G., 29
Willingham, D., 198
word families, 150–151
wordplay, 43–44
word walls, 154–155
working with administration and making curriculum work for you
    about, 25
    administration and, 25–27
    chapter assessment and answers, 36–37
    curriculum and, 27–34
    four ways of teaching and, 34–35
    in a nutshell, 36
    reproducibles for, 38
writing. *See also* teaching literacy
    independent writing, 169–173
    writing progression, 167–169
writing folders, 170–171
Handwriting Without Tears, 172

Z

zone of proximal development (ZPD), 160

Reading and Writing Instruction for PreK Through First-Grade Classrooms in a PLC at Work®
Erica Martin and Lisa May
Edited by Mark Onuscheck and Jeanne Spiller
Prepare your collaborative team to fully support and encourage every learner's literacy development. Written specifically for teachers of preK through first grade, this practical resource includes tools and strategies for designing standards-aligned instruction, assessments, interventions, and more.
BKF901

Mathematics Unit Planning in a PLC at Work®, Grades PreK–2
Sarah Schuhl, Timothy D. Kanold, Jennifer Deinhart, Nathan D. Lang-Raad, Matthew R. Larson, and Nanci N. Smith
Discover how to fully answer PLC critical question one in your mathematics classroom: What do we want all students to know and be able to do? With this resource, your teacher team will acquire detailed model mathematics units, learn how to perform seven collaborative tasks, and more.
BKF964

Success for Our Youngest Learners
Barbara W. Cirigliano
Put preK learners on the path to a great education by embracing the PLC process. Designed specifically for early childhood educators, this practical resource details the foundational ideas and concepts of a successful PLC.
BKF892

What About Us?
Diane Kerr, Tracey A. Hulen, Jacqueline Heller, and Brian K. Butler
Early childhood learning is a critical launchpad for every student's social, emotional, and intellectual growth. With *What About Us?* discover how to achieve the full potential of preK–2 classrooms through proven best practices aligned to the PLC at Work® process.
BKF941

Solution Tree | Press

Visit SolutionTree.com or call 800.733.6786 to order.

Wait! Your professional development journey doesn't have to end with the last pages of this book.

We realize improving student learning doesn't happen overnight. And your school or district shouldn't be left to puzzle out all the details of this process alone.

No matter where you are on the journey, we're committed to helping you get to the next stage.

Take advantage of everything from **custom workshops** to **keynote presentations** and **interactive web and video conferencing**. We can even help you develop an action plan tailored to fit your specific needs.

Let's get the conversation started.

Call 888.763.9045 today.

SolutionTree.com